Educational Dilemmas

Educational Dilemmas uses cultural psychology to explore the challenges, contradictions and tensions that occur during the process of education, with consideration of the effect these have at both the individual and the collective level. It argues that the focus on issues in learning overlooks a fundamental characteristic of education: that the process of educating is simultaneously both constructive and disruptive.

Drawing on research from Europe, America and Asia, chapters in this volume present and analyse different experiences of the tension between disruption and construction in the process of education. Situating educational discontent within the wider context, the book demonstrates how this issue can be exacerbated by the tension between the commodification and democratisation of educational systems. This book demonstrates that these issues permeate all levels of education and, as a result, emphasises how vital it is that educational discontent is considered from a new perspective.

Educational Dilemmas is essential reading for academics, researchers and postgraduate students in the fields of psychology and education. It should also be of great interest to school psychologists, teachers and therapists.

Luca Tateo is Associate Professor at Aalborg University in Denmark. He is a member of the Research Center for Cultural Psychology, Member of the Centre IBEF (Ideas for the Basic Education of the Future), ECNU in Shanghai, and visiting professor at the Federal University of Bahia in Brazil.

Cultural Dynamics of Social Representation
Series Editor: Jaan Valsiner
Centre of Cultural Psychology, Aalborg University, Denmark

The series is dedicated to bringing the scholarly reader new ways of representing human lives in the contemporary social sciences. It is a part of a new direction – cultural psychology – that has emerged at the intersection of developmental, dynamic and social psychologies, anthropology, education, and sociology. It aims to provide cutting-edge examinations of global social processes, which for every country are becoming increasingly multi-cultural; the world is becoming one 'global village', with the corresponding need to know how different parts of that 'village' function. Therefore, social sciences need new ways of considering how to study human lives in their globalizing contexts. The focus of this series is the social representation of people, communities, and – last but not least – the social sciences themselves.

Books in this series:

Persons and Their Minds
Towards an Integrative Theory of the Mediated Mind
Svend Brinkmann

Culture and the Cognitive Science of Religion
James Cresswell

An Interdisciplinary Approach to the Human Mind (Open Access)
Subjectivity, Science and Experiences in Change
Line Joranger

Educational Dilemmas
A Cultural Psychological Perspective
Edited by Luca Tateo

For more information about this series, please visit: www.routledge.com/Cultural-Dynamics-of-Social-Representation/book-series/CULTDYNAMIC

Educational Dilemmas

A Cultural Psychological Perspective

Edited by Luca Tateo

LONDON AND NEW YORK

First published 2019
by Routledge
2 Park Square, Milton Park, Abingdon, Oxon OX14 4RN

and by Routledge
52 Vanderbilt Avenue, New York, NY 10017

Routledge is an imprint of the Taylor & Francis Group, an informa business

© 2019 selection and editorial matter, Luca Tateo; individual chapters, the contributors

The right of the editor to be identified as the author of the editorial material, and of the authors for their individual chapters, has been asserted in accordance with sections 77 and 78 of the Copyright, Designs and Patents Act 1988.

All rights reserved. No part of this book may be reprinted or reproduced or utilised in any form or by any electronic, mechanical, or other means, now known or hereafter invented, including photocopying and recording, or in any information storage or retrieval system, without permission in writing from the publishers.

Trademark notice: Product or corporate names may be trademarks or registered trademarks, and are used only for identification and explanation without intent to infringe.

British Library Cataloguing-in-Publication Data
A catalogue record for this book is available from the British Library

Library of Congress Cataloging-in-Publication Data
Names: Tateo, Luca, editor.
Title: Educational dilemmas: a cultural psychological perspective/
 Edited by Luca Tateo.
Description: Abingdon, Oxon; New York, NY: Routledge, 2019. |
 Series: Cultural dynamics of social representation | Includes
 bibliographical references
Identifiers: LCCN 2018043436 (print) | LCCN 2018045805
 (ebook) | ISBN 9781315101095 (E-book) | ISBN
 9781138125605 (hardback) | ISBN 9781315101095 (ebook)
Subjects: LCSH: Educational psychology – Cross-cultural studies. |
 Educational sociology – Cross-cultural studies.
Classification: LCC LB1051 (ebook) | LCC LB1051. E344 2019
 (print) | DDC 370.15 – dc23
LC record available at https://lccn.loc.gov/2018043436

ISBN: 978-1-138-12560-5 (hbk)
ISBN: 978-1-315-10109-5 (ebk)

Typeset in Times New Roman
by Apex CoVantage, LLC

Contents

List of contributors vii

Introduction: the inherent ambivalence of educational trajectories and the zone of proximal development with reduced potential 1
LUCA TATEO

1 **Intrinsic education and its discontents** 22
EUGENE MATUSOV AND ANA MARJANOVIC-SHANE

2 **Stress – between welfare and competition** 41
THOMAS SZULEVICZ, LÆRKE KROMANN KURE AND
LILLITH OLESEN LØKKEN

3 **Problems from discontinuity of children's environment and development in Japan** 56
YORIKO OKAMOTO OMI

4 **Mental health 101: interpreting emotional distress for Canadian postsecondary students** 76
KAREN H. ROSS

5 **Counseling for university students** 98
GIULIA SAVARESE, ORESTE FASANO, NADIA PECORARO,
MONICA MOLLO, LUNA CARPINELLI AND PIERPAOLO CAVALLO

6 **The discomfort of writing in academia** 112
NOOMI MATTHIESEN AND CHARLOTTE WEGENER

7 **In deep water: university students' challenges in the processes of self-formation, survival or flight** 126
CASPER FEILBERG

8 **Corporal punishment in extracurricular sports activities (*bukatsu*) represents an aspect of Japanese culture** 139
YASUHIRO OMI

9 **"I see stress in many places around me, but as such, I'm over it": understanding psycho-cultural dimensions of university students' experiences** 146
PERNILLE HAMMER, THOMAS MADSEN AND LUCA TATEO

10 **Internship as liminal zone in education** 171
ENRICA MELE AND GIUSEPPINA MARSICO

Afterword on educational dilemmas 193
LUCA TATEO

Index 196

Contributors

Luna Carpinelli (PhD) is a clinical psychologist and a psychotherapist. She is a research fellow at the Medical School of the University of Salerno (Italy). Her research interests are focused on prevention of individual diseases and promotion of psychological well-being as well as the detection of child abuse and maltreatment.

Pierpaolo Cavallo is Assistant Professor of Public Health at the University of Salerno, Italy. He has been Guest Scholar at IMT – School for Advanced Studies, Lucca, Italy and currently is Research Associate at the ISC-CNR, the Complex Systems Institute of the National Research Council, Rome, Italy. His research interests are devoted to the study of Complex Systems in Public Health, Epidemiology, Environmental Health and Food Control.

Oreste Fasano (PhD) is a clinical psychologist and systemic relational psychotherapist. He carries out his professional activity at the Mental Health Unit of the Local Health Authority "ASL Salerno". He collaborates in research, training and counseling activities at the University of Salerno (Italy).

Casper Feilberg, PhD, is an Assistant Professor in the Department of Communication and Psychology at Aalborg University, Denmark. His main fields of research are higher learning, the academic study of psychology, Bildung perspectives and the professional role of the psychologist.

Pernille Hammer is a Masters student at Aalborg University Centre for Cultural Psychology where she is also working as a student assistant. She is also editorial assistant of *Human Arenas. An Interdisciplinary Journal of Psychology, Culture and Meaning* (Springer).

Lærke Kromann Kure graduated in Psychology at Aalborg University and is research assistant in the research group of Processes and Learning in Organizations at the Department of Learning and Philosophy, Aalborg University.

Thomas Madsen is a Masters student and student assistant at the Centre for Cultural Psychology at Aalborg University.

Ana Marjanovic-Shane is an Independent Scholar and a deputy editor-in-chief of *Dialogic Pedagogy: An International Online Journal* (http://dpj.pitt.edu). She graduated from the "Interdisciplinary studies of human development" program at the University of Pennsylvania, and has been interested in sociocultural, Bakhtinian approaches to dialogic meaning-making, democracy in education and critical and creative authorship.

Giuseppina Marsico is Assistant Professor of Development and Educational Psychology at the University of Salerno (Italy); Affiliated Researcher at the Centre for Cultural Psychology, Aalborg University (Denmark); Visiting Professor for the PhD in Psychology, Federal University of Bahia (Brazil); and Honorary Associate Professor in the School of Psychology, University of Sydney (Australia). She has 18 years of experience as a researcher, with a proven international research network. She is Editor-in-Chief of the book series Cultural Psychology of Education (Springer) and Latin American Voices – Integrative Psychology and Humanities (Springer); Co-Editor of SpringerBriefs Psychology and Cultural Developmental Sciences (together with Jaan Valsiner) and Annals of Cultural Psychology: Exploring the Frontiers of Mind and Society (InfoAge Publishing, NC, USA, together with Carlos Conejo and Jaan Valsiner). She is also Co-Editor of *Human Arenas. An Interdisciplinary Journal of Psychology, Culture and Meaning* (Springer); Associate Editor of *Culture & Psychology* (Sage) and *Social Psychology of Education* (Springer); and a member of the editorial board of several international academic journals (i.e. *IPBS – Integrative Psychological & Behavioral Science*, Springer).

Noomi Matthiesen is Associate Professor in Educational Psychology at the Department of Communication and Psychology at Aalborg University in Denmark. Her research interests include the impact on neo-liberal logics and practices in education.

Eugene Matusov is a Professor of Education at the University of Delaware. He was born in the Soviet Union and studied developmental psychology with Soviet researchers working in the Vygotskian paradigm. He worked as a schoolteacher before immigrating to the United States. Now he investigates and works with sociocultural and Bakhtinian dialogic approaches to education.

Enrica Mele graduated in clinical psychology from the University of Naples Federico II (Italy) in 2017. She spent six months at the Centre for Cultural Psychology in Aalborg in order to deepen her knowledge in some topics that are the object of this study. Now she is pursuing a master's degree in Work Psychology at the Catholic University in Milan (Italy) and is completing the traineeship for abilitation in a psychological profession in a hospital (Psychological Unit) and in an enterprise (Customer Care Training Unit).

Monica Mollo (PhD) is Researcher in Development and Educational Psychology at the University of Salerno (Italy). Her main research interests are: Argumentation; Self and Identity; Construction of Professional Identity in University and Schoolteachers; Elicitation Interview; Professional Practices; Construction of Logic/Mathematical Thinking in Children; Social Representations; Cultural Psychology.

Yoriko Okamoto Omi, PhD (Psychology) is Professor at Rissho University in Japan. Her research interests focus on the transition to parenthood and the communication development on asymmetric relationship, including Parental Proxy Talk for nonverbal infants, interpretation to fetal movements, and early childhood education and care.

Lillith Olesen Løkken is a research assistant at Aalborg University in Denmark. She is a teacher and supervisor at the psychology department. In practice she works with meditation and mindfulness in treatment of stress and promotion of mental health among university students.

Yasuhiro Omi is Professor of Psychology at the University of Yamanashi in Japan. He was a visiting fellow at Australian School of Environmental Studies at Griffith University and a visiting scholar at Frances L. Hiatt School of Psychology at Clark University in the United States.

Nadia Pecoraro is psychologist-psychotherapist, PhD in Methodology of Research in Education. She is lecturer in Developmental Psychology at the University of Salerno–DISUFF and she is psychologist and psychotherapist at the Counseling Center "M. Cesaro" of the same University. Her main research interests are the family transitions, the rule of family cultures in educational training, the risk and resource factors, as well as the discomfort of the students in the university studies.

Karen H. Ross is a PhD Candidate in Counselling Psychology at the Werklund School of Education, University of Calgary, Canada. She has served as a counsellor on three Canadian university campuses as well as at the Calgary Family Therapy Centre. She is an associate of the Taos Institute and lives in Vancouver, BC.

Giulia Savarese (PhD) is Assistant Professor of Development and Education Psychology at the University of Salerno, Italy. She is Director of the Counseling Psychological Center at University of Salerno. Her research interests are devoted to the study of attachment patterns, of typical and atypical development and of the child abuse and neglect.

Thomas Szulevicz, PhD, is an Associate Professor and Head of Studies in the Department of Communication and Psychology at Aalborg University, Denmark. His main fields of research are educational psychology, educational psychology practice and critical educational psychology.

Luca Tateo is Associate Professor in Epistemology and History of Cultural Psychology at Aalborg University. His research interests are the study of imagination as higher psychological function, the epistemology and history of psychological sciences, and revisiting the work of scholars such as Vico,

Cattaneo, Wundt, Lewin, Moscovici in order to reflect upon the future trends of psychological research and related methodological issues.

Charlotte Wegener is associate professor at Department of Communication and Psychology, Aalborg University, Denmark. She is interested in cross-boundary activities between practice, education and research, and these fertile yet difficult collaborative spaces for learning and development. She has developed "Open Writing" – a project devoted to the creation of a new research field and writing practice that explores the role of writing in academia and beyond.

Introduction

The inherent ambivalence of educational trajectories and the zone of proximal development with reduced potential

Luca Tateo

The process of education is always the arena of dramatic ideological changes in human collectives. Nowadays, a growing interest for the pathology of learning is signaling that there is a common understanding that attributes school failure or learning problems mainly to defective students. Cultural psychology, in the approach we promote at the Centre for Cultural Psychology in Aalborg, is sometimes blamed as too theoretical, and not as useful as other approaches for providing empirical models of application or intervention. I will argue that instead the perspective of cultural psychology has extremely direct consequences for the practice of psychology, if one really wants to accept its challenges and its critical reflections. This volume indeed explores the antinomies and tensions of the process of education with the powerful conceptual tools of cultural psychology. The aim is to draw a critical model able to account for the complexities and ambivalences of education, in which discomfort and tension, stress and fear seems to be part of the process of education, as well as self-confidence, passion and motivation.

What is not part of an acceptable process of education, instead, are the creation and maintenance of social and cultural inequalities. All the emphasis on special needs and learning problems overlooks one fundamental characteristic of education: the process of educating is at the same time constructive and disruptive. As with any other developmental process, it implies the emergence of new structures and a higher level of organization together with the demolition or reconfiguration of the previous state of the system. This is an overlooked aspect of teaching/learning processes and has profound implications for educational and developmental psychology. I will start by defining the philosophical and epistemological fundaments of my argumentation and will then illustrate the developmental dimension of educational processes in relation to cogenetic logic using the example of Vygotsky's *zone of proximal development* (Valsiner & van der Veer, 1993, 2014).

Philosophical fundaments: irreversibility

The first assumption is that living systems, as open systems, inevitably go through cycles of birth, life and death. It is what Valsiner calls the principle of irreversibility of time. In other words, ontogenetic development always takes place (Tateo, 2014, 2015; Tateo & Valsiner, 2015; Valsiner, 2001, 2014). What changes are the forms and times of development: some can be very short in time, as in the case of early childhood death (Figure 0.1).

Some other organisms can follow uncommon developmental paths. The famous scientist Steven Hawking, for instance, at the age of 21 was a brilliant young PhD student diagnosed with amyotrophic lateral sclerosis and given no more than 24

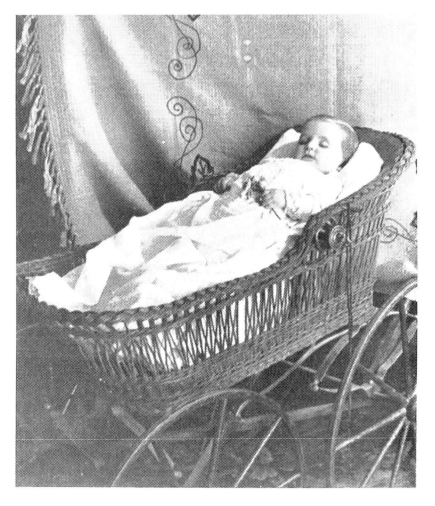

Figure 0.1 Phillips New Gallery, Main Street, near Sixth, Lafayette, Indiana. Deceased child in buggy. ca. 1900. 7V4 × 5V4 in. photograph on 9% × 6% in. cardboard mount

Quoted from Ruby, 1984, p. 211

months to live (White & Gribbin, 2002). However, he managed to follow a quite remarkable developmental path until the age of 87 (Figure 0.2).

We usually acknowledge that nature (or God, for some people) sets up an acceptable range of developmental pathways that lead to a temporary survival. Yet, what is undeniable is that living organisms trade with their surroundings (including other organisms, environmental parameters, etc.) in order to develop their ontogenetic cycle of birth, existence and death. If the system operates within a range of acceptable parameters, the life period will be longer and more prosperous. On the contrary, if the system falls outside those parameters, the ontogenetic cycle will fall short.

When it comes to human ontogenesis and sociogenesis, things become slightly different. Indeed, any human collective sets up a different window of

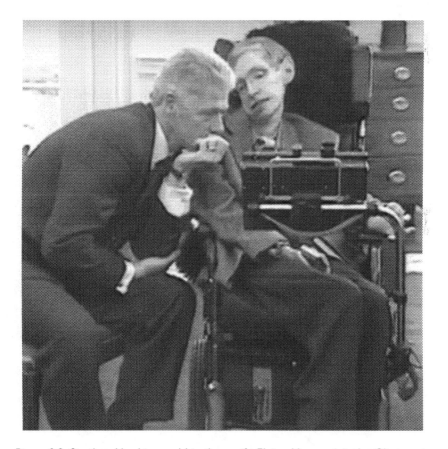

Figure 0.2 Stephen Hawking and his then-wife Elaine Mason visit the Clintons in the Oval Office. March 5, 1998

By White House Television Crew – Clinton Presidential Library. www.youtube.com/watch?v= 2UU8zM77twk, Public Domain, https://commons.wikimedia.org/w/index.php?curid=51560068

acceptability, a different set of parameters which are also based on a system of values. Thus, there are more or less historically situated "valued" or "acceptable" forms of development (Tateo & Valsiner, 2015). In a different time, for instance, a developmental trajectory as the one in Figure 0.2 would have been considered impossible, and the person would have had a much shorter life.

Human collectives sometimes value developmental trajectories that focus on the body strength or appearance (Figure 0.3). Some other collectives value other qualities, such as the ability to build social relationships or to produce goods.

Yet, even the most progressive human collectives create a hierarchy between the different potential forms of developments, promoting some and inhibiting others. In some historical cases, human collectives have decided to also set up the window of surviving that was a prerogative of nature and God, inventing eugenics. The idea of inevitability of development is somehow more general than the idea of adaptation. Indeed, adaptation supposes that the organism has to change in relation to its environment, while the notion of development includes that of adaptation but also that of exaptation (change preceding change) and of

Figure 0.3 Robert Cheeke at a natural bodybuilding competition at Clackamas High School in Oregon

By Mikkei at English Wikipedia, CC BY-SA 3.0, https://commons.wikimedia.org/w/index.php?curid=19497094

Introduction 5

mutuality (an organism can change the environmental parameters as form of development). Human collectives often choose the two latter forms rather than changing themselves.

In sum, the philosophical fundaments of a cultural psychology of developmental and educational trajectories can be defined as follows (Figure 0.4):

a   Living systems inevitably develop in a specific form and in trade with their surroundings;
b   Different forms of development have different durations;
c   Some forms of development fall within and some outside given parameters;
d   Human collectives establish value-laden parameters (windows of possibility) that are hierarchically organized and historically changeable;
e   Some forms of development can fall within and some outside the established parameters of the human collective;
f   Some forms of human development fall on the border of the window of possibilities;
g   Human agency turns ontogenetic development into teleogenetic development (Tateo, 2014, 2017)

Figure 0.4 illustrates four different hypothetical developmental trajectories of human development. As assumed in (a), development always takes place even though (b) they can have different durations. In Figure 0.4 we have trajectory "A", which can exemplify the life of the unfortunate child in Figure 0.1. A trajectory begins following the commonly accepted developmental parameters, and then suddenly stops before time. Indeed, the early death of a child is one of the events that we feel as extremely unnatural and unjust nowadays. However, this

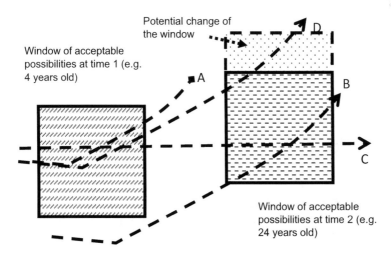

Figure 0.4 Windows of possibilities and development

was not necessarily the case a hundred years ago, when parameters of a healthy childhood were different, and the window of possibilities was narrower. Trajectory "B" describes the opposite trajectory: a person who in young age is outside the acceptable social parameters (e.g. a puny or unhealthy child, or one diagnosed with ADHD) but later develops as a healthy and fully functional (according to the social window of acceptable developmental parameters) adult.

Trajectory "C" hypothetically illustrates what in social sciences would be considered an average individual. Interestingly enough, this kind of trajectory is the most socially valued. In pediatrics, infant and children trajectories are constantly monitored according to their fitting percentiles. At school, average is still a more or less implicitly valued parameter; consider "excellence" and "special needs" are considered as marginal cases in the window of possibilities. Finally, as an adult, the "average" individual is the point of reference of social sciences.

The case of Steven Hawking nicely illustrates trajectory "D". A person, apparently conducting the ordinary life of a brilliant university student, is suddenly struck by an unexpected life event. At this bifurcation in life (Sato, Mori, & Valsiner, 2016), he acted in such a way that a potential trajectory of type "A" in Figure 0.4 turned out to be completely different. By the age of 24, Hawking had indeed already undertaken a developmental trajectory outside the currently acceptable parameters for a diagnosis of sclerosis in that specific human collective. His case describes the relevance of principle (g) and the role of human agency as teleogenetic force in the life of the open system. At the same time, through his trajectory, Hawking contributed to modify the existing window of possibilities, making familiar a form of development that was not previously considered acceptable (see the dashed part of the window in Figure 0.4).

The philosophical principles presented in (a) to (g) describe the ontological bases of my proposal for cultural psychology, yet we still need to discuss the forms through which we come to understand and conceptualize those principles in the everyday life. For this, we also need to develop some epistemological fundaments. What forms of knowing do we need in order to understand these forms of developing?

Epistemological fundaments: systemic cogenetic logic

What Giuseppina Marsico and I have called the "window of possibilities" in developmental trajectories follows a cogenetic logic (Marsico & Tateo, 2017; Tateo, 2016b). It means that when a human collective establishes the acceptable parameters of a window of possibilities, this immediately implies the emergence of its complementary negation and of the border between them (Tateo, 2016a). For instance, when a human collective establishes how a "healthy" person *should* develop, this immediately implies how a person *should not* develop. We often overlook the cogenetic nature of human systems and do not build suitable cogenetic concepts (Tateo, 2016b). Indeed, the cogenetic principle states that any time we create a distinction, this operation generates a systemic relationship between three elements ("A", "non-A" and the border). In the case of a window of possibilities, we can observe how human collective systems devoted to development (e.g. childcare, socialization, education institutions) always imply guidance about what is "proper" or "ought to be", what "should" happen at a given time and what is acceptable, but also what "should not", "ought not to be", is not "ordinary" or is "quasi-acceptable" or completely unacceptable (Figure 0.5). Very importantly, the system also implies the "border", that is, the way of producing the distinction and, at the same time, the requirements to change from one condition to the other.

Figure 0.5 shows the features of a cogenetic system (Tateo, 2016b) in the case of a window of possibilities in a given socially guided developmental trajectory. First of all, cogenetic logic tells us that once the idea of proper development is established, two other elements emerge. The forms of "non-proper development" imply all the forms which are not "ordinary". This means that "non-A" is not "non-development", but rather contains all the forms that do not correspond to the socially accepted parameters. The second important element that emerges is the border zone between "A" and "non-A". Each human collective produces forms of distinction-making (e.g. stages of development, developmental tasks, age distinctions, percentiles, gender roles, etc.) that regulate the relationship between "A" and "non-A". But these distinctions also set the rules for moving a single trajectory from "non-A" to "A". For instance, we establish developmental tasks (e.g. if a child learns to tie his shoes at a proper age) and checkpoints (e.g. school assessments) through which a developmental trajectory can become "proper".

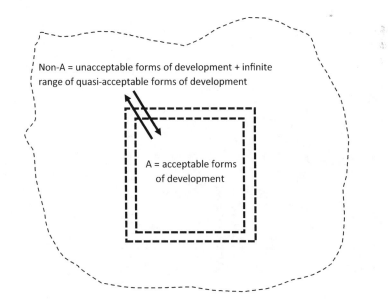

Figure 0.5 Cogenetic system in the case of socially guided development

8 Luca Tateo

Yet, most important of all, *any distinction also creates a relation*. What is "A" can be defined only in relation to what is "non-A". We usually treat these elements as mutually exclusive, but they are in fact *inclusively separated* (Valsiner, 2014). Thus, "A" and "non-A" constitute a new system, in which parts are at the same time distinguishable but interdependent. The production of a distinction defines what is contained in the "A" zone (Tateo, 2018a). In a school setting, for instance, the curriculum defines only what must be learned. Yet at the same time, the cogenetic principle implies that defining "A" creates an infinite number of "non-A", which form part of the system. So, by defining what must be learned, the curriculum also implicitly defines what must not be learned at school (e.g. inappropriate language or behavior). In addition, "non-A" includes an infinite number of "quasi-A", that is, elements that are not completely unacceptable but can be more or less acceptable depending on the contextual conditions. For instance, in many Western countries there is currently a debate over whether some content, such as art or religion, must be included in the curricula. These are not "inappropriate", of course, but have historically been considered "quasi-appropriate" or not completely appropriate for today's schooling. In the past, military training, including use of weapons, was an accepted part of the regular curriculum in some schools, while today it is considered "inappropriate". For the moment, it is perfectly integrated in the Chinese school system (Figure 0.6).

Figure 0.6 Photos of military training on a Shanghai school billboard
Photo by Tateo, 2017

The curriculum of Chinese public middle schools includes a week of military training for students. When you visit the school, you can easily find a billboard with a picture from the last training days. Between drawings of leaves and trees, pictures of kids marching and using firearms are proudly pinned up. Perhaps this will come back in the near future in the curricula of American or Russian schools as well.

The cogenetic principle is so important because it is both an empirical and an epistemological concept. It serves not only to understand phenomena but also to create the theoretical concepts we use to understand those phenomena. Indeed, we tend to create pseudo-oppositions of concepts based on implicit assumptions. Social sciences are full of such "themata" (Holton, 1975), such as nature/nurture, individualistic/collectivistic, normal/abnormal, quantitative/qualitative, cooperation/competition, etc. It would be instead more productive to elaborate cogenetic concepts (Tateo, 2016b). In this way, the theoretical concept we use would reveal a more nuanced view of phenomena in the field of development and education. The concept formulated through cogenetic logic would be able to account for both the observed phenomena and the non-observed, revealing the underlying process at stake (Tateo, 2016b). In the next section, I will discuss Vygotsky's *zone of proximal development* as an early example of a cogenetic concept (Vygotsky, 1997, 1998). I will try to apply both the philosophical and epistemological principles I have discussed to the concrete cases of educational settings in order to show how cultural psychology can directly illuminate psychological processes and suggest concrete forms of intervention.

Developmental fundaments: cogenetic and temporality

So far, I have only discussed the implications of the concepts of *window of possibilities* and *cogenetic logic*, mainly as synchronic sub-parts of a system (Figure 0.5). Yet, one of the fundamental elements of any developmental process is time (Tateo & Valsiner, 2015). No development is conceivable without introducing a temporal dimension, and this expands the notion of cogenetic logic into a *temporal* logic. In this way, the triadic system, viewed diachronically, becomes "A" + "not-yet-A" (or "no-longer-A") + the border, which becomes the temporal border at the present time (Figure 0.7).

In Figure 0.7, the window of possibilities is represented as an arrow, signifying irreversible time, and corresponds to the synchronic cogenetic forms of development. The present moment should not be understood as a duration, as it does not have its own extension; rather, it is codefined by the past and future forms (Tateo & Valsiner, 2015). The present should be understood as the border element of the triadic system. Thus, in the present state, a person can present forms that are within or outside the window of possibilities (as in Figure 0.5). But these forms are also in cogenetic relation with previous and potential future developmental trajectories. Actually, Figure 0.7 is not a linear process; it develops along at least

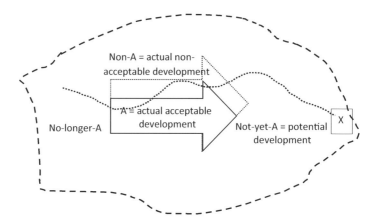

Figure 0.7 Cogenetic system in a diachronic perspective

three dimensions. Any personal developmental trajectory "X" can diachronically unfold in different ways, sometimes within and sometimes outside the window of possibilities. This zooming into a particular *tranche* must of course be contextualized in a different temporality of the personal life trajectory (Tateo & Valsiner, 2015).

In a model like Zittoun (2008), this is conceptualized in terms of ruptures and transitions during the life course, which are institutionally set, promoted or inhibited and guided by educational agencies. Another example is Valsiner's (1987) concept of development as organized by bounded indeterminacy. This is set by interpersonal constraint systems that, once internalized, orient the direction of the future development. Such constraint systems are constantly signified and reorganized by the co-constructive actions of both the developing person and her partners in particular situations. Valsiner (1987) identifies two different sub-parts of the bounded system: the Zone of Freedom of Movement (ZFM), which defines the set of possibilities that can be actualized at a given time, and the Zone of Promoted Actions (ZPA), which includes the set of possibilities, the actualization of which is promoted at the time by the persons involved in the interaction. The trajectory "X" in Figure 0.7, according to Valsiner (1987), would thus be the vector resulting from the different influences of socially constructed opportunities and constraints over time. This concept is very close to the idea of window of possibilities, though the latter also focuses on the process of co-definition of the triadic system – in which "A" and "non-A" maintain each other in a state of existence and constructive tension – and the rules of transition between the different zones of the cogenetic areas (Marsico & Tateo, 2017). Both Valsiner (1987) and Zittoun (2006, 2008) find their inspiration in the concept of *zone of proximal development* (from Russian: *zona blizhaishego razvitia*, ZBR) (Valsiner & van der Veer, 1993, 2014; Vygotsky, 1998). The theoretical tenet of Vygotsky's ZBR[1] is based on the dialectical process of development over time. What is not yet observable, potential and fully developed is as important as what is already observable or actual. Vygotsky's criticism of the approaches to development based on the observation of the actual state could be reformulated (using my terminology) in terms of monological concepts (Tateo, 2016b). The kind of "symptomatic diagnostics based on the study of symptom complexes of child development" (Vygotsky, 1998, p. 204) indeed focuses only on the "A" part of the window of possibilities and leads to a normative view of development "depending only on establishing external traits" (Vygotsky, 1998, p. 204) and socially set standards. A cogenetic approach would instead aim "to elucidate the given state of development characterized from the aspect of both the finished ['A' type] and the unfinished ['non-A' or 'quasi-A' type] processes" (Vygotsky, 1998, p. 204). In addition, the cogenetic nature of ZBR is evident in the idea of sociogenesis of mental functions. Development takes place in the boundary space between a subject-system ("A") and her social others ("non-A") in the shape of neoformations "of personality and its activity" (Vygotsky, 1998, p. 190), which can be considered border zones and subject to temporal modification, creation and disappearance. It is also important to note that in the person/other relation, according to Vygotsky (1997), the dynamic tension is between the sociogenesis of activities and the purposefulness of the person's actions. The examples of developmental trajectories above show how the co-constructive dialogue between socially guided and personally striven for development can lead to complex and more or less socially accepted outcomes.

This further cogenetic aspect of ZBR emerges with more clarity during the periods of crisis that characterize development at different ages (Valsiner & van der Veer, 1993). Development, far from being a linear, cumulative process, is a dynamic movement between the actual state ("A") and the not-yet ("non-A") established neoformation. The border moves in time in a process of co-definition between what is created and what is demolished: what at a certain time becomes the new state (from "not-yet-A" to "A") and what is deconstructed (from "A" to "no-longer-A").

> Progressive development of the child's personality, the continuous construction of the new, which had been so prominent in all stable ages, is seemingly attenuated or temporarily suspended. Processes of dying off and closure, the disintegration and breakdown of what had been formed at preceding stages and distinguished the child of a given age move to the forefront. During the critical periods, the child does not so much acquire as he loses some of what he had acquired earlier. The onset of these age levels is not marked by the appearance of new interests of the child, of new aspirations, new types of activity, new forms of internal life.
>
> (Vygotsky, 1998, p. 192)

Finally, the third cogenetic aspect of ZBR is identified by Valsiner and van der Veer (1993) in the idea that psychological processes develop along central/adjunct dialectic lines of development.

> The same psychological function – speech, for instance – may play an adjunct role in development in infancy, become central in early childhood, and again become adjunct in the following age periods. The actual dialectical synthesis at crisis periods leads to the reorganization of the structure of central and adjunct psychological functions in ways that give rise to novel functions on the basis of loss and reorganization of the previous ones.
>
> (Valsiner & van der Veer, 1993, p. 41)

Taking into account educational activities, one can see how the central/adjunct dialectic can be framed by socially oriented ranges of acceptability. The window of possibilities, indeed, provides guidance about the relative central or peripheral value of psychological functions by setting, for instance, the temporal lines of development of language use.

As Valsiner and van der Veer (1993) remark, the epistemological power of ZBR lies in the fact that it allows not only what is "visible" but also what is "non-visible" and would potentially never be observable to be conceptualized and included in the teaching/learning work. Once we observe cognitive development, reached for instance with the support of a more expert adult, we are already observing the "actual" development, and there is no way to know whether the developmental trajectory of that specific person would have been different or similar in the case of another partner. This cannot be observed empirically, as one cannot make a child unlearn language and then teach it again under different conditions. In other words, what becomes fundamental is the moment of "preparation" for qualitative developmental movements. In a more recent development of the idea, Valsiner and van der Veer (2014) have further elaborated their ideas within the context of developmental sciences. Given the theoretical paradox of the impossibility of both retrospective and predictive understanding of personal development, "the phenomena of *emergence*, *becoming* and *transformation* become the objects of investigation in developmental science" (Valsiner & van der Veer, 2014, p. 151, original italics).

In the context of educational intervention (Figure 0.8), the crucial space–time for observing educational intervention is exactly in the transition phase, when neoformations begin to emerge; some of them will be promoted by the intervention while others will be inhibited.

According to Valsiner and van der Veer (2014), "psychology is blind to the study of development by eliminating developmental phenomena at the outset – through treating the fuzzy 'borders zones' between A and B as an 'error'" (p. 152). Educational approaches based on meta-cognitive and reflexive skills – such as visible learning (Hattie, 2008), problem-based learning (Dolmans, Loyens, Marcq, & Gijbels, 2016) or self-regulated learning (Zimmerman & Schunk, 2013) – must deal with the paradox of ZBR: once a psychological function is

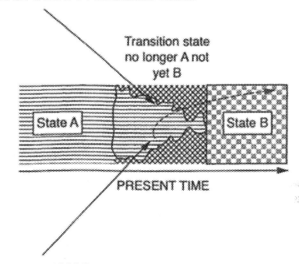

Figure 0.8 The locus of development in education
Valsiner & van der Veer, 2014, p. 152

consciously mastered by the student, it is already out of the transitional zone. Of course, the new level of development allows the student to use the mastered function to engage in more complex problems, yet assessment of the new skill still takes place retrospectively.

In addition, any educational intervention is meant for a non-yet existing child (a child-to-be), assuming that the real child *must* change in the future as result of the pedagogical action (Figure 0.9).

The intervention is focused on what the child *should be* (promoting some features) but at the same time defines what the child *should not be* (inhibiting other developmental features). Vygotsky reminds us that the intervention is useless if it only takes into account observable features. Indeed, what is relevant is the promotion or inhibition of the preparatory moment before the neoformations become visible. For instance, if at a given age a child *manifests* some special inclination towards an activity (e.g. music or math), she will be oriented towards a school trajectory, on the basis of socially valued criteria, that will promote and reinforce this already visible tendency; in the aftermath, it is impossible to know whether this choice inhibited some other potentialities that were, at the given moment, not yet observable (e.g. drawing or sports).

Intervention occurs within the acceptable range of potential developmental trajectories established by the system of values and the contextual conditions in a specific community

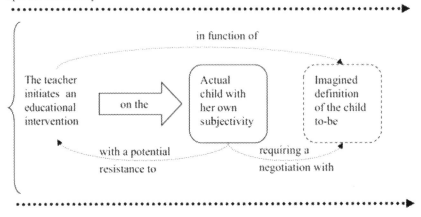

Figure 0.9 Educational intervention in function of an imagined child
Tateo, 2018b, p. 161

Cogenetic logic at school: a thought experiment

We can now try to take a step further by integrating the idea of window of possibilities and the temporal dimension of the ZBR. Let's perform a little thought experiment and imagine the educational trajectories of two children in a public school of a random country. According to the above-mentioned principles, the educational institution will set up a window of possibilities framing acceptable, unacceptable and quasi-acceptable developmental trajectories. For instance, according to cogenetic logic (Tateo, 2016b), the educational system will define the system of "A" + "non-A" + the border; this will emerge together, for instance, in:

- learning goals at a given age + non-learning goals + the way to assess them;
- appropriate behavior in class + non-appropriate behavior + the rules for observing it (when, how frequently, with whom, etc.);
- independence of the child + non-independence of the child + limits of the independence;
- playtime + non-playtime + temporal border of playtime.

The triads can be observed starting with any of the three elements. For instance, the way of assessing also makes the appropriate or non-appropriate conduct emerge. On the other hand, if the educational system sets some learning goals, this will also define the way of observing them. In addition, each of the triads can be further understood as a potential new border. Very often in educational practices, the triads produce ambivalent messages for the students (Tateo, 2018b), who need to negotiate and navigate these ambivalences. Messages like "be independent" but "always behave" or "enjoy studying" but "study time is different from play time" convey contradictory ideas.

Let's try to imagine that student "Y" is a girl from a middle-class family of a given country and student "X" is the daughter of a migrant family from a different country (see Figure 0.10). For both of them, the school sets up learning, developmental and social goals. The window of possibilities will frame the range of acceptable developmental trajectories for what they *should* or *should not* become in the future. For instance, they shall both learn the use of some linguistic features, but also forget some ways in which they "ought not" to use language – some forms of independent behavior but also some forms of non-independent or not-too-much independent conduct.

Student "Y" will probably have some ups and downs at school, but in the end, these are perfectly acceptable within the window of possibilities. "Y" will be what the school calls an "average" student: the reference of any educational institution. Student "X" could have a different trajectory. As her family migrated to a "developed" country from a "less developed" one, she will probably be subject to more attention, maybe involved in activities of school "inclusion". Also, for her, the school sets up what *ought to be* and what *ought not to be* to do with language. She will be encouraged, for instance, to speak the language of the host country, because early integration is important and her actual state of (native) language development is not appropriate to the acceptable range. The teaching/learning activities will then be focused on promoting some linguistic uses, and inhibiting

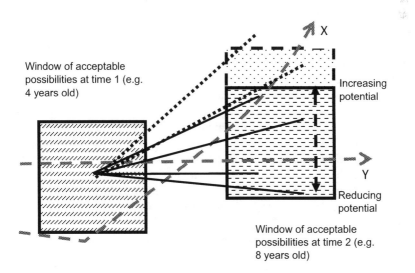

Figure 0.10 Windows of possibilities in the zone of proximal development

some others (like the use of her mother tongue). In terms of developmental zone, her bilingual potentialities are reduced by constraints, which are not strictly pedagogical but rather political. The use of a language at school is indeed a matter of "inclusion", in the sense that if you do not speak the dominant language, you will be "not included". The ambivalent message here is "we want to include you" but "leave your native culture at home". Thus, any form of resistance (Figure 0.9) by student "X" will be interpreted as non-compliance, a non-developmental zone, by the institution, rather than a potential further developmental trajectory (Figure 0.10) outside the window of possibilities. Indeed, if the school did not promote the monolingual view, which sees inclusion as a monodirectional acquisition of the dominant language (*ZBR with reduced potential*), it would consider the possibility of making the second language of student "Y" a source of further development (*ZBR with increasing potential*). The restriction of the use of a single language at school is indeed only a function of the narcissistic cultivation of national identity by the educational institution rather than a real promotion of learning. In developmental terms, it represents a reduction of potential of the ZBR (continuous triangle in Figure 0.10) to fit an "average" understanding of educational trajectory.

In the continuation of our thought experiment, let's imagine that the presence of student "X", expert in a different language, would become an opportunity for development. Instead of merely "teaching" the dominant language to student "Y", the school could decide to "learn" the second language and give the opportunity also to student "X" to learn it. Thus, both "X" and "Y" students would benefit from working "beyond" their current state of development. They could learn two languages instead of one and expand their understanding of the world, and their educational trajectories would contribute to widening the window of opportunities provided by the school (dotted triangle in Figure 0.10). This would represent an increase in the potential of ZBR. We should seriously consider whether any educational intervention, aimed for instance at reducing stress and making learning "smoother", does not actually create a ZBR with reduced potential. The good news is that this kind of educational practice exists (Figure 0.11).

The Castle Bridge School,[2] directed by Julie Zuckerman, is located in Washington Heights, New York, in the middle of multicultural neighborhood with a relevant Latino presence (Au, 2017). The whole curriculum is bilingual, in the sense that Castle Bridge offers instruction in English and Spanish as languages of equal status. Children of Latin ancestry, especially Dominican, share classes with children of African-American and white background. Teachers alternate between speaking English to their students half the time and speaking Spanish, with the goal of having children reading, writing and speaking fluently in both languages. When I visited the school in 2017 (Figure 0.11), I was impressed by the atmosphere of care and joy and by the fluidity with which everything was experienced by the children. The richness of the activities and of the school environment provided an enormously powerful context for developing *ZBR with increasing potential*. The bad news is that these are still *experiments* and are not widespread. Children are perfectly aware of their differences and their cultural identities, but thanks to the absence of linguistic dominance, they are able to make sense of

Figure 0.11 The door of a classroom at Castle Bridge School, New York
Photo by Tateo, 2017

those differences as resources for dialogue and tools for learning rather than for perpetuating social inequalities.

Educational dilemmas worldwide

The main limit of this book is its heterogeneity. The reader will find a number of different contexts – countries, continents, schools, approaches to cultural psychology; a number of different approaches – from phenomenology to social constructivism, from psychoanalysis to cultural–historical; different ages – from preschool to university, and issue discussed – discomforts, stress, abuse, creativity, transitions, among others. It is indeed a big problem in current psychology, which is oriented toward consistent, ready-made and omni-comprehensive solutions. We firmly believe, however, that education is a heterogeneous arena, in which there are no solutions good for everyone everywhere. So, the main virtue of this book is its heterogeneity. We try to create a polyphony – though not always harmonic – that represents the polyphony of education, providing a different angle from the current trend towards a monological and standardizing view. This volume provides different experiences of the study of the tension between construction and disruption in the process of education as it has been observed in Europe, America and Asia. The commodification of education and the instrumental dimension of learning is gaining ideological relevance worldwide, generating processes that sometimes overlook the real protagonists of the process of education, that is, the student and the network that supports her learning, including teachers, parents and peers. On the one hand, the focus on assessment and competition affects the life of the emerging generations, creating psychological discomfort, instead of cultivating passion, motivation and commitment (Valsiner, Lutsenko, & Antoniouk, 2018). This is clearly described in the chapters of this volume at all levels of education, from kindergarten to university. On the other hand, without effort and labor there is no learning. Education takes place outside the comfort zone of the actual level of development in the ZBR where the person is confronted with new difficulties and new challenges. The risk is that we support a *ZBR with reduced potential* for the sake of protecting an imagined child.

The window of possibilities produces a number of dilemmatic situations that the authors of the book have explored worldwide, including changes and challenges in the process of education. The phenomena of educational discomfort and resilience assumes many facets in several contexts (Denmark, Brazil, Canada, USA, Japan and Italy), including amazing ways of coping with them.

Chapters 1 and 2 analyze the contemporary crisis of education. Of course, depending on the perspective one takes, the crisis is at our backs, as the neoliberalist ideology has introduced a healthy competition that will improve the commodity of education as any other. It will identify the weak parts of the system and find an accountable solution to allocate economic resources to only the profitable schools. If you take a different perspective, like Matusov Marjanovic-Shane or Szulevicz, Kromann Kure and Olesen Løkken does in their respective chapters, the picture is quite different.

In Chapters 3–10, we try to provide an excursus across different cultural contexts and different kinds of education, from basic to higher. There is no cross-cultural comparison, just the attempt to provide a critical and articulated gaze on the many forms of education in different human communities. For instance, it seems paradoxical that one can detect signs of stress even in early-age pupils, or that university student must be led by the hand like kids through academic life. It sounds worrisome to observe aggressive and oppressive practices in educational contexts. It is still a relief to observe the many resources teacher and learners can use to cope with difficulties. The overview is an attempt to create a different picture, from preschool to the transition between education and the job market. The ultimate goal of this book is to show how all these elements exist side by side as inherent contradictions in any educational system.

Conclusion

I have discussed the main theoretical focus of this book, which is how development can be conceptualized as a process that inevitably takes place in open systems. Development can come to an end only if the system becomes *food or mud*, that is, if the system is terminated by inclusion into another system or if it exhausts its trade with its surroundings. In human collectives, different forms of development are hierarchically organized according to their social value. Some developmental trajectories are more acceptable than others. However, a person finds her own trajectory by negotiating with social suggestions about her future condition (window of possibilities).

My second point is that the window of possible developmental trajectories follows a cogenetic logic. Anytime the human collective establishes an acceptable condition, it immediately evokes the "non-acceptable", the way to distinguish these and the conditions for transition. The triadic system "A" + "non-A" + border develops both synchronically as logic and diachronically as process.

I then took Vygotsky's zone of proximal development as an example of a theoretical concept that responds to the conditions of cogenetic logic. Finally, I tried to develop a thought experiment in which the zone of proximal development, the window of possibilities and cogenetic logic can be combined to understand a concrete educational trajectory and to foresee the possible corrections to its limitations.

Going through the chapters, the reader will hopefully find more and better organized theoretical suggestions and will also become aware of the fact that teaching/learning is neither a linear process nor cumulative progress. We can learn disruptive things; we can even "unlearn" to be human. At the same time, we receive suggestions about what is worth learning and what is not, how we should become and how we should not. Teaching/learning can be as destructive as it is constructive. This is a fundamental dilemma of which we should be aware. Dilemmas have no definite solution; they are, rather, a cultural tool that human collectives use to develop new forms of systemic organization.

Notes

1 I will use the abbreviation ZBR, from the Russian original, as suggested by Valsiner and van der Veer (1993), to distinguish it from the later theoretical developments.

2 A special thanks goes to Angela Di Giulio, a great friend and colleague, who introduced me to this wonderful school where she is teaching. She gave me the opportunity to visit the school and meet the teachers, the students and the principal.

References

Au, W. (2017). What the resistance to high-stakes testing can teach us about urban classrooms. In G. Sirrakos & C. Emdin (Eds.), *Between the world and the urban classroom* (pp. 35–42). Rotterdam: Sense Publishers.

Dolmans, D. H., Loyens, S. M., Marcq, H., & Gijbels, D. (2016). Deep and surface learning in problem-based learning: A review of the literature. *Advances in Health Sciences Education, 21*(5), 1087–1112.

Hattie, J. (2008). *Visible learning: A synthesis of over 800 meta-analyses relating to achievement.* London: Routledge.

Holton, G. (1975). On the role of themata in scientific thought. *Science, 188*(4186), 328–334.

Marsico, G., & Tateo, L. (2017). Borders, tensegrity and development in dialogue. *Integrative Psychological and Behavioral Science, 51*(4), 536–556. doi:10.1007/s12124-017-9398-2

Ruby, J. (1984). Post-mortem portraiture in America. *History of Photography, 8*(3), 201–222. doi:10.1080/03087298.1984.10442223

Sato, T., Mori, N., & Valsiner, J. (Eds.) (2016). *Making of the future: The trajectory equifinality approach in cultural psychology.* Charlotte, NC: Information Age Publishing.

Tateo, L. (2014). Beyond the self and the environment: The psychological horizon. In K. R. Cabell & J. Valsiner (Eds.), *The catalyzing mind. Beyond models of causality. Series: Annals of theoretical psychology* (Vol. 11, pp. 223–237). Springer Verlag.

Tateo, L. (2015). Continuity and discontinuity of the educational context. In G. Marsico, M. V. Dazzani, M. Ristum, & A. C. Bastos (Eds.), *Educational contexts and borders through a cultural lens: Looking inside. viewing outside* (pp. 29–54). New York: Springer.

Tateo, L. (2016a). What imagination can teach us about higher mental functions. In J. Valsiner, G. Marsico, N. Chaudhary, T. Sato & V. Dazzani (Eds.), *Psychology as the science of human being: The Yokohama manifesto* (Vol. Part II, pp. 149–164). New York: Springer (*Annals of Theoretical Psychology*, Vol. 13). doi:10.1007/978-3-319-21094-0_9

Tateo, L. (2016b). Toward a cogenetic cultural psychology. *Culture & Psychology, 22*(3), 433–447. doi:10.1177/1354067X16645297

Tateo, L. (2017). Tensegrity as existential condition: The inherent ambivalence of development. In I. Albert, E. Abbey, & J. Valsiner (Eds.), *Trans-generational family relations* (pp. 3–20). Charlotte, NC: Information Age Publishing.

Tateo, L. (2018a). Affective semiosis and affective logic. *New Ideas in Psychology, 48C,* 1–11. doi:: 10.1016/j.newideapsych.2017.08.002.

Tateo, L. (2018b). Ideology of success and the dilemma of education today. In A. C. Joerchel & G. Benetka (Eds.), *Memories of Gustav Ichheiser* (pp. 157–164). Cham: Springer. doi:10.1007/978-3-319-72508-6_9

Tateo, L., & Valsiner, J. (2015). Time breath of psychological theories: A meta-theoretical focus. *Review of General Psychology, 19*(3): 357–364.

Valsiner, J. (1987). *Culture and the development of children's action.* Chichester: Wiley.

Valsiner, J. (2001). *Comparative study of human cultural development*. Madrid: Fund Infancia y Aprendizaje.

Valsiner, J. (2014). *An invitation to cultural psychology*. London: Sage.

Valsiner, J., Lutsenko, A., & Antoniouk, A. (Eds.) (2018). *Sustainable futures for higher education: The making of knowledge makers*. Cham: Springer.

Valsiner, J., & van der Veer, R. (1993). The encoding of distance: The concept of the 'zone of proximal development' and its interpretations. In R. R. Cocking & K. A. Renninger (Eds.), *The development and meaning of psychological distance* (pp. 35–62). Hillsdale, NJ: Lawrence Erlbaum Associates.

Valsiner, J., & van der Veer, R. (2014). Encountering the border: Vygotsky's zona blizaishego razvitya and its implications for theory of development. In A. Yasnitsky, R. van der Veer, & M. Ferrari (Eds.), *The Cambridge handbook of cultural-historical psychology* (pp. 148–173). Cambridge: Cambridge University Press.

Vygotsky, L. S. (1997). *The collected works of LS Vygotsky, Vol. 4: The history of the development of higher mental functions*. Ed. and Trans. R. W. Rieber & M. J. Hall. New York: Plenum Press.

Vygotsky, L. S. (1998). *The collected works of LS Vygotsky, Vol. 5: Child psychology*. Ed. and Trans. R. W. Rieber & M. J. Hall. New York: Plenum Press.

White, M., & Gribbin, J. (2002). *Stephen Hawking: A life in science*. Washington, DC: Joseph Henry Press.

Zimmerman, B. J., & Schunk, D. H. (Eds.) (2013). *Self-Regulated learning and academic achievement: Theoretical perspectives*. New York: Routledge.

Zittoun, T. (2006). *Transitions: Symbolic resources in development*. Charlotte, NC: Information Age Publishing.

Zittoun, T. (2008). Learning through transitions: The role of institutions. *European Journal of Psychology of Education, 23*(2), 165–181.

Chapter 1

Intrinsic education and its discontents

Eugene Matusov and Ana Marjanovic-Shane

Introduction

Recently, in one of my (the first author) classes for preservice teachers, my students and I discussed diverse approaches to arranging classroom life, which my students initially interpreted as "classroom management." Very quickly, our discussion started revolving around the notions of punishment and rewards. What is more effective? Pure punishment? Pure rewards? Or some kind of combination of both? What kind of punishment is more effective? What kinds of rewards are more effective? Also, manipulative and non-manipulative organizational educational techniques were introduced in our discussion. For example, asking students to write something – it does not matter what – pulls them away from activities the teacher deems undesirable, without any use of punishments or rewards. This pedagogical manipulation seems to be based on affordances of dictation. Designing seating arrangements provides different psychological and social affordances: whether it is easier or more difficult for the students to get involved in discussions, collaboration on projects, or listening to a teacher. Finally, we labeled this approach to arrangement of classroom life as "classroom management" and focused on its purposes. The students listed the following purposes of classroom management: "keeping students on task," "keeping control," "controlling students' attention," "preventing acting out," and "keeping children safe."

I then put to my students that in all these goals it is the teacher (or school administration, or even the entire society) who defines what is good for the students and what is bad. The teacher defines unilaterally what is the task for the students and what is not; what is worthy for them to pay attention and what is not; what is learning and what is not; what is safe and what is not; what they must do and what they must not; and so on. As one of my students formulated, "the main goal of classroom management is to conform the students to the teacher's expectations." I formulated it slightly differently: "the main goal of classroom management is to make students do what the teacher wants them to do." I also introduced the psychological theory of behaviorism with its primary goal of controlling and predicting behavior through a smart design of punishment and rewards, and their schedule.

My students got very excited about learning more about behaviorism when I abruptly introduced a new theme – alternative ideas – to them. I told them that some educators criticized classroom management not because it is inefficient, but because it is efficient! These educators disagree that the primary goal of education in a democratic society should be to make students obedient to the authority's (teacher's) orders. Thus, when we discussed their own examples and cases of classroom management, they focused on the notion of student "responsibility." "Responsibility," in my students' view, meant children's conformity to the teacher's orders and expectations. I challenged this notion by claiming that true responsibility must start with children's own decision making about what is good and what is bad. However, "classroom management" does not involve children in decision making. As an illustrative example, I told my students that when fascism and Nazism came to power in Europe, some psychologists and educators became concerned that children learned a disposition to fascism in school through classroom management techniques of unconditional obedience. Thus, famous psychologist Kurt Lewin, a German Jewish immigrant from Nazi Germany to the USA, did his famous study of "three teaching styles" to explore this phenomena in 1939 (Lewin, Lippitt, & White, 1939).

I showed them a fragment from Lewin's video (Lewin, Lippitt, & White, 1953/1939), which portrayed three experimental situations of clubs of 10-year-old boys in a summer camp with an adult, using authoritarian, democratic and laissez-faire styles of arranging and guiding the clubs. Each club was involved in carpeting craft activities. In each situation, a teacher left the children alone at some point. After watching the fragments, I asked my students to predict which group finished the project quicker, which produced better quality work, which group generated more aggression and chaos when the teacher left, which group demonstrated more creativity. After the student's guesses and discussion of the reasons of their guesses, I reported Lewin's research results about these inquiries. The students started to realize that different "teaching styles" generated their own systems of values and, thus, their own "efficiencies." The questions for them shifted from how to control their future students more effectively to what value system is more desirable for them and their future students, education-wise. I asked my students which one of these approaches they liked more. All but one student preferred the democratic approach. The student who preferred the authoritarian approach said that she needed certainty based on control because she would become very anxious in her life. The students who preferred the more democratic approach provided reasons for their preference, such as "making choices," "creativity," and "quality of work." One of these students mentioned that it is very difficult to implement a democratic approach in modern classrooms because teachers are required to achieve educational standards, and for that, one needs an authoritarian approach. She elaborated that in a democratic approach, students must engage in judgment and decision making about what they should study and why. With sadness, she said that it is often impossible in a "real" classroom.

Indeed, the mainstream school not only prevents students from engaging in, developing, and utilizing their own judgments but also puts teachers in the position of technicians, executing somebody else's decisions, goals, and values. The technician inquiry of "how" prevails over the professional inquiry of "why" for the teachers. Mainstream schools rob the teachers of professionalism, which is based on developing authorial, practice-rooted judgments. In its own terms, technological pedagogies demand authoritarian approaches, i.e., "classroom management," to classroom life. Democratic and communal decision making and governance become very difficult under the regime of technological pedagogies of "covering curriculum" and "delivering educational standards."

In this chapter, we discuss and analyze impossibilities of genuine intrinsic education on a mass scale in our current society. We define genuine intrinsic education as having a goal in itself, as basic human craving for reflective self-actualization, self-transcendence, and self-realization. In contrast, we define mainstream institutionalized education, both conventional and some innovative, as instrumental, as a servant to other practices and societal spheres like economy, democracy, patriotism, nationalism, societal cohesion, social mobility, and so on. Conventional institutionalized education is often aimed at students' arrival at curricular endpoints – knowledge, skills, attitudes, values – preset by the teacher and society (Matusov, 2009). However, we argue that genuine education is an inherent and existential human need and right, involving human self-realization, self-actualization, and self-inspiration (Greenberg, 1992). We found two bases for intrinsic education: 1) creative authorship and 2) critical authorship. Both involve promoting students' authorial agency and voices. Creative authorship is primarily interested in production of new culture. Meanwhile, critical authorship is primarily interested in deconstruction of ready-made culture in a critical dialogue. We abstracted six types of academic freedom that support both kinds of intrinsic education: curricular, instructional, participatory, valuative, ecological, and role-based. These academic freedoms of the students are currently violated almost in all educational institutions. In our view, this is because current society is survival- and necessity-oriented and not leisure-based (Arendt, 1958). Modern societal and mainstream institutional conditions distract students and teachers from their focus on intrinsic education and their fundamental existential needs. Thus, these conditions produce discontent and a feeling of lifelessness in the participants. "They suck life out of you," commented a student, who moved from an innovative middle school that promoted a love of learning to a conventional high school that promoted credentials, about his new conventional school (DePalma, Matusov, & Smith, 2009, p. 945). However, changes in technology and economy may create new societal conditions for genuine education in the future, orienting the society on authorial agency and leisure (Markoff, 2016). We will ground our critical discussion in our pedagogical experimentation with genuine education.

Intrinsic vs. instrumental education

Traditionally, the purpose of education, and especially institutionalized education, has been defined instrumentally. The primary instrumental goal of education is for education to serve the economy, to prepare students for current and future jobs (Livingstone, 2009). Thus, sociologist and historian of education David

Labaree (1997) abstracted three major publicly announced purposes of education. He called the first purpose "social efficiency," which is to reproduce society economically and promote even more economic advancement. The second purpose of education, as defined by Labaree, is "social mobility," which is to ensure students will have better, or at least the same, economic and social life as their parents. This instrumental goal of education is the basis of educational credentialism (Hoskins & Barker, 2014). These educational credentials will open gates for students to diverse opportunities: educational, jobs, and so on. Finally, Labaree's third main purpose of education is "democratic participation." This instrumental goal of education is for education to serve to promote skillful participation in in a democratic society (Dewey, 1966).

In our view, these three publicly announced instrumental goals of education are not exhaustive. There are other instrumental goals of education that have circulated in public discourse, such as patriotism (Straughn & Andriot, 2011); nationalism (Bénéï, 2007); moral character; social cohesion (Babacan, 2007); social justice (Cochran-Smith, 2010); elimination of poverty (Ribich, 1968); political, cultural, and religious tolerance (Wain, 1996); and so on.

> Education should be a means to empower children and adults alike to become active participants in the transformation of their societies. Learning should also focus on the values, attitudes and behaviors which enable individuals to learn to live together in a world characterized by diversity and pluralism.
> (UNESCO, 2017, March)

The primary purpose of instrumental education is to make all students predictably arrive at preset curricular endpoints (i.e., important knowledge, skills, attitudes, dispositions, values) by the end of the educational term (e.g., lesson, semester, school year, school level). Besides these primary instrumental purposes, there are secondary instrumental purposes that may have little to nothing to do with education per se (except, maybe, creating conditions for education). These secondary instrumental purposes of schooling may include: babysitting, preventing child labor, preventing juvenile delinquency, promoting universal immunization, providing food for children from poor families, promoting desegregation, exposing children to diversity, providing security for children, and so on. These are secondary reasons why students must attend school.

Although in conflict with intrinsic education, instrumental purposes of education can be legitimate (Dumitru, 2018, in press). However, in our view, there is a problem when instrumentality is either the only or the predominant goal of education as opposed to intrinsic purposes of education. An intrinsic purpose of education is rooted in education itself. "I want education because I enjoy education, because education is part of my life, because without education my life is not fulfilled." My colleagues and I (the first author) (Matusov, Baker, Fan, Choi, & Hampel, 2017) conducted the following study of intrinsic education based on Isaac Asimov's novella *Profession* (Asimov, 1959). Asimov envisioned a future society in which education is replaced by direct modification of the brain so that people can acquire necessary knowledge, skills, dispositions, and attitudes almost instantaneously without any effort by reprogramming the brain according to preset templates. This procedure has two phases. First, experts examine a young child's brain for predispositions to certain professions, and then when the child becomes a late teenager, his/her brain is transformed accordingly – a newly certified professional emerges. However, for the main character of the novella, who wanted to be a space-craft pilot, things did not work well. In phase one, the experts discovered that, for some reason, his brain could not be molded into any profession. Instead, the teenage boy was placed in the custody of certified psychologists at a special orphanage for children like him, surrounded by books. Reading books was useless, since it would take a lot of time to learn from books to become a competent professional. After several crises, the boy persevered in studying though the books and finally understood that, instead of having a disability, he belonged to a hidden elite group who designed and controlled the entire society. The inventors are those who enjoy learning for the sake of learning.

Our study ignores Asimov's story's elitism and, instead, focuses on the phenomenon of "learning for the sake of learning." We interviewed diverse participants from three different countries, asking about an imaginary scenario of a "magic learning pill." Taking the "magic learning pill" would allow someone to instantaneously acquire desired knowledge and skills. The quality of the knowledge and skills acquired through the magic pill and the best learning would be the same. The participants were asked about their important past learning experiences in and out of school and which of these learning experiences they would replace by taking a magic learning pill and which they would not. Based on the responses, my colleagues and I interpreted that when the participants wanted to take a magic learning pill, their learning was instrumental, and when they did not want to take the pill, their learning was "ontological" (i.e., intrinsic). According to our findings, almost all research participants have some important learning experiences for which they would take a magic learning pill and some for which they would not. As Matusov and colleagues describe, non-instrumental, intrinsic education is education that constitutes the participants' life and, thus, its shortening is undesirable for its participants. In this education, the process is more important than its outcomes (rather, the emerging outcomes are subordinated to the process):

> [Take MLP?][1] No, [I would not take the MLP,] because the process is important. . . . I feel like I would be losing something, because the actual learning of something is interesting. . . . Well the gradual interaction with some material, when you think about it every day, and start to view it differently. Immediately, now you don't know it, now you don't, you go through these stages and understand it completely differently, like something else. And moreover, when you're immediately there, you don't have the feeling that the material is something social, with that you lose some of the color, even some of the lines. Do you understand? So, when initially English was something foreign to me,

it's important, because now I hear it through someone else's ear, as well as with my own. Maybe with mine not as well, as the carriers, but on the other hand, a lot better with that of the other. It becomes kind of like a stereo effect.
(Sasha, Russia, adult, BS) (Matusov et al., 2017, p. 8)

In contrast to instrumental education, which serves other spheres of practice (e.g., economy, nation building, upward social mobility, mastery of a desired practice), ontological education is an end in itself (Dumitru, 2018, in press). It is education for education's sake. Using Aristotle's terminology, we could say that education is "the final cause," irreducible to any other cause. That is why intrinsic education is a basic human right, without which life is incomplete. Intrinsic education constitutes life itself – that is why it is ontological. The primary outcome is to be an important part of the person's life, valued by the person him/herself. Ontological education is eventful, existential, experiential, relational, and dialogic. It is based on an authorial meaning-making process (Matusov, 2009).

Intrinsic ontological education is always and primarily personal business, rather than societal. "Education is the discovery and drawing out of the best that is in a person" (de Grazia, 1962, pp. 360–361). Although intrinsic education may have important instrumental implications and outcomes, they are secondary to its intrinsic value for the participant. Intrinsic education may involve some instrumental education – technological and/or authorial – but these aspects are subordinated to the existential values of intrinsic education. For example Sasha, a Russian participant in our research, experienced learning English as intrinsic education. He benefited instrumentally from this education by being able to read English literature and communicate with English-speaking people. However, these instrumental benefits did not outweigh the existential value of the process of learning English for him.

In contrast to instrumental education, in intrinsic education, curriculum cannot be preset but rather emerges through dramatic events constituting the participant's life. This emerging curriculum is a never-ending process, as it essentially a relationship between past educational experiences and the present circumstances. It is the participants – and not the teachers, test designers, curriculum experts, politicians, the state, the whole society – who are the final authority for defining the value of their educational experiences.

So far, we have abstracted two main types of intrinsic education (Matusov, 2019, in preparation). The first is *creative authorship* intrinsic education and the second is *critical authorship* intrinsic education. In the creative authorship intrinsic education, the focus is on the collaborative or individual production of culture and meaningful life in communities of practice. Existing, ready-made knowledge and culture become material for production of the unknown, emerging ways of existence and experience (Matusov & Marjanovic-Shane, 2016a). The creative authorship type of intrinsic education is about creative participation in projects that promote meaningful life and "learning in our own sociocultural, historically grounded world" (Lave, 1991). Learning in such education is often secondary to living; it is a byproduct of an unfolding, meaningful communal activity (Matusov, 2009).

Many good examples of creative authorship intrinsic education can be found in drama education (Heathcote & Bolton, 1995; O'Neill, 1995). As most of the "drama pedagogues" claim, drama in education is about making a meaningful transformation for the whole person, "not *for* the aesthetic experience, but *through* it" (cf. Taylor & Warner, 2006, p. 29, italics in the original). Thus, in a drama workshop, "The Prisoners of War Camp,"[2] Dorothy Heathcote enters a classroom of 14 boys aged between 10 and 13 years, students in a residential school, and in a few minutes, invites them to engage in making a play. After some discussion, the children and Dorothy choose to create a "prisoners of war camp" (3m:46s).[3] Dorothy assumes various leading imaginary play roles, changing her voice and posture, to help the students build creatively this phantasy world of the camp. As the "senior commanding officer," she dramatically tells the "new recruits": "NOW!!! Pick up your guns!!! . . . It matters! . . . It's all there is between you and the Germans with their guns, isn't it? . . . Really!" (4m:40s) The students are quickly transformed into "soldiers defending their country against a powerful enemy, then captured and put into a prison camp." In this imaginary prison camp, some of the students play the German guards and the others play the English inmates. Unbeknownst to the students who played inmates, Dorothy secretly nominated one of the "inmates" to be a spy for the "guards." At one point, a few "inmates" steal the keys form another "prison guard" (10m:30s). At "night" all the "inmates" start making plans how to escape (12m:24s). The "spy" is among them, included in plotting the escape. At that moment in the play, another "guard" enters and asks the "spy" to hand him the keys (13m:18s). The "spy" gets up and points to one of the inmates, saying, "He's got them, sir!" and, thus, he also gives himself away. This is an actual shock for the students who play the "inmates." The boy to whom the "spy" pointed, stands up, glares at the "spy," and emphatically says, "Swine! You, swine!" (13m:36s). The "spy" kneels down, crouches to the floor and puts his hands over his head, deeply shamed. Other "inmates" start pushing him and yelling "Get out! Move! Get out!" (14m:00s) After the play, the students analyzed what they did and why. The student who played the "spy" said, "I did not really want to betray them" and seemed somewhat embarrassed. In the filmed interview that Dorothy Heathcote gave to other drama educators, she made the following comment about this drama episode:

> It looks a bit like an adventure tale, as if everybody is just pretending to be prisoners, and so on. And I think if you would ask the boys about this, they would think that they had a good adventure, you know, it was grand, we didn't do ordinary lessons, for a start. . . . It would take a little time for them to begin to be very honest and say to themselves, 'Well, actually, that was *me* talking. . .'

Why does this example represent intrinsic education? Why does it involve creative authorship?

In our view, in this dramatic play, the boys intrinsically own the situations they play-craft. That is why we see this activity as intrinsic, as a final cause in itself. They are deeply involved in their improvisations, which carry them on their own. After the improvisation starts, they do not need any more outside prompts, a teacher, or an authority to tell them what to do next – they are fully authoring it on their own. We are not sure if this is education or not for the children themselves, that is, whether they considered this activity as educational. Although Dorothy Heathcote thinks that it is – because, in her view, the children were only half playing but also half acting as themselves, and the time will come when the students will realize something about themselves, some deep truth, which may be transformational for their whole person – we do not know that for sure. If it is education, it might involve children's reflection, but this reflection is not guided and necessarily critical. This is why we argue that this is an example of genuine intrinsic education based on creative, but not on critical, authorship.

In contrast, critical authorship intrinsic education involves deconstruction of ready-made concepts and ideas, often dear to participants, by testing them against alternative ideas in a critical dialogue. It is a critical examination of the life, self, world, and society in "internally persuasive discourse" (Bakhtin, 1991; Matusov & von Duyke, 2010). The critical dialogue of intrinsic education is often messy, involving heterodiscoursia of the participants jumping from on discursive theme to another (Matusov, 2011b) and interrupting each other (Nikulin, 2010; Yakubinsky & Eskin, 1997). The first author provides a good example of critical authorship intrinsic education, as he worked at a Latin-American Community Center afterschool program with his undergraduate students, future teachers. The described events that occurred in a computer room where most of the Latino children of diverse ages played computer games or worked on diverse projects of their choices after their homework was already done:

> An LACC[4] [9th grade] teenager asked the LRM[5] instructor (Eugene Matusov) to help him with his homework, which involved writing a structured summary of a newspaper article about science; listing the source, the place, three details, and so on. [The LRM instructor reluctantly accepted this request – just because this young man asked him, not appreciating the meaninglessness of this homework.] The LRM instructor asked the LACC boy if he had already chosen the article. The boy nodded and showed a short article [from a local newspaper] about melting ice in the Arctic. The instructor asked why he had chosen this particular article and the boy replied that it was the shortest article he could find on a science topic, and that he wanted to finish the homework assignment as soon as possible to go to play computer games [in the room]. In order to promote LACC children's meaningful participation in social and educational activities that eschew school tasks, the LRM

instructor asked the child if he would mind spending more time and efforts on the homework if they turned it into something interesting and fun.[6] The boy replied that he would be happy to do so if the homework were fun and added that he did not mind spending time and efforts on playing computer games that sometimes were very difficult and frustrating.

The LRM instructor asked the boy what he was currently interested in and the boy said that he was interested in downloading music [of his choice] from the Internet [as he wanted to become a hip-hop musician]. The LRM instructor went to the *New York Times*' website and searched for "music pirating." [He] found an article about a retired dyslexic schoolteacher who was sued by [several] record companies for illegally downloading music. The article stated that the accused schoolteacher's son [who was a computer programmer] proved that the record company used static Internet Protocol (IP) addresses to look for perpetrators while his retired mother had a dynamic IP address. In addition, the schoolteacher's old computer could not handle current Peer-To-Peer (P2P) software required for music pirating. The LRM instructor read and discussed the article with the boy. The article was very long with very difficult vocabulary and grammar but the child was very interested in it and did not mind working through this difficulty. The article generated an avalanche of [diverse] issues for the boy:

- what dyslexia is,
- how a dyslexic could become a teacher,
- what an IP address is and [what is] the difference between static and dynamic IP addresses,
- why it is difficult to discover people who are accessing a web site if they use a dynamic IP address,
- why an old Apple II computer cannot handle P2P software,
- what copyright protection is, and, finally,
- whether or not it is fair to share and download copyrighted music from the Internet.

The LRM instructor demonstrated how to find the IP address on a computer connected to the Internet, discussed dyslexia and the purpose of education, and the old versus new computer operating systems. Another topic of discussion was that many LACC kids want to become successful musicians in future earning a lot of money and yet still want to be able to download music for free.

Very soon, many LACC children in the computer room stopped playing computer games and joined their discussion, as well as some UD students[7] present in the computer room. [The LRM instructor problematized music pirating for the children, many of whom wanted to become famous hip-hop musicians: "How will you earn money if your fans pirate your music from the Internet?!" To the instructor's surprise, the children started asking him about what he was doing at the LACC in their response.] The children asked why the LRM instructor from UD spent so much time at LACC and who paid him for that. When they learned that it was UD that paid the instructor for his academic work, teaching, research, and scientific articles and that his publications were openly available in libraries, the children suggested that musicians should also have tenure and be paid by a university so their music could also be available in libraries for free. That was a very interesting and fresh idea even for the LRM instructor and later he discussed this issue in his University class. The teenage boy wrote two summaries of the article: one according to the teacher's rigid structure and the other based on the [entire] LRM discussion. Fortunately, the teacher appreciated his second summary. She awarded him with an A (the highest grade in the US schools) and invited him to read his article summary on the school's public-address system for the entire school. The LRM instructor created a learning community around the article about music pirating in which all the participants, including himself, were peripheral participants.

Unfortunately, it is not always possible to "hijack" traditional, decontextualized school homework and turn it into something meaningful for the children.

(Matusov & Smith, 2011, pp. 29–30)

Why does this example represent intrinsic education? Why does it involve critical authorship? The evidence that the described activity was intrinsic for the children is because it successfully competed with other intrinsic activities – computer games, free chatting, and projects – that the children chose of their free will and were final causes in themselves. The activity was eventful for the children as they remembered it many years after, and for not only its interesting outcomes but also its intensity of "being together" with each other and me. The experience was also educational for everybody, including me. Mateo (a pseudonym for the teenage boy) told me later that for him there were two most striking lessons: 1) academic learning can be fun and powerful (his second essay was read over school intercom) and 2) we invented a viable system, in which musicians can be paid while their music was free to download. Through our collective guidance, we all involved ourselves in critical deconstruction ideas about dyslexia, IP, music pirating, and so on. One of the inquiries for our collective critical deconstruction was why teachers could not make this deep, eventful, and fun learning, similar to described above, an everyday school experience.

Conditions for intrinsic education: seven students' academic freedoms and rights

Why indeed? Why cannot conventional and even most innovative schooling make students experiences eventful, deeply meaningful, and fun (even if it is difficult and frustrating)?

First of all, intrinsic education starts with open appreciation of a learner's authorship of his/her own learning and education in general by the learner and the relevant others (Matusov, 2011a). Intrinsic education is not about reproduction of a ready-made culture in a new generation as conventional and even some innovative schooling assumes. Rather, intrinsic education is about production of a new culture, culture-making, on small or large scales (Berlyand, 2009; Bibler, 2009). A production of a new culture can occur through either learners' creative authorship or critical reflective authorship. This authorship can be self-initiated by the learner in some short-term (e.g., a stand-alone question) or long-term (e.g., a long-term project or journey) self-assignment or responsive to a teacher's or peer's or somebody else's dialogic provocation. This highly contrasts with conventional and some innovative schooling where most learning activities are constantly assigned by the teacher (Matusov, 2015). In intrinsic education, a learner's authorship can be assisted by the teacher (or by other people) or autodidact. This important characteristic of intrinsic education demands an important educational right – the right of the student to define his/her own curriculum, instruction, and valuation (what to value in his/her education). In intrinsic education, guidance starts with the learner request for help addressing others, self, texts, Internet, and so on.

The learner's right of defining his/her own (intrinsic) education is based on the learner's multidimensional academic freedoms. These multidimensional academic freedoms and rights involve:

1. Curriculum: Freedom to decide what to learn;
2. Instruction: Freedom to decide how, when, where, and with whom to learn and ask for guidance;
3. Participation: Freedom to engage or disengage, freedom to learn or not to learn, freedom of a no-fault divorce from any teacher or learning community;
4. Valuation: Freedom to determine what is or is not important for the learner to study or to do, the quality, and the purpose of his/her education;
5. Ecology: A right to have access to and opportunity for a rich educational environment, pregnant with and supportive of diverse discourses, practices, and values;
6. Role: Freedom to define what kind of student the learner wants to be in every particular situation and overall (e.g., a credential student, a self-responsible critical learner, an other-responsible critical learner, a creative learner, an autodidact, an apprentice);
7. Leisure: Freedom from necessities and needs such as hunger, sickness, concerns about shelter, concerns about safety, concerns about future well-being, and so on.

Curricular academic freedom involves a learner's right to pursue his/her own academic interests, questions, inquiries, needs, and passions. These interests, questions, inquiries, needs, and passions may pre-exist in the learner or emerge in an interaction with the teacher, peers, other people, texts, experiences, observations, activities, and so on. For example, in our classes, we provide our college students with Curricular Maps. Initially, a Curricular Map involves a list of topics that we have developed based on our own authorial judgments, on authorial judgments by colleagues teaching similar courses around the world (via their syllabi posted on the Internet), and our past students' interests. Finally, during the class term, our current students can and do amend the course's Curricular Map at any time. At the end of each class, our students are engaged in selecting a topic for the next class. Often our students vote on the topics, but at times they want to decide by consensus, or by accepting several topics and splitting the class into smaller groups, or by asking the instructor to make a choice for them, or by flipping a coin on the several most popular topics of their choice. Also, students often try to convince their peers to join them in voting for the topic of their choice. Recently, we started experimenting by offering our students a list of themes within chosen class topic to start our discussion, which the students can always amend with their own themes. The Curricular Map creates an image of the vast, rich, and growing field of study – representation of the rich and inexhaustible learning environment – for the students. This democratic process of selecting topics to study or themes to discuss promotes both students' activism and ownership of their own learning and education. It discursively and powerfully forms their educational desire, "I want to study/learn" (Matusov & Marjanovic-Shane, 2017). In intrinsic education, curriculum is always emerging, surprising, and, thus, cannot be preset. In contrast, in many conventional and some innovative schools, it is up to educational authorities to define and mandate curricular topics, themes, and their sequence, disabling students' educational activism, desire, and ownership. Curriculum is imposed on the students. Students do not have a legitimate right to define their curriculum, often justified by their ignorance to do so. Their educational desires are tabled until after school is over. Efforts are made to motivate students to engage in the school-imposed curriculum and/or to make school-imposed curriculum attractive to the students, such as, for example, in progressive innovative education (e.g., Dewey, 1956).

Instructional academic freedom involves a learner's right to organize his/her own study in whatever way may fit the learner. Classes, guidance, and learning activities cannot be imposed on the student, only offered and suggested by teachers or initiated by the students. The student has a right to be the final authority to accept, reject, or modify these guiding offers, suggestions, or invitations. Students must have a right to choose or create their own classes, to choose or invite teachers or peers with whom to study. As in the case of the Curricular Map, a teacher can develop a list of possible diverse rich learning activities and projects that the students can choose from, modify, or amend with their own. Guidance cannot be imposed on the students by the teachers (or peers, or institutions) but only can be offered. Of course, the students can ask for guidance. In contrast, in many conventional and some innovative schools, classes, guidance and learning activities are determined by school authorities and imposed on the students. Students' instructional choices are illegitimate there. This often leads to insensitive guidance that generates resistance in the students, to which many teachers reply with oppression or bribing. It also often undermines the students' educational interests, desires, and confidence in their own educational aspirations and abilities.

Participatory academic freedom involves a learner's right to move freely, in and out, to and from learning and educational activities and communities. The students' right of non-participation and disengagement has to be respected and valued. The students' non-participation, disengagement, and divorce from activities and communities must not be punished, as is often the case in many conventional and innovative schools. This right creates an opportunity for a self-correcting process in educational practice, where the students can vote by their feet when educational practice or guidance becomes insensitive for their educational (or other) needs or meaningless for them (Matusov & Marjanovic-Shane, 2016b). In contrast, in many conventional and some innovative schools, participation is mandatory and unconditional. Students' non-participation is viewed as illegitimate and punishable. It makes the educational practice insensitive and leaves it without feedback based on the primary benefactor of the educational practice – the student him/herself. Using accountability as a feedback loop creates parasitic practices of summative assessments that undermine the trust between the teacher and the student and the educational process itself (Matusov, 2009; Matusov, Marjanovic-Shane, & Meacham, 2016).

Valuative academic freedom involves a learner's right to define the values, quality, and purpose of their own learning and education. In intrinsic education, purpose, value, and quality of the educational activity emerge in the activity itself (i.e., "praxis" in Aristotelian terms) and do not pre-exist the educational practice (i.e., "poiesis" in Aristotelian terms). Before learners become involved in a particular educational activity, the purpose, value, and quality of this activity does not exist but rather emerges from within it. In the example described above, my undergraduate students, preservice teachers, wanted to study classroom management, mostly focusing on how they can most effectively control their future students. However, in our discussions of the goals of "classroom management," with my guidance, we came across the difference between the notions of students' responsibility and students' unconditional obedience. My preservice teachers became perplexed about their previous commitment to classroom management with its goal of students' unconditional obedience. They became interested in the notion of responsibility and its promotion through engaging their future students in their own investigation of diverse values and in democratic governance of their own education. In their Exit Reflections at the end of the class, when my preservice teachers summarized what the class was about, they referred to "building a classroom community" and to "democratic governance," not to "classroom management."

Another inherent aspect of intrinsic education, evident in the example, is students' realization, examination, and transformation of their educational values, desires, and goals. They started the semester wanting to study classroom management but ended up wanting to study democratic governance, building learning communities, and promoting students' responsibilities. This was important learning and had an educational value in its own turn for them. Learners' realization of transformation of learners' educational goals, values, desires, and qualities in education can be called a meta-learning.

Finally, it is the learner, not the teacher, who is the primary and final authority for educational evaluation of the quality of the learner's work, setting educational purposes, and defining its educational values. The teacher does not have a right to see the student's work without the student's permission (Matusov et al., 2016). In contrast, in many conventional and some innovative schools, valuation is exclusively done by the school authority, which increasingly includes private testing companies. Often the quality of education is predefined as all students successfully arriving at curricular endpoints, preset by society, school authorities, teachers, and testing agencies. The hidden curriculum of such schooling involves students learning how to please this school authority rather than to engage in genuine education.

The *ecological* right for a learner's education involves both the access to diverse resources and the legitimacy to pursue diverse practices, discourses, and values. Thus, at the Latin-American Community Center at Wilmington, Delaware, USA, a computer instructor, Mr. Steve Villanueva, has organized a Lego-Logo Club for Latino/a children of very diverse ages from 5 to 18 years old as a part of their afterschool program (Matusov, 2009, Chapter 10). The Club settings involved a computer room with some children playing computer games or engaging in other activities unrelated to the Lego-Logo Club. In the center of the room, there were big desks with the Lego-Logo blocks and settings for robots designed by the children. Mr. Steve was preparing the children for the national competition. This was an extremely rich and diverse learning environment. Some children were involved exclusively in engineering tasks of the robotics competition, some exclusively in programming the robots, and some in-between; some were interested in the aesthetics of robots; some were videotaping the work. However, some children were involved in robotics projects outside of the competition promoted by Mr. Steve (e.g., making robot-cars that could "dance" to the music, like their favorite Latino wrestler Eddie Guerrero). A few very little children were sitting under the long desks with Lego-Logo settings and playing with little cars that they made out of Lego-Logo blocks. A few teenage girls were discussing romance and pregnancy symptoms. A few young boys were engaged in horse-play and teasing. One boy engaged in an engineering task suddenly said that he was bored and wanted to go play basketball. Mr. Steve commented that the boy should have left for basketball a half hour before, when his team had left. The boy left and came back after about a half hour. There were many discourses: separate, overlapping, and dynamically emerging and shifting. Children moved freely among diverse activities and discourses. The learning environment was heterodiscursive, affording very diverse activities and discourses (Matusov, 2011b). Everything was legitimate. At times, Mr. Steve or other children asked for help from those children who were not engaged in the preparation for the competition, but they were free to move back to their activities after they helped (some did and some not). All in all, the children loved to come to the Club and could come and work on their activities even when

Mr. Steve was not with them for whatever reason (Matusov, 2009, Chapter 10). In contrast, in many conventional and some innovative schools, the learning environment is either sterile or highly limited, mono-discursive, and controlled by the teacher. The students are expected to be on-task or on a few tasks, well defined by the teacher (and if not, the teacher may be punished by the school administration). The tasks and subjects are purified from "contamination" by other discourses, practices, and values (often couched in the moniker "best practice"). In a conventional school, tomato is always a fruit, as defined by the biology science practice, and never a vegetable as defined by the culinary practice.

Role academic freedom involves a learner's right to define his/her own mode of participation in each particular area, educational activity, or topic. It is up to the learner to determine their own approaches to their own interests. A student may determine his/her overall educational goals as, for example, to become recognized by society or by a practice's experts as a competent and capable practitioner through receiving a license or certificate – i.e., to assume a role of a practice-based credential student. In this case, the goal of education for a credential student is to pass some qualifying tests set by the practice's experts. It does not matter how the credential student will prepare for these qualifying tests: alone or with a help of somebody or by going to school. Passing the qualifying tests is the most important. In contrast, a student may want to be a good authorial professional, who learns in a community of other professionals as an apprentice. Alternatively, a student may want to engage in a critical dialogue about the life, self, world, and society. All these and other possibilities for students' roles in education have to be available and legitimate. Also, there should be a possibility for a student to combine or shift between and among these roles. In contrast, in many conventional and some innovative schools, the legitimate role of the student is single and predefined by school authorities, mostly (but not always!) involving the role of a school-based credential student, who successfully jumps through all hoops that the school sets for the students.

We will discuss leisure academic freedom in our conclusion.

In sum, most conventional and some innovative schools deny freedoms and rights to students because they view education instrumentally and not intrinsically. Mass education was designed as the right of society to impose education on the people for economic, political, nationalistic, and other societal goals. The right of a person for such education is nothing more than a right of society to impose its unilaterally designed curriculum on the person. At its best, the right for education in our society is the right of the person to fit into our society, in a way that society defines it. However, there is no right for education for the person's self-actualization, self-realization, and self-determination – i.e., there is no right for intrinsic education in our society.

Conclusion: why is instrumental education so ubiquitous?

The word "school" (σχολείο) in Greek means leisure (σχολή) – time that one can dedicate to examination of the self, the others, and the world. Aristotle argued that we should seek education for our children and ourselves "not as being useful or necessary, but because it is liberal and noble" (Aristotle & Barker, 1958, pp. viii, 3, 1–13). He viewed genuine, i.e., intrinsic, education as a basic existential craving of a free citizen in a democratic society, a free citizen who does not work and whose basic needs are fulfilled. For Aristotle, instrumental education is mostly needed by those who are not free from labor and survival. Of course, in Ancient Greece, intrinsic education of citizens, free from labor and concerns of necessities, was possible through slavery and exploitation of women, peasants, and artisans. In our times, intrinsic education still remains a luxury that can be affordable by very few.

However, with the emergence of robotics, telecommunication, and automatization, things might change (Markoff, 2016). A time may be coming when fewer and fewer people will be needed to engage in the world economy. A few economists predicted the rise of so-called technological unemployment (Gorz, 1989; Keynes, 2016; Marx, 1868). Although it is not necessarily guaranteed (see, Blacker, 2013, for an alternative, dystopian, possibility), technological unemployment may lead to an emergence of a leisure-based society, in which a growing number of people do not need to work, while they are all receiving growing universal income. In this leisure-based society,[8] intrinsic education may be able to take root and become a universal human right, while instrumental education may become subordinated to intrinsic education (Matusov, 2019, in preparation).

In sum, we argue that the past and present ubiquity of instrumental education is caused by a necessity-based society, in which people do not have genuine leisure on a universal basis. Intrinsic education is a form of genuine leisure, leisure that is based on people's self-actualization and self-realization. Modern educational institutions are built to promote instrumental education and non-educational functions (e.g., health, babysitting and so on) at the expense of intrinsic education. Unless our society changes to allow a spread of genuine leisure, we do not expect spread of intrinsic education despite its being a fundamental existential human need.

Notes

1 The Magic Learning Pill for learning English the language.
2 This particular drama workshop was filmed and presented within a documentary movie, *Three Looms Waiting*, by the BBC producer Ron Smedley (1971), about the work of Dorothy Heathcote, one of the most known teachers and scholars of drama in education. The video is available at http://www.youtube.com/watch?v=owKiUO99qrw.
3 Through our summary, we point the minutes and seconds when these events take place in the video.
4 Latin-American Community Center (LACC).
5 "La Red Mágica" (LRM) – a university–community partnership between LACC and University of Delaware (UD).
6 Although at the moment, I was improvising and did not know if I could deliver "something interesting and fun."
7 University of Delaware (UD) undergraduate teacher education students who had a practicum at LACC as a part of their class on cultural diversity in education.

8 Of course, this type of leisure-based society will never be based purely on leisure, but will also involve work for a decreasing number of people (Matusov, 2019, in preparation).

References

Arendt, H. (1958). *The human condition*. Chicago: University of Chicago Press.
Aristotle, & Barker, E. (1958). *The politics of Aristotle*. New York: Oxford University Press.
Asimov, I. (1959). Profession. In I. Asimov (Ed.), *Nine tomorrows: Tales of the near future* (1st ed., pp. 17–74). Garden City, NY: Doubleday.
Babacan, H. (2007). Education and social cohesion. In J. Jupp, J. Nieuwenhuysen, & E. Dawson (Eds.), *Social cohesion in Australia* (pp. 142–157). Port Melbourne, VIC, Australia: Cambridge University Press.
Bakhtin, M. M. (1991). *The dialogic imagination: Four essays by M. M. Bakhtin*. Trans. C. Emerson & M. Holquist. Austin, TX: University of Texas Press.
Bénéï, V. (2007). *Manufacturing citizenship: Education and nationalism in Europe, South Asia and China*. London: Routledge.
Berlyand, I. E. (2009). A few words about Bibler's dialogics: The school of the dialogue of cultures conception and curriculum. *Journal of Russian & East European Psychology*, *47*(1), 20–33. doi:10.2753/RPO1061-0405470101
Bibler, V. S. (2009). The foundations of the school of the dialogue of cultures program. *Journal of Russian & East European Psychology*, *47*(1), 34–60. doi:10.2753/RPO1061-0405470102
Blacker, D. J. (2013). *The falling rate of learning and the neoliberal endgame*. Blue Ridge Summit, PA: Zero Books.
Cochran-Smith, M. (2010). Toward a theory of teacher education for social justice. In A. Hargreaves, A. Lieberman, M. Fullan, & D. Hopkins (Eds.), *Second international handbook of educational change* (pp. 445–467): Springer.
de Grazia, S. (1962). *Of time work and leisure*. New York: The Twentieth Century Fund.
DePalma, R., Matusov, E., & Smith, M. P. (2009). Smuggling authentic learning into the school context: Transitioning from an innovative elementary to a conventional high school. *Teachers College Record*, *111*(4), 934–972.
Dewey, J. (1956). *The child and the curriculum and the school and society* (Combined ed.). Chicago: University of Chicago Press.
Dewey, J. (1966). *Democracy and education: An introduction to the philosophy of education* (1st Free Press paperback ed.). New York: Free Press.
Dumitru, A. (2018, in press). Neither end, nor means, but both – why the modern university ought to be responsive to different conceptions of the good. *Educational Philosophy and Theory*. doi:10.1080/00131857.2018.1449105
Gorz, A. (1989). *Critique of economic reason*. Trans. G. Handyside & C. Turner. London: Verso.
Greenberg, D. (1992). *The Sudbury Valley School experience*. Framingham, MA: Sudbury Valley School Press. Retrieved from www.sudval.com/05_underlyingideas.html#05.
Heathcote, D., & Bolton, G. M. (1995). *Drama for learning: Dorothy Heathcote's mantle of the expert approach to education*. Portsmouth, NH: Heinemann.
Hoskins, K., & Barker, B. (2014). *Education and social mobility: Dreams of success*. London: Institute of Education Press.

Keynes, J. M. (2016). Economic possibilities for our grandchildren *Essays in persuasion* (pp. 321–332). New York: Palgrave. doi:10.1007/978-1-349-59072-8

Labaree, D. F. (1997). *How to succeed in school without really learning: The credentials race in American education.* New Haven, CT: Yale University Press.

Lave, J. (1991). Situating learning in communities of practice. In L. B. Resnick, J. M. Levine, et al. (Eds.), *Perspectives on socially shared cognition* (pp. 63–82). Washington, DC, US: American Psychological Association.

Lewin, K., Lippitt, R., & White, R. K. (1939). Patterns of aggressive in experimentally created "social climates". *The Journal of Social Psychology, 10,* 271–299.

Lewin, K., Lippitt, R., & White, R. K. (1953/1939). Experimental studies in social climates of groups [video recording]. Iowa City: University of Iowa.

Livingstone, D. W. (2009). *Education & jobs: Exploring the gaps.* Toronto: University of Toronto Press.

Markoff, J. (2016). *Machines of loving grace: The quest for common ground between humans and robots.* New York: HarperCollins Publishers.

Marx, K. (1868). On the reduction of the working day. In K. Marx & F. Engels (Eds.), (Vol. 21). Brussels: The Bee-Hive.

Matusov, E. (2009). *Journey into dialogic pedagogy.* Hauppauge, NY: Nova Science Publishers.

Matusov, E. (2011a). Authorial teaching and learning. In E. J. White & M. Peters (Eds.), *Bakhtinian pedagogy: Opportunities and challenges for research, policy and practice in education across the globe* (pp. 21–46). New York: Peter Lang Publishers.

Matusov, E. (2011b). Irreconcilable differences in Vygotsky's and Bakhtin's approaches to the social and the individual: An educational perspective. *Culture & Psychology, 17*(1), 99–119. doi:10.1177/1354067X10388840

Matusov, E. (2013). Chronotopes in education: Conventional and dialogic. *Pedagogies: An International Journal.*

Matusov, E. (2015). Chronotopes in education: Conventional and dialogic. *Dialogic Pedagogy: An International Online Journal, 3,* A65-A97, doi: 10.5195/dpj.2015.107. Retrieved from http://dpj.pitt.edu/ojs/index.php/dpj1/article/view/107/91.

Matusov, E. (2019, in preparation). *Education in the jobless age of leisure.*

Matusov, E., Baker, D., Fan, Y., Choi, H. J., & Hampel, R. L. (2017). Magic learning pill: Ontological and instrumental learning in order to speed up education. *Integrative Psychological and Behavioral Science, 51*(3), 456–476. doi:10.1007/s12124-017-9384-8

Matusov, E., & Marjanovic-Shane, A. (2016a). Dialogic authorial approach to creativity in education: Transforming a deadly homework into a creative activity. In V. P. Glăveanu (Ed.), *The Palgrave Handbook of Creativity and Culture Research* (pp. 307–325), doi: 10.1057/978-1-137-46344-9_15. Hampshire, UK: Palgrave Macmillan Publishers Ltd.

Matusov, E., & Marjanovic-Shane, A. (2016b). The state's educational neutrality: Radical proposal for educational pluralism (Editorial). *Dialogic Pedagogy: An International Online Journal, 4,* E1–E26. Retrieved from http://dpj.pitt.edu/ojs/index.php/dpj1/article/view/170/114. doi:10.5195/dpj.2016.170

Matusov, E., & Marjanovic-Shane, A. (2017). Promoting students' ownership of their own education through critical dialogue and democratic self-governance (Editorial). *Dialogic Pedagogy: An International Online Journal, 5,* E1–E29. Retrieved from https://dpj.pitt.edu/ojs/index.php/dpj1/article/view/199. doi:10.5195/dpj.2017.199

Matusov, E., Marjanovic-Shane, A., & Meacham, S. (2016). Pedagogical voyeurism: Dialogic critique of documentation and assessment of learning. *International Journal of*

Educational Psychology, 5(1), 1–26. Retrieved from http://hipatiapress.com/hpjournals/index.php/ijep/article/view/1886/pdf. doi:10.17583/ijep.2016.1886

Matusov, E., & Smith, M. P. (2011). Ecological model of inter-institutional sustainability of after-school program: The La Red Mágica community-university partnership in Delaware. *Outlines: Critical Social Studies, 5*(1), 19–45.

Matusov, E., & von Duyke, K. (2010). Bakhtin's notion of the internally persuasive discourse in education: Internal to what? (A case of discussion of issues of foul language in teacher education). In K. Junefelt & P. Nordin (Eds.), *Proceedings from the second international interdisciplinary conference on perspectives and limits of dialogism in Mikhail Bakhtin Stockholm University, Sweden June 3–5, 2009* (pp. 174–199). Stockholm: Stockholm University.

Nikulin, D. V. (2010). *Dialectic and dialogue*. Stanford, CA: Stanford University Press.

O'Neill, C. (1995). *Drama worlds: A framework for process drama (The dimensions of drama)*. Portsmouth, NH: Heineman.

Ribich, T. I. (1968). *Education and poverty*. Washington, DC: Brookings Institution.

Smedley, R. (Producer). (1971). Dorothy Heathcote: Three looms waiting. Retrieved from https://www.youtube.com/watch?list=PLB1E6842FAF6BBA6B&v=f5jBNIEQrZs#t=136

Straughn, J. B., & Andriot, A. L. (2011). Education, civic patriotism, and democratic citizenship: Unpacking the education effect on political involvement. *Sociological Forum, 26*(3), 556–580.

Taylor, P., & Warner, C. (2006). *Structure and spontaneity: The process drama of Cecily O'Neill*. London: Trentham Books Limited.

UNESCO. (2017, March). Role of education. *Social and Human Sciences*. Retrieved from http://www.unesco.org/new/en/social-and-human-sciences/themes/fight-against-discrimination/role-of-education/.

Wain, K. (1996). Education and tolerance. *Higher Education in Europe, 21*(1), 13–24.

Yakubinsky, L. P., & Eskin, M. (1997). On dialogic speech. *PMLA, 112*(2), 243–256.

Chapter 2

Stress – between welfare and competition

Thomas Szulevicz, Lærke Kromann Kure and Lillith Olesen Løkken

Introduction

In a recent Danish student life study, 47% of the questioned students considered themselves stressed. This might not be surprising since most Western societies are witnessing epidemics of psychological problems. Even so, it is interesting to take a closer look at why so many Danish university students consider themselves stressed. In many ways, Danish students can be considered privileged: there are no tuition fees at universities, every Dane over the age of 18 is entitled to public support for his or her further education – regardless of social standing – and job prospects are fairly good in Denmark with relatively low rates of graduate unemployment.

Based on an empirical study, this chapter will discuss the phenomena of stress and well-being among university students. The empirical material in the article portrays how university students feel distressed, lonely and pressured. The article analyses and discusses student stress and well-being in relation to 1) new neoliberal university reforms and societal changes where many countries have moved from the model of welfare state to that of the *competitive state*, 2) whether (Scandinavian) students generally lack resilience and 3) whether universities themselves might play an active role in the cultivation of distressed and vulnerable students.

We conclude the chapter by claiming the need for insisting on an educational agenda within higher education. Over the last years, higher education has changed rapidly, with a significant expansion of the monitoring of educational outcomes, by increased political regulation and by a neoliberal logic of markets. One of the consequences has been that educational and pedagogical questions have been marginalised on behalf of administrative, political and economic ones, and we argue that problems related to a growing number of distressed students both have to be understood and solved from an educational perspective.

University life and stress

On 9 October 2017, a big conference on stress and well-being among university students was held at the seat of the Danish parliament, Christianborg Palace. In the press coverage of the conference it was stated that:

> Alarmingly many students are plagued by stress and distress across the country. This has to be addressed. Therefore, a number of student organizations

invite to a conference where experts and politicians together will find solutions to the problems related to student distress.
(www.djoef.dk/presse/pressemeddelelser/2017/konference-om-stress-og-studietrivsel-p-aa – christiansborg.aspx, our translation)

The conference was held as the culmination of a vague concern being raised over the general mental health condition of Danish university students, with almost half of them experiencing stress in their everyday lives.

The current attention to student stress is noteworthy because university students often are perceived of as a group full of resources and strengths. In Denmark, it also seems to have been a globally held view that university students are privileged with very good study and working conditions, and as a consequence, students haven't received much public or political sympathy and backing when it comes to their general mental state or well-being. This is, for example, evidenced in former Danish Minister of Higher Education Esben Lunde Larsen's quote from a Danish newspaper in 2015:[1]

> When a large number of students talk about stress it can't solely be because they need to attend to their full-time studies. People have done that for generations.

Lunde Larsen commented on the paradox that many university students feel stressed while different in-depth analysis show that Danish universities do not seem to spend enough time on their studies on a weekly basis. In the same article, Lunde Larsen stated:

> When you are a student at a Danish education institution and you get a free education with [the student stipend] SU on top of that, then society should have a clear expectation that you at the very least are a full-time student and show up prepared. It doesn't do any good if there is an expectation that you can just have a cozy time and have five full years to finish your education. It is completely unacceptable if the educators don't send the signal that one needs to show up for an education.

Lunde Larsen's quotes are interesting as they also refer to another paradox, namely that politics on one side have identified that university students in general do not spend enough time studying and that the students at the same time seem to be increasingly stressed. And Lunde Larsen's thoughts about students' estimated time spent on their studies are also evidence of the increasing politicisation of education in which universities follow politically guided trajectories marked by growing political intrusion and accountability, commodification, control, measurement etc. This politicisation, or neoliberalisation, as it is also often referred to, shapes both academic subjectivities and identities among teachers/researchers and students. Among teachers, we are witnessing a growing academic precariat of non-tenure track teaching staff with uncertain career perspectives, a rise of competitive logics with competition over-funding, a general marketisation of education with consumer logics and far-reaching quality assurance procedures to ensure documentation of satisfying teacher and student output. For the students' part, an increasing number of them seem to suffer from a 'performativity regime' marked by 'CV-competition', résumé building, career-planning, employability and increased competition on academic achievement.

In Denmark, students have been notoriously tardy in finishing their degrees. As a consequence, the Danish government enacted a 'Study Progress Reform' in 2015. Together with changes in study regulations and the national study grant structure, the ambition of the reform was to force Danish students to start and finish their university studies earlier. From a political perspective, the reform has been a success. The students have pulled themselves together, and we now have a marked reduction in the average age on graduation among Danish students. On the other side, critics have stressed that the reform has been implemented concurrent with a period of budget cuts in the university sector. Furthermore, the study progress reform makes it much more difficult for students to alter their educational direction; students have less liberty of choice, have less time for immersion in the topics and feel stressed with less time to finish their studies.

If we go back to Lunde Larsen's claims about students being spoiled and the fact that they don't seem to be sufficiently resilient, there are also growing signs that both politicians and universities recognise and pay increasing attention to the apparent rising mental health issues among university students (as evidenced by the conference on student stress and well-being at the Danish Parliament).

We already have a lot of quantitative data from different surveys on student well-being. But we still lack in-depth qualitative research that sheds light on the complex relations between the study context of students and increased levels of stress among university students. In the following section, we aim to answer the call for more qualitative research by including data from an ongoing project instigated by the faculty of humanities at a Danish university to improve the socio-psychological student environment. The empirical data is the result of the project's initial phase of mapping the students' well-being and identifying important contributing factors, and consists of interviews with various student counselling organisations at the university.

Everyday life and struggles of university students

The different organisations and institutions occupied with guiding and counselling students differ considerably in both aims and means for servicing the students who need it: the General Student Guidance Centre and the Decentral Student Counsellors attached to the individual study programmes are internal organisations mainly focused on helping students with formalities in relation to the university (dispensation applications, internships, studying abroad etc.), whereas external organisations such as the Student Counselling Service and the University Chaplains offer both workshops and lectures as well as individual and group sessions of more of a counselling nature. Their combined efforts thus offer a great variety of services and have a wide contact area across faculties, study programmes, classes etc. In the following, we will outline some of the most prevalent themes emerging from interviews with these organisations.

Expectations and performance

The newcomer phenomenon has been researched thoroughly in the field of education and employment and is also identified as a prevalent risk factor in developing stress. For university students, the transition from high school is a natural and inevitable part of adapting to a new identity as a university student. It involves a change from the role of a high school pupil and a structured and guided learning process to that of a university student with increased responsibility for own learning achievements as well as learning to navigate between the often diffuse expectations of a large organisation with multiple aims – education being just one of them. Bearing this in mind, it is not surprising that the newcomer phase is considered as both a potentially troublesome period and an important establishing factor for students' well-being later on.

The issue of transition is addressed by various and often tradition-bound start-up activities for the first-year students, especially during the first semester. These activities differ greatly between the different study programs, but usually include practical tasks (a tour around campus, activation of library card etc.) as well as support for the formation of study groups and the arranging of extracurricular activities such as parties or field trips. Start-up activities are thus meant to welcome new students to the university and reduce the gap between life as a high school pupil and life as a university student. When enrolling at university, first-year students often appreciate and embrace the social and practical focus of the start-up activities but are faced with new challenges when the 'honey moon' period is over. Although the start-up activities do seem to reduce the gap between high school and university on social and practical levels, they often fail to reduce the gap academically, and many students struggle with adapting to a new setting and a new set of expectations. When students turn to the various counselling organisations, it is often because they fail to form realistic expectations regarding their role as university students:

> When commencing at university, many students have this idea about swotting constantly, expecting to know and do everything, e.g. writing academically, right away – It has to be perfect from the beginning. But it cannot be so. They cannot be swotting all the time and they cannot remember everything they read.
>
> (Student counsellor)

First-year students thus begin their life at university with a slightly misconstrued idea about what is expected from them, as the objective of learning in many cases seems secondary to the perceived objective of performing. One might argue that misaligned expectations is an inherent and inevitable part of the newcomer phenomenon, and that first-year students are likely to adjust appropriately in due time as they settle in and slowly become more familiar with the setting and themselves in it. However, indications are that misaligned expectations regarding the level of performance affect students' sociality, insofar as they spark a sense of insecurity leading to increased shyness and a lack of volition to participate actively in lectures, group work, academic discussions etc. Consequently, first-year students risk missing out on forming valuable social relations that can aid in the process of expectation alignment as well as academic, social and personal support later on.

> We recognise that the students are very cautious, that they feel very insecure and that they are afraid of confronting their fellow students. For example, if students feel themselves writing inadequately and cannot find their contribution in a common project, rather than asking 'What do you think?' they take it to heart and think 'Well, perhaps I do not belong here'.
> (Student counsellor)

When first-year students begin at university, they are thus faced with the difficult task of bridging the transition from high school to university. Although many start-up activities during the first couple of semesters are meant to lessen the gap, indications are that a lack of or insufficient focus on academic integration might balance out the social benefits in the long run. Not being able to identify the often diffuse and formal expectations posed by the university, combined with an experience of also not living up to one's own expectations, leaves students at risk of never properly settling in at university and therefore struggling with forming an identity as a university student, acquiring adequate study techniques and experiencing a sense of self-efficacy.

Performance and competition

One of the prerequisites for understanding the daily life and struggles for universities is the organisation of the Danish educational system, as all universities are publicly funded and have free admission. This aims to ensure equal access to the educational system regardless of socioeconomic background. Admission is instead regulated by different requirements adjusted to the specific study programmes, e.g. a minimum grade or level in relevant subjects or a certain grade point average. Consequently, Danish high schools have in recent years experienced a rather excessive focus on grades among high school pupils. The discussion of whether the increased focus on grades is intentional or indeed desirable falls outside the scope of this chapter; for present purposes, it will suffice to note that the issue is prevalent enough to cause the coining of the term '12-girls', which in recent years has become a well-known part of the Danish vocabulary. The term aims to describe a certain type of person (mainly girls) who gets straight 12s (the highest grade on the Danish grading scale) – implying both skills and ambition but also excessive perfectionism and exceptionally high expectations.

In the case of university students, however, this issue is particularly relevant when it comes to the study programmes with particularly high grade point average admission requirements, for example psychology, medicine and law, which are renowned for attracting these so-called 12-girls. As one student counsellor puts it:

> They come from a high school, where they really have to improve and to get high grades in order to be enrolled at university. But when they are admitted they are hit by reality, because it is not always the grades that matter, but they do not know what else to do.
>
> (Student counsellor)

Typical '12-girls' have been exceptionally diligent in high school, which ensured the grades necessary to be enrolled at university, and they expect to keep performing at the same level. They maintain high expectations for excelling despite the change of setting, extended curriculum, fewer classes etc., but are sometimes faced with grave disappointment in themselves when realising that they are no longer able to keep up their high standards. The quote also emphasises another important consequence of an excessive focus on grades: it happens at the expense of learning. Students report attempting to memorise the curriculum before an exam using memo techniques but do not care whether they remember it the following day. They speculate in failing exams on purpose by not attending if they do not feel they have prepared enough to secure a top grade. Or they show up to meetings with their supervisor with only one question: 'What do I have to do in your classes in order to get 12?' When students are faced with the task of adapting to the admittedly higher expectations at university, this excessive focus on grades prompts them to engage in insufficient study techniques that first and foremost are incompatible with the educational objectives of the university, to educate people for a labour market that requests skilled employees that can apply as well as acquire knowledge.

Furthermore, this excessive focus on grades affects students' well-being, insofar as top grades become the only important means of measuring success. With expectations of getting only top grades in every class, students set themselves up for inevitable disappointment; at the same time, they cut themselves off from finding any consolation in having learned from the process, met new people or acquired new knowledge. When students thus seek help, they report very low self-esteem and see themselves as failures unable to perform adequately:

> They report of an enormous pressure and an environment that dictates a certain way of being. . . . They are afraid of the consequences if they do not perform well enough. I suspect that they are dealing with massive anxiety about not sufficing. And when we talk to them we realise that this is not only about their studying – they are afraid to fail as a human being.
>
> (Student counsellor)

In some ways, students find themselves trapped in a vicious circle, constantly chasing top grades and at the same time fuelling a culture of increasingly high expectations of perfectionism. Despite the somewhat obvious negative consequences on well-being that result from cultivating expectations at a practically unobtainable level, the excessive focus on grades fuels a competition culture in which students not only have to excel but also deal with concerns about positioning themselves in relation to their fellow students – who in some instances become tactical collaborators and competitors rather than potential friends or means of reciprocal academic and social support. For example, students report being less willing to share notes and thereby give fellow students an advantage that they have not 'earned', and fight vigorously to be assigned responsibility for parts of a common project that are perceived as more important:

> I think there is a strenuous tendency, insofar that the students are not willing to share things because of this underlying competition culture. In a very unconstructive fashion where everyone is closest to themselves and sitting at home studying alone.

The university thus potentially becomes a battle ground, where students struggle to identify expectations and position themselves in the most favourable way, leaving little inducement to participate in social events and engage in activities related to societies or associations. The result is a sort of double negative effect, as it has a direct and immediate impact on the students' well-being and an indirect one insofar that the psychosocial study environment suffers, leaving students with even poorer possibilities of forming social relations to aid them throughout their time at university.

Why are university students increasingly stressed?

Although this outlining of prevalent themes is by no means exhaustive, it does allow for some insight in the daily life and struggles of Danish university students. However, the questions still remain: Why are an increasing number of seemingly privileged, young and skilled students experiencing increasing levels of stress and problems with well-being?

A common-sensical perspective would be to attribute the increasing levels of stress and problems with well-being to the students themselves: they are spoiled, not resilient enough, too occupied with themselves and their appearances on social media and too easy to shake up. This is evidently way too simplistic, as it ignores the complex relationships between university (educational system) and its students (human beings), and in the following sections, we will discuss some different explanations regarding why stress seems to be a growing problem among university students.

The neoliberal condition

In the empirical section above, we described how psychology students are struggling with issues of adaptation, belonging, performance, high expectations, peer-competition etc. Many of these struggles are timeless and universal, and have thus always been part of student life at universities. There are, however, also signs that some of the struggles could be the result of recent changes in higher education; thus, one of the questions we will pursue is whether recent quality and standards-based reforms in higher education are leading to greater stress and less well-being among university students. Globally, the nature of higher education has been changing rapidly, with a significant expansion of the monitoring of educational outcomes both globally and locally (Zajda & Rust, 2016), and as already described, the neoliberal logic of markets has entered the realm of higher education.

The neoliberalisation of education has led to a discourse on the benefits of education being positioned almost exclusively in terms of their effect on income and their ability to produce a valuable outcome for society. The discourse of producing valuable outcomes also seems to have been internalised by students and might be one explanation for their increasing levels of stress. Education is a complex and moral endeavour that, according to educational philosopher Gert Biesta (2016a), consists of three dimensions: qualification, socialisation and subjectification. However, the recent outcome-orientation in educational policy and practice increasingly treats education like a technical process in which the dominant questions are about how to achieve given ends. And in modern day higher education, these given ends are termed almost exclusively in terms of student learning (outcome). Biesta goes on and (nick)names this development a 'learnification', meaning that education in general has developed a technical and fragmented view of learning and that education as a consequence has become too preoccupied with producing visible learning outcomes. This is the case when subjects taught in universities are fragmented into knowledge, skills and competences and when the objects of a course are described with zealous precision in study regulations. In this paradigm, the student goes from being a scholar to a consumer, and with consumerism, what is taken for good education is converted into what satisfies the desires of the stakeholders, as consumers (Gibbs, 2017, p. 13). Gourlay (2017) makes a similar point in her analysis of recent changes in higher education. She describes how the term 'student engagement' has become ubiquitous in mainstream higher education discourses. And although student engagement obviously is desirable, Gourlay still argues that the term places a lot of responsibility on the individual student:

> This apparently benign discourse 'wears the clothes' of progressivism, but could be critiqued for offloading the responsibility onto the students and indirectly reinforcing the marketised view that the student carries sole responsibility for their learning as a customer who makes a financial investment for personal gain. In a policy environment such the present one in the UK and beyond where assessment of 'teaching excellence' is likely to lead to far-reaching financial and reputational consequences for students, academics and institutions, this standpoint calls for rigorous and sustained scrutiny.
>
> (Gourlay, 2017, p. 29)

Gourlay refers to Biesta and argues how higher education generally has moved toward learnification; she attributes this shift to postmodern critiques of authority as well as to the neoliberal imperative that the individual should take responsibility for their own learning.

The self-responsible learner is a general neoliberal ideal in which students are expected to be self-evaluating, responsible and self-monitoring. This is, for example, the case with the notion of self-regulated learning (SRL), which has been promoted as a pedagogy associated with empowerment, agency, democratic participation and personal responsibility (Vassallo, 2012; see also Szulevicz, 2018). And, just as the 'engaged student' might on the surface look like an ideal, Vassallo argues that teaching students to regulate their learning represents a hidden curriculum that can be associated with obedience, subordination and oppression.

Our empirical material clearly illustrates how students battle with notions of individualisation and how many students seem to have internalised current educational discourses that, on one hand, enhance competition among students, while on the other hand lead to conformity and subordination with students more or less following the same kinds of student trajectories. This is what has happened with the current focus on employability in higher education, for example, where students have complied and now get stressed because they have to build the best possible CVs while studying. Gibbs (2015) goes on and analyses what this university context driven by employability and efficiency measures means for student well-being and 'happiness', arguing that current higher education strategies aim (too much) at the expedient, developing skills that lead to employment.

If we go back to Biesta's claims about a learnification of (higher) education, it could be argued that current university pedagogy focuses on 'facilitation of learning', but following Biesta (2016b), the consequence potentially is that content and teaching are being devalued. This is exactly the point in a recent book written by educational psychologist Simon Gibbs, who analyses student well-being in the educational system in general; his point is that if we want to improve student well-being, we should start with the teachers. And from Gibbs' point of view, we are moving in the wrong direction at the moment:

> One way of framing my enquiry is, therefore, with reference to the question 'If we care about education (and the future), how should we treat teachers?' Thus my premise is that as schools become increasingly commercialised and teachers held closely to account for their performance, the aim and purpose of education, its philosophical heart, becomes less clear. As a result, teachers' autonomy, agency, and their professional identity, are all disregarded, and a major function of education, helping young people learn how to be human, is degraded. We have been seduced into asking the wrong questions about education and what we want for society.
>
> (Gibbs, 2018, p. vi)

Claiming that university teachers' autonomy and professional identity are disregarded is, from our perspective, an exaggeration. But the point that student wellbeing also is related to university teachers' working conditions and professional identities is definitely very important, and there is no doubt that current changes in the nature of higher education also are affecting teacher working conditions and teacher/researcher professional identities in substantial ways. As described in the empirical section above, these changes also seem to affect students in many and often subtle ways, with feelings of increased competition, loneliness and worries over career perspectives as some of the most prominent features.

A (Scandinavian) lack of resilience?

We quoted former Danish Minister of Higher Education, Esben Lunde Larsen, who said that Danish students' stress-related problems couldn't solely be ascribed to the fact that they attend full-time university studies, because people have done so for generations – and without being stressed.

By saying this, Lunde Larsen insinuates that students are whining and that they lack sufficient resilience. Our empirical data clearly illustrates how competitive the study environment is among students, and basically this competitiveness is in stark contrast to some of the fundamental values in the Scandinavian educational system. Scandinavian countries have traditionally held a very strong belief in education as a means of creating democracy, and there has generally been a strong commitment to equality, social justice and inclusion, which is evidenced, for example, in a vision of a comprehensive school for all students (Nevøy, Rasmussen, Ohna, & Barow, 2013). This educational equality ideal is also expressed in the fact that there are no tuition fees at Danish universities and that every Dane over the age of 18 is entitled to public support for his or her education.

However, our claim is that the educational equality ideal is in many ways being challenged these years, which partly has been triggered by the fact that Denmark and the neighbouring Scandinavian countries have been characterised by a movement from the model of a universal welfare state to that of the *competitive state* (Pedersen, 2011). The term 'competitive state' refers to the fact that the state acts within international competition in order to create economic growth. The competitive state is developed with a view to optimising national competitiveness in order to strengthen the economy and the country's position vis-à-vis other competitive states. The competitive state has transformed Danish society in many ways, including the educational system, which has been widely marked by the already described shift towards neoliberal governance.

An interesting hypothesis would thus be that the change towards more neoliberal governance is experienced differently among Scandinavian university students, because these changes break up some fundamental values in those countries. A counter-argument on the other side would be that university students globally seem to be increasingly distressed, and there are no clear indications that stress problems in the university population are bound to specific regions.

Moreover, the notion of resilience is often problematised as inappropriate for capturing the complexity of social problems. Among other things, it is highlighted how resilience has become a buzzword and a powerful technology of the self (often associated with positive and behavioural psychology). In this context, resilience is conceptualised in a way that focuses on how individuals beat the odds or bounce back from difficult circumstances. In this way, resilience easily becomes a matter of individual strength. Harrison (2012) also argues that the dominant resilience discourse may overemphasise people's ability to bounce back and that it often shifts responsibility for dealing with problems and crisis away from the common and public sphere (Szulevicz, 2018).

The vulnerable student

In the previous sections, we have discussed how student well-being and increased levels of stress could be understood in light of 1) neoliberal societal and educational changes and 2) a general (and probable Scandinavian) lack of resilience. In this section, we will discuss how universities themselves might play an active role in the cultivation of distressed and vulnerable students.

In his unusually scathing book, *What's Happened to the University*, Furedi (2017) describes how universities since the 1980s increasingly have occupied a paternalistic role by treating students as not fully capable of exercising the responsibilities associated with adulthood. Furedi argues that university has gone through a process of infantilisation, where students are depicted as vulnerable characters that become dependent on (institutional) parenting. According to Furedi, this is a consequence of a rising parenting culture in Western societies, where parents have become over-protective and less open to encouraging their children to take risks and to be autonomous, independent and free. Moreover, this risk-aversion is accompanied by a tendency to consider and treat existential problems as psychological ones. This is exactly the case when university students are considered stressed and not just burdened or busy. When treating a great percentage of university students as stressed or potentially stressed, we also regard them as subjects of pathology. In this frame of reference, a natural measure for universities has become to focus on study environment and the affective aspects of student learning, and over the last years, we have seen a massive increase in the promotion of well-being, therapeutic interventions and emotional awareness in higher education. On one side, these measures have been needed and appropriate since the alarming rise of stressed students calls for action. On the other side, a therapeutic frame of reference has subtly gained a footing in higher education. From Furedi's perspective, this therapeutisation implies that the affective aspects of learning might trump the need for intellectual understanding and rigour in higher education and that the greater purpose of education is at risk of being replaced.

If we once again turn our attention to the empirical section of the chapter, there is no doubt that many students feel lonely, under pressure, hopeless and so on.

According to Furedi, however, these signs of vulnerability among students are maintained or maybe even promoted by universities themselves:

> Campus life has been reorganized around the task of servicing, supporting and in effect infantilizing students, whose well-being allegedly requires institutional intervention. Many universities provide so-called well-being services, presuming that students need the intervention of professional service providers to manage the problems they encounter. Unfortunately, the tendency to treat students as children can incite some young people to interpret their predicament through the cultural script that infantilizes them. As we discuss in later chapters, mental fragility, and a disposition to emotional pain, often becomes integral to the ways in which some students make sense of their identity. It is how they have been socialised to perceive themselves.
> (Furedi, 2017, p. 8)

According to Furedi, universities are cultivating vulnerable students. The image of the vulnerable student is backed by a stream of surveys and reports that document how students are psychologically distressed, and a growing trend among universities is to refer psychologically distressed students to a third party for help (Furedi, 2017). We are thus seeing a growing well-being and therapeutic industry within universities. Furedi also argues that the language of vulnerability is often also used by the students themselves to legitimate different causes.

While not all university students have internalised the prevailing narrative of vulnerability, the point is that the therapeutisation of higher education is part of a general societal trend. However, this trend is also fuelled by different forces within higher education.

Concluding thoughts: so what's next?

When almost half of university students are stressed or fail to thrive, it obviously calls for reflection and also some sort of action. We have discussed different reasons for increased levels of stress and argued how they could be understood in light of 1) neoliberal, societal and educational changes, 2) a general (and probable Scandinavian) lack of resilience and 3) a tendency towards universities being more paternalistic. Our discussions also reflect how psychology for years has been the privileged partner of education (De Vos, 2015), and it now seems that neoliberal trends have accompanied psychology in this privileged partnership. We thus have a very complex interplay between psychology and neoliberal thought that influences and dictates educational practices.

Over the last couple of years, some of the responses to the apparent mental state crisis among students in higher education have been addressed by different approaches. One of these approaches is so-called positive education (White & Buchanan, 2017), which is an umbrella term for educational practices that try to promote empirically validated interventions and programs from positive psychology that have an impact on student well-being.

Likewise, so-called contemplative pedagogies have recently gained a footing in higher education as they are considered to have mental health and stress-reducing benefits by addressing specific cognitive dimensions as well as a general sense of well-being among students (Oberski, Murray, Goldblatt, & DePlacido, 2015).

From our perspective, an interesting reflection is that many of the approaches launched to address well-being issues among students are non-educational in nature. This is not to say positive education, contemplative pedagogies or other approaches and pedagogies that seek to maximise student well-being have no legitimacy. Our standpoint is rather that they might overemphasise the notion of well-being and that educational criteria often get relegated to the background.

Korsgaard and Mortensen (2017) have written a paper on inclusive education in which they urge researchers and practitioners to begin to ask educational questions of inclusion, as opposed to inclusive questions of education. In the same vein, our point is that we should start asking educational questions of well-being instead of well-being questions of higher education. Ecclestone (2015) suggests that well-being is not something to be broken down and taught in parts. Well-being is rather something that emerges as a by-product from being part of a stimulating and rich learning environment. The trivial point is thus that the best way to ensure well-being among students is to create strong and sound learning environments and to formulate educational criteria for educational processes. This is not to make light of the well-being issues among students, but rather to claim that a great deal of the well-being and stress-related problems in the student population potentially would have different prospects if the questions raised to higher education were more of an educational character than what we see today. One of the consequences of what Busch (2017) terms 'The Neoliberal Takeover of Higher Education' is that, namely, economic, bureaucratic, commercial and administrative, rather than educational, considerations have restructured universities.

The neoliberal takeover has thus resulted in a marginalisation of educational considerations, and according to Busch, universities need to develop means to resist neoliberal policies and practices. The Danish study progress reform is a good example of a political (and neoliberal) incentive that might make sense from a political perspective, but from an educational one is completely counter-productive.

In educational thinking, the notion of the student capable of autonomous moral judgement has been hailed for years. But this autonomy is not absolute. The student always also needs some kind of guidance from a master/teacher, and this is the fundamental educational premise that we refer to as the pedagogical paradox: discipline the student, but don't make her/his mind slavish. If we go back to Furedi's identification of an increasing infantilisation of higher education, where students are treated as if they are not autonomous or capable of exercising the responsibilities associated with adulthood, we may also subtly be undermining the pedagogical paradox. And while Furedi might be too alarmistic, he still addresses some interesting consequences of a non-educational invasion of higher education:

> There are powerful cultural forces that underpin the infantilisation of the university. The socialisation of young people has become increasingly reliant on therapeutic techniques that have the perverse effect of encouraging children and youth to interpret existential problems as psychological ones concern with children's emotions has fostered a climate where many young people are continually educated to understand the challenges they face through the language of mental health. Not surprisingly, they often find it difficult to acquire the habit of independence and make the transition to forms of behaviour associated with the exercise of autonomy.
>
> (Furedi, 2017, p. 7)

Note

1 www.thelocal.dk/20150828/higher-education-minister-to-danish-students-shape-up

References

Biesta, G. (2012). Giving teaching back to education: Responding to the disappearance of the teacher. *Phenomenology and Practice*, 6(2), 35–49.

Biesta, G. (2016a). *Beautiful risk of education*. London: Routledge.

Biesta, G. (2016b). The rediscovery of teaching: On robot vacuum cleaners, non-ecological education and the limits of the hermeneutical world view. *Educational Philosophy and Theory*, 48(4), 374–392.

Busch, L. (2017). *Knowledge for sale: The Neoliberal takeover of higher education*. Cambridge: The MIT Press.

De Vos, J. (2015). Deneurologizing education? From psychologisation to neurologisation and back. *Studies in Philosophy and Education*, 34(3), 279–295.

Ecclestone, K. (2015). Well-being programmes in schools might be doing children more harm than good. *The Conversation*, 23 January.

Furedi, F. (2017). *What's happened to the university? A sociological exploration of its infantilisation*. New York: Routledge.

Gibbs, P. (2009). Adopting consumer time: Potential issues for higher education. *London Review of Education*, 7(2), 113–124.

Gibbs, P. (2015). Happiness and education: Troubling students for their own contentment. *Time & Society*, 24(1), 54–70.

Gibbs, P. (2017). *Why universities should seek happiness and contentment*. London: Bloomsbury.

Gibbs, S. (2018). *Immoral education: The assault on teachers' identity, autonomy and efficacy*. London: Routledge.

Gourlay, L. (2017). Student engagement, 'Learnification' and the sociomaterial: Critical perspectives on higher education policy. *Higher Education Policy*, (30): 23–34.

Harrison, E. (2012). Bouncing back? Recession, resilience and everyday lives. *Critical Social Policy*, 33(1), 97–113.

Korsgaard, M. T., & Mortensen, S. S. (2017). Towards a shift in perspective for inclusive education research – a continental approach. *International Journal of Inclusive Education*, *21*(12), 1245–1260.

Nevøy, A., Rasmussen, A., Ohna, S. E., & Barow, T. (2013). Nordic upper secondary school: Regular and irregular programmes – Or just one irregular school for all. In: U. Blossing, G. Imsen & L. Moss (eds.), *The Nordic education model. 'A school for all' encounters neo-liberal policy*, 191–210. Dordrecht: Springer.

Oberski, I., Murray, S., Goldblatt, J., & DePlacido, C. (2015). Contemplation & mindfulness in higher education. In P. Layne & P. Lake (Eds.), *Global innovation of teaching and learning in higher education. Professional learning and development in schools and higher education*, vol 11. Cham: Springer.

Pedersen, O. K. (2011). *Konkurrencestaten [The Competitive State]*. København: Hans Reitzels Forlag.

Szulevicz, T. (2018). Psychologists in Neo-liberal schools – What kind of marriage? *Journal of Psychological and Behavioural Sciences*, *52*(3), 366–376.

Vassallo, S. (2012). Critical pedagogy and Neoliberalism: Concerns with teaching self-regulated learning. *Studies in Philosophy and Education*, *32*(6), 563–580.

White, M. A., & Buchanan, A. (2017). Why we need positive education 2.0. In M. White, G. Slemp & A. Murray (Eds.), *Future directions in well-being*. Cham, Switzerland: Springer.

Zajda, J., & Rust, V. (2016). Current research trends in globalisation and Neo-Liberalism in higher education. In J. Zajda & V. Rust (Eds.), *Globalisation and higher education reforms*. Switzerland: Springer International Publishing.

Chapter 3

Problems from discontinuity of children's environment and development in Japan

Yoriko Okamoto Omi

Japanese system in young child education and care

In Japan, the nine-year compulsory education starts at the age of 6 years. This means that parents must send their children to school (e.g. elementary and junior-high school) from April after their children turn 6 years of age. This compulsory education, of course, is free of cost. In other words, Japanese parents' obligation is legally established and all children at the age of 6 years must be enrolled in a public or private elementary school. In fact, the number of children enrolled in elementary school is 6,449 thousand; the number of those not enrolled for special reasons is fewer than 3,000 across Japan, so that the retention rate of elementary school is also approximately 100% (Ministry of Education, Culture, Sports, Science, and Technology (MEXT, 2017). This shows that in Japan fundamental education is guaranteed and basically executed. On the other hand, the number of students with long-term absences in elementary school is 63,089, of which the number of school non-attendance is 27,581 (MEXT, 2016). School non-attendance is defined as students who do not or cannot go to school due to some psychological, emotional, physical, or social reasons or background (MEXT, 2016), and is recognized as one of the serious social problems of Japanese children. Although proper support in different aspects for students who cannot unwillingly go to school has been discussed, some children withdraw from society continually or intermittently at junior high or high school age, sometimes even into adulthood. This is known as "*hikikomori*" in Japanese, which means social withdrawal; withdrawing oneself from society and staying at home is considered another social problem related to school non-attendance.

Before they enter elementary school, Japanese children can go to a preschool facility and gain experiences outside the home with those of the same or a similar age group. The preschool system in Japan provides both education and care; these are not compulsory and free, although discussion regarding making preschool education free of cost has already begun. This system is complicated because the government is transitioning it to a newer, simpler system at the moment, and has three types of facilities: (1) day care centers (nursery schools) (*hoiku-sho* in Japanese), (2) kindergartens (*yochi-en* in Japanese), and (3) accredited early childhood care centers (*nintei kodomo-en* in Japanese).

Historically, only two types of day care centers and kindergartens have been developed in different contexts, viz. welfare and education. Day care centers are facilities under the jurisdiction of the Ministry of Health, Labor and Welfare (MHLW) to provide day care services and education to preschool children (aged 0–6 years) who could not receive sufficient care from parents who work during the day. The day care services are basically a full day, approximately eight hours. Kindergartens are facilities under the jurisdiction of the MEXT in order to provide education and care to preschool children aged 3–6 years. They provide approximately four hours of service. Previously, these facilities were established with different aims, such as welfare and education. Hence, day care centers have assessments for admission regarding the need for day care mandated by each town and city from the welfare necessary for each family. For instance, if at least one of the parents does not work and can stay with their children at home or if they cannot stay with their children but can find someone like grandparents living close to them, their children would not be accepted into the day care centers. On the other hand, kindergartens may have criteria for admission like first-come first-served or examinations stipulated by each kindergarten. They provide learning activities but previously, they did not include care like potty-training or teaching how to use chopsticks.

Recently, however, times have been changing, and the importance of both education and care for every young child before entering school has become more focused. The increase in the number of educated working mothers without serious economic reasons has led an increased demand for education at day care centers. Day care centers have integrated educational functions into care functions. However, the increase in the number of nuclear families in Japan has led to a lack of helpers like grandparents and opportunities to learn child-rearing, thereby increasing demand for care in kindergartens. Kindergartens have added care functions to educational functions. These two types of preschool facilities, day care centers and kindergartens, are becoming almost the same in terms of programs and practice. With this changing, the government decided that day care centers and kindergartens should be integrated into accredited early childhood care centers. Therefore, this is currently in a period of transition, and there are three types of preschool facilities. Accredited early childhood care centers are supposed to function as both child care centers and early childhood education services (Cabinet Office, 2008) under the jurisdiction of the Cabinet Office, which aims to provide equal preschool services to every child whether they have a need for day care or not. However, since it is still in the transition phase, three facilities exist together. The admission systems, teacher's licensing, and criteria for day care centers and kindergartens are not integrated. As a result, accredited early childhood care centers take day care children and kindergarten children together but with different fees; these centers include children who are enrolled by assessment on the basis of day care need and provide an eight-hour program, but also have children who do not need such an extensive program.

Out of all preschoolers, the percentages of day care children and kindergarten children aged 0–5 years are approximately 35% and 25%, respectively; it is approximately 45% and 55% for 5-year-old children in their last year before school, respectively (Cabinet Office, 2016). Almost all children have opportunities for education and care in group settings for at least one year before entering school, i.e., compulsory education.

Collectivism in Japanese preschool facilities

Each preschool facility plans and conducts programs and practices for education and care based on guidelines mandated by the government. The basic daily schedule is planned as shown in Figure 3.1. In many preschool facilities, group setting activities are conducted for two hours in the morning as the main activity of the day, following "circle time (morning greeting time)," and they sometimes conduct corner setting and free play activities. The group setting activities involve all

	Day care centers	Kindergartens
7:00 (–9:00)	Arrival	
8:30	Free play	Arrival
9:00	Circle time	
	Main activity	
11:30	Lunch	
13:00	Nap	Free play
14:00		Dismissal
15:00	Snack	
	Free play	
(16:00–) 19:00	Dismissal	

Figure 3.1 Basic daily schedule in day care centers and kindergartens

children in the same homeroom (maximum 30–35 children in a classroom) under the instructions of the teacher(s); they play group games, soccer, and pretend, play with toys, make things using craft paper, draw pictures, learn reading, writing letters, counting, and so on. All children in the same homeroom do the same activity at the same time. The guidelines for preschool facilities recommend "learning through play" and suggest the importance of "learning through experience," so that playing and learning are not distinguished clearly in the daily schedule.

This considerable emphasis on group setting activities certainly comes from collectivism in Japan. Both teachers and parents accept this because they believe that young children should learn how to be harmonious and cooperative with their friends; this is the most important thing for them. For instance, if they find a child playing alone, teachers gently ask the child to join the other children. In fact, it was shown in a survey of kindergarten parents that parents are likely to be the most worried about their children's relationships with friends at the ages of 3 and 4 (Fujisaki, 2013).

Group setting activities, however, could be presumed to have another practical reason for limited space in Japan. In Japan, many people share small amounts of space. Many preschool facilities lack enough space; children's play toys sprawl on the floor in the same areas in which they learn, dance, do gymnastics, have lunch, and then take naps. For every activity change, they tidy up the space by organizing the toys, setting up tables and chairs, and then taking away the tables to set up beds for naps. Some preschool facilities, especially in urban areas, have no yard to play outside. Therefore, classes often take a walk around the neighborhood. It is easier for teachers to handle all their children together rather than allowing a few children to do different activities or stay in the homeroom.

Japanese children are basically submissive and accustomed to staying in a group (of course, this depends on the child) because they receive many opportunities from earliest childhood to spend time with friends of the same or a similar age group and to join play groups before entering the preschool facility. It is still not easy, however, for a teacher to control 30 or 35 young children to do the same activity together. In this cultural context, teachers must have important skills for organizing and controlling a group of young children. Teachers strive to avoid boredom in young children and to maintain their focus on instructions by singing songs with gestures, speaking loudly and clearly, using funny expressions at times, and occasionally giving strict warnings to those who do not listen. In addition, teachers often play with children by running together outside, climbing the jungle gym, or digging in a sandbox. This is done so that teachers can regulate relationships among the children and resolve conflicts between them up close when they occur.

Making use of children's relationships with others

A typical skill of Japanese teachers is how they make use of a child's relationship with the teacher, other children, or the group. An example of proper involvement is described below in a scenario in which a teacher had a child with special needs and a possible developmental disorder in her homeroom (Suetsugu, 2012).

When the child hit another classmate, the teacher quickly attended to the classmate who had been struck and then brought the child who hit the classmates in front of the other children. The teacher said, "I do not like such behavior." The child looked uncomprehending and grinned. The teacher replied to him, "Look at your friends. Nobody is grinning." Then one of the other children said, "You should not do what you do not want someone else to do against you." The teacher agreed, "Yes, that is right."

This kind of involvement is common in Japanese preschool practices. In this case, the teacher did not directly mention "you should never hit your friend." Japanese teachers generally expect children to think for and control themselves when the teacher does not mention explicitly what the child should or should not have done; they believe their children already know what is good or wrong. This teacher's words, "I do not like such behavior," would be followed by "and then, what you think? You do not like such behavior, do you?" Observational research on Japanese kindergarten children has shown that when there are conflicts in children's peer relationships, teachers are unlikely to interrupt and directly instruct them. Instead, teachers are likely to choose indirect intervention (indirect strategies), such as first helping the children to calm down and then deliberately do nothing so that the children resolve the conflict together themselves (Tanaka, 2015). This practice is known as "*mimamori*," in which "mi" means to watch and "*mamori*" means to protect; in other words, it means the teacher will wait and watch in order to provide the children the autonomy to resolve their issues, while being ready to help and interrupt if the situation worsens – for instance, if the children almost hit or kick each other.

In addition, children need to get rid of persistent and stubborn thoughts so that they can think by themselves. Many teachers in preschool facilities know that it will be effective to encourage children to use the eyes (perspective) of others in the group setting; the teacher's words, "Look at your friends. Nobody is grinning" is an example that shows her expectation that the child might notice the other children's eyes and monitor himself from their perspective. In research on a day care center in Japan, Ito (2013) has shown that when teachers had a child who exhibited improper eating behavior, they were likely to make the child aware of their classmates and encourage the children to offer support to each other when eating food which they disliked; of course, teachers also provided direct support to the child when the need arose.

Although "untold rules" are implicit language epitomized in Japanese communication, in these Japanese contexts, it could be understandable that children get to read and use the untold rules until they are grown up. This can be related, for instance, to a typical phrase (e.g., "I am sad") used by Japanese teachers and parents to discipline a child when s/he engages in mischievous behavior or behaves badly. They try to teach the child that although the child's bad behavior does not seem to be directly related to the adult's emotion (sadness), it can nevertheless have an effect on another's feelings. Teachers and parents also teach their children typical prosodic notation like "*Ka-shi-te!*" ("Let me use it!") and "*I-i-yo!*"

("Yes!") at an earlier age, sometimes by using popular video characters. This request–answer prosodic notation is common when children share toys in Japan; therefore, even 2-year-old children are able to share their own toys with other children semi-automatically. Although Japanese children often have rich opportunities to get along with their friends, they can have fewer opportunities to think about their own wants and desires if the regulation with others is too emphasized.

It should be noted here that when adults hope children will learn how to control themselves, they lead the children to think by themselves in line with their relationship with other children and teachers, instead of thinking of themselves as they please.

Being independent, or being cooperative?

Of course, spontaneous self-control is important for any child. Japanese young children are generally organized and harmonious with their friends. Being cooperative can be more important than being independent in Japan, and learning cooperativeness can be preferred over learning independence. A principal of an Australian day care center that the author visited mentioned that:

> If you find five children play together around the slide, it could be too many. Some of them may just follow the other children and may not choose what they really want to do. So, a teacher tells them to look at the sand box and trampoline, where nobody is playing. Some of the children may realize what they want to do and can independently decide what to do.

This suggests that it is important for children not to play without thinking about what s/he wants but instead by deciding what they want to do.[1] While Japanese teachers basically invite a lonely child to play with others, Australian teachers encourage them to play differently from others.

In kindergartens in the USA that the author visited, preschoolers took part in corner setting activities, where some corners (zones) in a classroom were separated by tables, carpets, or shelves; each corner could be assigned an activity, such as a blocks corner, play pretend corner, writing corner, drawing corner, and so on. A teacher prepared a small sheet in which every colored shape – a red circle, a blue rectangle, and so on – indicated a specific corner from the shape of its table, and the children moved to each corner and checked its box (Figure 3.2; these photos were permitted by the kindergarten principals). The teacher mentioned that each child moves to corners in whichever order they like, but with this sheet, the child can move to corners that they have not experienced by him/herself and thus experience them all (Figure 3.3). In addition, other teachers used a rule of "capacity," which refers to the largest number of children that each corner can hold; this was indicated by a capacity board or notices on a wall (Figures 3.4 and 3.5). The children check the available corners that have not reached capacity so that they can move from one corner to another by themselves, and may sometimes negotiate to switch places with a child who has stayed in a corner too long.

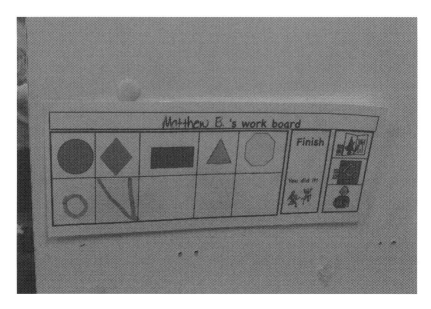

Figure 3.2 A sheet for corner

Figure 3.3 Short stay with the sheet in a writing corner

Figure 3.4 Capacity board

It shows each corner's name and its capacity by number of black magic tapes, where a child put his/her name tag. Two children are discussing which corner has black magic tapes without any name and they want to visit

Figure 3.5 Notices of capacities on the wall

Home living corner has a capacity of 4 children and Sensory Table has a capacity of 2 children

These corner-setting activities are conducted based on the assumption that every child chooses a different activity. If a child follows the others and chooses the same activity, s/he might not be able to join because the capacity might be exceeded. These practices promote children's ability to move differently and become independent.

Stressed leader: April-born pressure

Teachers want all the children to get together, even with different roles for the same activity, in order to help each other achieve something and to share toys, space, or ideas and emotions. Therefore, teachers sometimes use the children's relationship with their peers. For instance, if a child does not remain seated and runs away from the classroom, the teacher might ask a steady, obedient child to bring their classmate back, because as the teacher they have to take care of the rest of the class. Thus, a responsible child helps the teacher by aiding a child who cannot follow his/her group, for example, "help him to clean up," "talk to her and go together to washroom,"[2] or "teach him how to make it."

A traditional Japanese phrase, "children's world" ("*kodomo no ryobun*"),[3] means that children have their own world without adult intervention. This is a cultural value wherein children group together to plan and do something or to solve problems without getting help from adults. Compared to an individualistic culture, the independence that children develop can have different meanings. It is considered not "my" independence but "our" independence and is known as shared/mutual independence. As Valsiner (2014) mentioned, Japanese culture does not contrast the self and the other like European culture; as a result, Japanese children may develop their self accorded to the others.[4]

This practice of making use of children's relationships, however, sometimes leads to excessive pressure on the responsible child asked by the teachers to help or to control another child, although this is common in Japan. The children who are asked are likely to be relatively more mature among their classmates, and these few children are likely to be stabilized by the beginning of the year. The school term in Japan starts in April (even for preschool), and children are classified according to their age on 1 April. Thus, children born in April (or May) are older than their classmates and may find it relatively easier to comprehend things; they tend to be more talkative, steadier, and more skillful. Such children are likely to have more opportunities, as the teachers rely on them, and may be given some authority. The children, of course, feel proud of themselves and develop their leadership skills. However, it is not easy to control children, even for adults. April/May-born children may find it more difficult to manage and feel frustrated. Furthermore, their developmental differences due to the month in which they were born diminishes during the year and over the years. Some of the April-born children feel pressured and exhibit problematic behaviors when children take over the teacher's expectations or when expectations are not high. April/May-born children may try to be too good in the group; they may gradually become a substitute for teachers and perceive their group as a target for monitoring rather than enjoying. Some of these children might get nervous and unexpressive and then sometimes become cowed due to the situation of the group.

This not limited to April- or May-born children; more mature children, especially linguistically developed children, may face similar situations in which they have more opportunities to be relied on. For instance, girls generally are faster in developing linguistics skills than boys; Kashiwagi (1988) found that girls in 3- to 4-year-olds class have a higher frequency of self-control in their peer relationships than boys of the same age, while boys and girls in the same class have no differences in self-actualization. This is not confined to the situation only in Japan; some traditional ideas on gender may influence the lives of children as well as those of adults. Furthermore, the problem is not only that these children feel pressures and cowed but also that teachers can unwittingly construct a static relationship of leader–follower, even though this relationship should be flexible in early childhood. As for this finding (Kashiwagi, 1988), we will have to rethink the possibility that adults who take care of children guide them automatically and unconsciously in the points of the cultural reproduction of gender bias since such early childhood.

Teachers have noticed problems like April-born pressure. Therefore, they provide education and care by carefully observing every child in the class and trying not to be biased toward a few children by relying on them. For instance, teachers utilize a rotation system, wherein children play a facilitator's role during circle time in the morning and one or two children in turns provide thanks for the meal.[5]

The following is a typical routine:

The teacher asked, "Who are today's facilitators?" and called out the names on the rotation name tag. "Come here, Kota and Moe [children's names]." The children stood in front of their classmates and said, "Good morning, teacher." The class followed together, saying, "Good morning, teacher." The child-facilitators said again, "Good morning, everyone." The class repeated, "Good morning, everyone." Thereafter, the child-facilitators said, "Today is the 8th of June. The weather is good. Let us play and enjoy today!"

In some homerooms, the child-facilitators have other tasks or roles like taking attendance and conveying this to the principal and workers at the meal center, wearing aprons and masks and serving meal to each child in the classroom, and taking care of small animals like rabbits that the facilities breed.

In addition, public support from the government has also developed. In Japanese preschool facilities, one teacher can have 30–35 children or fewer in a class for 5-year-olds. If one teacher is required to control 35 children, s/he would require an assistant and may ask a few mature children to help. In addition, there has been a recent emphasis on inclusive education and care even in preschool facilities, which all children with or without a disorder can attend and the class can have additional teachers. The additional teacher is assigned to a child with special needs, including those with a possible disorder. Due to this support, classroom dynamics have changed.

Hesitation to attend preschool

School non-attendance ("*futoko*") is a serious social problem for school students in Japan. "*Toen shiburi*," the hesitation to attend preschool – in which children refuse or hesitate to go to the preschool facility – can be considered similar to school non-attendance. This hesitation to attend preschool is also a typical maladaptation to preschool life and makes it tough for the children themselves as well as their teachers and parents who support the children. Some children freeze in front of the entrance and refuse to enter the preschool facility when they reach it in the morning, and they burst into tears when their parent tries to persuade them, pulls his/her hand, or carries them in their arm to try to take them to the classroom. Other children cry for a couple of hours and vomit or crouch in the corner of the classroom without involving themselves with anyone after their parent leaves the facility. Other children cannot have snacks or lunch and cannot get any sleep at nap time. This situation can continue for a couple of months in some cases. Furthermore, in serious cases, children may complain of stomachache when getting out of bed at home. Stomachache in the morning is a typical symptom of school non-attendance, and this is not malingering. The child really experiences stomachache, but the ache diminishes around noon.

However, it has generally been observed that, with regards to the hesitation to attend preschool, many cases are transient and can be distinguished from school non-attendance. Common hesitation to attend preschool can be attributed to transient separation anxiety due to proper, adapted attachment to the parents (Fujisaki, 2013). Especially in Japan, it is known that the rate of the secure type of parent–infant attachment is similar to many other countries such as the USA, England, and Sweden, while the rate of the ambivalent type in Japan is higher than in the other countries (Thompson, 1998). As stated by Rothbaum, Weisz, Pott, Miyake, and Morelli (2000), Japanese infants spend more time with their mothers at home. This is considered to be related to traditional Japanese values that mothers (but not fathers nor both parents) should stay with their children at home; therefore, many mothers do not work, at least when their children are young.[6] Some mothers take care of their children behind closed doors without meeting anyone outside of family members before the child enters the preschool facility; this is known as "capsuled mother–child" and is considered to be another social problem. The experimental Strange Situation to estimate the attachment type can be too shocking for the children who are in this situation to cope with. In other words, for children with a hesitation to attend preschool, there may be difficulties for them when meeting strangers. Recently in Japan, the number of nuclear families has been increasing,[7] and the inclusion of individualism has been promoted, leading to the isolation of each family, yet children are still required to adapt to the group quickly in a collective culture. In order to support children struggling between traditional collectivism and increasing individualism, facilities help children to take enough time to adapt through methods such as having the child stay for a shorter time at the facility and allowing the child to be alone in another location, such as the staff room, with additional staff.

However, hesitation to attend preschool should not be understated; some cases seem to have serious results later on, at school age. Some children who looked too recovered from their hesitation to attend preschool are unable to go to school again when they in elementary or junior high school, and some children repeat non-attendance or possibly experience "*hikikomori* (social withdrawal)" in early adolescence. When considering cases of school non-attendance, not only transient separation anxiety but also the more serious separation anxiety disorder, hidden developmental disorder, and poverty have recently been emphasized as causes of serious hesitation to attend preschool (e.g., Imanishi et al., 2012; Nishihara, 2006; Harada & Matsuura, 2010). Especially at the preschool age, any hidden developmental disorders that remain undiagnosed need to be observed and followed up by teachers in cooperation with counselors, medical institutions, and parents. The expert roles and skills of preschool teachers are thereby rediscovered, as they are expected to understand the problems of each child. Training programs for preschool teachers have been developed in order to widen the occupational range and improve to a higher degree the expertise of each teacher.

In Japan, if a child does not attend the preschool facility, it has a significant effect. As already mentioned, approximately 100% of children go to preschool at the age of 5, and this collectivist culture places value on children getting along with others and their group. This rate refers not only to the children who are educated and cared for but also the children who gain experiences with the same age group, get involved and negotiate with other friends, and control themselves in line with group intentions before school. Furthermore, the rate of enrollment to higher education institutions after graduating high school has increased to about 80% (MEXT, 2017). This means that almost all children go to elementary school after attending preschool facility and then go on to junior high school, high school, and university or college, after which they become employed. In this cultural context, hesitation or refusal to attend preschool might be the first, wrong step that leads to another maladaptation or multiple problems.

School education in preschool facilities

The acceleration of "school education" in preschool facilities is contentious. Japan is known as an East Asian country with highly competitive entrance examinations; many parents are interested in providing education for their children, and some of them are highly obsessed with education. These parents demand that preschool facilities introduce "school education" such as reading, writing, calculating, and English language so that when children enter elementary schools, they are not behind in classes compared with future classmates from other facilities. In fact, some preschool facilities, especially some kindergartens that provide accelerated school education programs, are popular. In the collectivist Japanese society, although it may seem to aim at equalitarianism, it is easy to increase competition on the same criterion, like academic achievement, because it does not place value on children choosing unique courses for their future. Such competitiveness begins from an early age, and some preschool children may be involved in such competitions already.

It may seem good that children can gain different experiences early, but the quality of children's experiences is more important. Japanese guidelines for preschool facilities have emphasized that children should obtain rich, direct experiences of their own senses and feelings through play, which cannot be complemented by indirect routes such as classroom lectures (i.e., MEXT, 2008; MHLW, 2008). Here, the direct experiences of their senses and feelings are considered to build the child's intellectual curiosity and are the most important foundation for the child to learn in the future. For instance, when playing a game of tag, children must count the number of participants, run around, control their bodies, and discuss with each other keeping to the rules so that they can develop their curiosity about the meaning of the number, biology of body, mechanism of speed control, choice of proper language and expression, and the structure of society; this intellectual curiosity of the child will foster authentic learning in the future (Muto, 2001). Nonetheless, young children are gradually losing the opportunities of play to be guaranteed based on the guidelines for Japanese preschool facilities. This can increase the number of passive learners who just memorize answers and work seriously without any motivation; such individuals may lose the aim of their life when they realize their own passiveness.

"O-juken": taking entrance examinations for private elementary school

"*O-juken*" can also be considered a factor that leads to a decrease in the direct experience of young children.

"*Juken*" without "*o*" in Japanese refers to taking entrance examinations, and this term includes a preparation period of about one year in order to concentrate on examination studies by giving up other activities or hobbies. This term, "Juken," generically points to the entrance examination for entering high school and then university/college after junior high school of the last compulsory education period. Some children, however, choose to take these entrance examinations in order to enter private elementary and junior high schools or national/ private schools attached to a university/college instead of local, public schools that do not require any examinations. These schools have escalator systems to university/college or educational continuity programs to prepare students for well-known university/college entrance examinations. Therefore, some parents are likely to positively lead their children to have good environment in school life and good future, even with some difficulties, i.e., taking entrance examinations, in the earlier period.

Here, "*o-juken*," or taking entrance examinations for elementary school, is experienced by children during early childhood. "*O-juken*" is an ironic, Japanese word; "*o*," a prefix that means politeness and childishness, is attached to the word "*juken*"; the resulting word gives the idea that a wealthy family has their young child take this examination. Only 1.8% of elementary students go to national and private schools after passing the examination (MEXT, 2017), which means that many young children experience failing the examination.

"*Juken*" (without "*o*") can be tough and is considered one of the biggest life events even for students in junior high or high school. If a young child is faces with "*o-juken*," the child as well as his/her parents would be involved; in fact, the parents would have more initiative in having the child prepare for the examinations. These entrance examinations for elementary school include interview, written examination, behavioral observation, arts and crafts, exercise (P.E), lot,[8] and/or documentary examination, although it depends on the specific school. The interview is believed to be the most important phase of the selection process for many schools. Only the child or the child along with his/her parent(s) would be interviewed and asked about motivation for applying, family philosophy of raising the child, and the child's personality. The child and their parents are required to repeatedly practice how to answer the questions so that they converse fluently in a cultivated diction and give the interviewers a good impression. Some families assemble expected questions and discuss the answers beforehand according to the preference of the interviewers, and parents have their children memorize answers by rote learning. The behavioral observation aspect of the examination involves grouping children together and instructing them to play a group game or solve a simple task while cooperating with each other. Therefore, each child is observed and their behavior and cooperativeness in the group appraised. These examinations require proper answers, behaviors, and skills, and in some schools – those that are more famous and popular and have a higher rate of competition – extensive preparation is needed for 5-year-old children. Therefore, many families send their children to cram schools, English classes, cultural lessons like arts and piano, and sports clubs like swimming and soccer in order to take the entrance examinations. In Japan, there were originally many cram schools for junior high and high school students; recently, cram schools for younger children to take "*o-juken*" have been also increasing. In addition, there are increasing number of children who will not be taking "*o-juken*" but attend cultural lessons and sports clubs as after-preschool activities; some of them have two or three activities a week.

Some families prepare their children for the examination so eagerly that the child spends most of his/her time attending cram school, culture lessons, and sports clubs after preschool hours instead of playing and spending time with friends or families or simply relaxing. Some children with imbalanced "*o-juken*" preparation and too many after-preschool activities are always busy, making them more passive. They obey the adults' instructions and do not have their own independent ideas and opinions. They also may not be able to have opportunities to learn appropriate social skills and may be less socialized; others could be ostensibly too socialized. They might feel frustrated, tell lies, or exaggerate to draw their friends' and teacher's attention. Furthermore, the entrance examinations are supposed to have a high failure rate, but families are likely to avoid sending their child to public school in their local community after failing the "*o-juken*" because they worry that all the friends of their child will know about them failing and that this might make their child uncomfortable. Therefore, they always take examinations for several schools until they pass the examination. Some children who fail the examinations may lose confidence in themselves.

First-grader problems

For many children, entering elementary school is one of the biggest environmental transitions. Final-year children look forward to entering a new school after graduating from a now-familiar preschool facility; at the same time, they may feel nervous about a strange new environment. The following are examples from 5-year-old children:

> In elementary school, teachers tell us all the things in the beginning, don' they? If there is something I don't know, do teachers let me know perfectly? Is it true?
>
> (5-year-old girl)

> I think I will be alright, but I'm a little worried about elementary school. Now, I am trying to listen very carefully to what my teacher says. She always says, "I have tree things to tell you. The first is . . ." I remember the first one

when she talks about the first one, and I remember the second one when she talks about it . . . and when she talks about the third one, I try to remember it but I forget the first one. What if the elementary teachers talk too much at the same time? I don't know if I can get them all.

(5-year-old boy)

Teachers who take charge of the class for 5-year-olds also prepare over the final year to send the children to elementary school. They begin to treat them as independent and autonomous individuals by increasing their opportunities to make independent decisions and discussing and planning some events with children. Furthermore, they respect their children as the oldest in the preschool facility through planning shows and letting the older children take care of the younger children. Teachers try to develop the children's independence and self-confidence to help them to get through elementary school. As already mentioned, acceleration of school education in preschool facilities is supposed to help children transition to a new school life. The transition from preschool life, based on playing, to school life, based on classroom lectures, can be a big change for the children and, for some, it can be hard to adapt.

"First-grader problems" refers to the difficulties of some first-graders who cannot adapt to elementary school and engage in behaviors such as making noise or wandering around during class and causing disturbances (Kikuchi, 2008). This is a serious social problem in Japan, and the government should promote discussion regarding teachers' expertise and the educational system. It is also important to understand the viewpoint of children who experience this transition. This transition from preschool to elementary school may lead to a big change in the quality of the group to which the children belong, implicit and explicit rules that they follow, and their physical environments. For instance, elementary schools have timetables that clearly schedule classes and recess and assign each subject to a specific timeslot; a chime sound is used to control the children in accordance to the timetables. Preschool facilities have play-based programs and no clear borders between play and learning time. When the activities are changed, the teachers call the children. Children are allowed to use the washroom at recess time in elementary school, but in preschool, they are allowed to use it whenever they want. In school, children have to adjust to the classroom lecture style, in which one teacher talks and all students just sit and listen to the teacher for 45 minutes per class, while they can play freely without teachers during recess time (although teachers often watch the children from the window of the teacher's room). Since they are not yet used to recess time without teachers, children do not know what they can do and find it difficult to play without teachers at the start of elementary school.

These big changes unsurprisingly lead to children having difficultly adapting. Japanese preschool facilities might be too focused on collectivism; Japanese children might be good at being self-organized in line with their group but not as good at regulating their own behavior by doing what they want. Few opportunities to learn how to express oneself in preschool might make them confused when they want to build new relationships in a new environment. Of course, in some cases, a hidden developmental disorder may be exposed.

Elementary school teachers can also be confused and try to make their children obey them strictly. This can make children more confused and lead to a negative spiral. Due to the situation in which school and preschool systems function separately, elementary school teachers and preschool teachers may have little contact each other, even when they take charge of the same children in the same community. Elementary school teachers cannot know how younger children behave and could be confused in a new environment, and preschool teachers cannot imagine what is required from first-graders. Recently, based on this reflective consideration, cooperation between elementary school and preschool facility has been focused on, and cooperative programs have been developed within the same community.

Concrete cooperative programs between elementary schools and preschool facilities include preschool children visiting elementary schools to observe the elementary students taking part in a class and joining them for lunch and elementary students visiting preschool facilities to play with preschool children on the playground. Further, in the initial period of elementary school, teachers should not make new students remain seated for too long in their classroom; rather, children should be encouraged to observe the outside environment in order to promote learning through experiences, so that new students can have enough time to adapt to school (e.g., Kikuchi, 2008; Fukumoto, 2014). These programs enable preschool children entering elementary school to imagine themselves and expectations as elementary students.

Summary: growing up in an individualizing collective culture

In this chapter, it was suggested that group setting education and care in Japanese preschool facilities and elementary school are beset by common problems. These can be related to the discontinuity of children's environment and development, for example, discontinuity between home and the preschool facility and discontinuity between the preschool facility and elementary school, to which children have to transition.

Japan has a collectivist culture, and children are likely to enter the same age group earlier. Although children develop both cooperativeness and independence and learn to balance both, as in other cultures, in Japan cooperativeness in a group is likely to be more focused on and is expected to be developed earlier than independence. Development of children in Japan can be guaranteed by "lack of anonymity." Given that their proper development is likely to be promoted by making use of their relationship with others in their group, children can develop through being watched by others and monitoring themselves as they are watched. Their cooperativeness thus makes the group stable and peaceful, and even their independence might help them to take the initiative to control themselves in line with the expectations of other or the intentions they perceive. Children may be able to learn self-assertiveness or self-actualization without rejecting others.

Preschool education and care in individualizing collective culture must shift in a new direction in order to receive and understand unique personal or minor value. In young childhood, the practice of preschool education and care is attempted under a new concept of diversity in which the interests and curiosities of each child are respected while the group is simultaneously maintained. This concept has been focused on in such contexts as inclusive education and care and increasing multicultural practices, and Japanese preschool practices and programs should continue to develop this change.

Notes

1 The Australian principal also mentioned that decreasing peer conflict is important for teachers.
2 In many Japanese preschool facilities, the washroom break is set between activities, when most of the classmates go together to the washroom in a line or by holding hands.
3 The meaning of "*Kodomo no ryobun*" may be closely related to the good aspect of a(n) (gang) age group.
4 In fact, the recent increase in individualism and overprotection has made it hard for the "children's world" to sustain. Japanese adults still value it.
5 In Japan, there are typical phrases – "*Itadaki-masu*," which is said before the meal, and "*Gochisosama*," which is said after meal – used to express gratitude for food and for the people who prepare it.
6 Of course, it is just a traditional value and has been changing recently.
7 Japanese have opportunities to move away from their hometown as a result of entering university, getting married, and getting a job. In particular, many Japanese companies order transfers for their workers and many families have to move. Furthermore, there are many nuclear families.
8 Some elementary schools decide children who pass by lots.

References

Cabinet Office (2008). Reform of "kodomo-en" early childhood care centers.
Cabinet Office (2016). White Paper on children and young people 2016.

Fujisaki, H. (2013). Influence of children's kindergarten life on their homes, investigated through parents' attitudes. *Annual Bulletin of Institute of Psychological Studies. Showa Women's University*, *15*, 33–44.

Fukumoto, M. (2014). Trends and issues in the connective curriculum between preschool and elementary school: Two approaches in education policy. *The Japanese Journal of Educational Research*, *81*(4), 14–24.

Harada, N., & Matsuura, K. (2010). A study of school-refusal students with learning and/or behavioral problems and the development of a comprehensive support system. *Japanese Journal of Human Sciences of Health-Social Services*, *16*(2), 13–22.

Imanishi, M., Yoshikura, Y., Kawanishi, M., Koyama, A., & Tamamura, K., (2012). Students with developmental disorders who have a tendency toward non-attendance at school – Case study at the LD resource room. *Bulletin of Nara University of Education*, *21*, 203–208.

Ito, Y. (2013). The feature of a childcare teacher's approach at lunchtime in a nursery school. *Japan Society of Research on Early Childhood Care and Education*, *51*, 211–222.

Kashiwagi, K. (1988). *Development of self in early childhood*. Tokyo: Tokyo University Press.

Kikuchi, T. (2008). The mutual adjustment process between children and ecology in the transition from preschool to elementary school. *The Japanese Journal of Developmental Psychology*, *19*(1), 25–35.

Ministry of Education, Culture, Sports, Science, and Technology (2017). School basic survey 2017. http://www.mext.go.jp/component/b_menu/other/__icsFiles/afieldfile/2017/12/22/1388639_2.pdf (2018.10.31.)

Ministry of Education, Culture, Sports, Science, and Technology (2008). Course of study for kindergarten.

Ministry of Education, Culture, Sports, Science, and Technology (2016). Research on issues over teacher guidance toward student's misbehavior 2015. http://www.mext.go.jp/b_menu/houdou/28/10/1378692.htm (2018.10.31.) Ministry of Health, Labor and Welfare (2008). Guidelines for day care centers.

Muto, T. (2001). *Education and care to develop intellectual curiosity—Tree modes to learn*. Froebel-Kan.

Nishihara, N. (2006). "Yogo-type School-Refusal" and educational deprivation experienced by children from disadvantaged families—Need for compensatory education systems and collaboration with families. *Japanese Journal of Social* Welfare, 46(3), 87–97.

Rothbaum, F., Weisz, J., Pott, M., Miyake, K., Morelli, G. (2000). Attachment and culture—Security in the United States and Japan. *American Psychologist*. 55(10), 1093–1104. http://dx.doi.org/10.1037/0003-066X.55.10.1093

Suetsugu, Y. (2012). "Special Consideration" for the child with developmental disabilities in group nursing and its possibilities: On the basis of empirical data for coping with trouble between children. *The Journal of Educational Sociology*, *90*, 213–232.

Tanaka, A. (2015). Effects of Preschool Teachers' Refraining from Getting Involved in 3 to 4-Year-Olds' Emotion-Evoking Scenes. *Research on Early Childhood Care and Education in Japan*, *53*(3), 284–295.

Thompson, R. (1998). Early sociopersonality development. In W. Damon & N. Eisenberg (Eds.), *Handbook of child psychology* (5th ed., Vol. 3). *Social, emotional, and personality development* (pp. 25–104). New Jersey: John Wiley & Sons, Inc.

Valsiner, J. (2014). *An invitation to cultural psychology* (p. 31). Thousand Oaks, CA: Sage.

Chapter 4

Mental health 101
Interpreting emotional distress for Canadian postsecondary students[1]

Karen H. Ross

In September 2012, the cover story of a prominent Canadian news magazine warned that the country was facing a "mental health crisis on campus" (Lunau, 2012). Labelling contemporary undergraduates "The Broken Generation," the report deployed dire statistics and alarmist language to paint a picture of widespread hopelessness, depression, and anxiety among "our best and brightest students." Alongside ongoing popular media attention, academic and government messages have articulated student mental health as a pressing social problem; the Mental Health Commission of Canada (2012) called for increased investment in "comprehensive . . . post-secondary mental health initiatives that promote mental health for all students and include targeted prevention efforts for those at risk" (p. 27). As Rosenbaum and Liebert (2015) sardonically observe, postsecondary student mental health is "trending now" (p. 179).

Although ubiquitous, mental health discourse is far from neutral. Like all knowledge, it operates to organize social reality – in this case, student suffering and struggle – in particular ways. This chapter explores constructions of student mental health in relation to three prominent forms of discourse: biomedical, therapeutic, and recognition-based. Each discourse will be discussed in terms of its key affordances and critiqued for its occlusions and more insidious potentials. Consistent with the theme of this volume, I will highlight dilemmas or tensions that students describe in relation to each style of navigating mental health problems. Rather than denouncing any particular discourse, my aim is to suggest that – from individual to institutional levels – maintaining space for multiple "languages of suffering" (Brinkmann, 2014) can maximize possibilities for creative responding to student distress.

Situating the inquiry

At Canadian postsecondary institutions, an overwhelming gamut of activities is underway to define, improve, and manage student mental health. High-ranking administrators disseminate risk management policies; wellness teams advertise stress-relief dodgeball and "puppy therapy" sessions; counsellors, psychiatrists, and mid-level managers develop evidence-based "stepped care" models to meet demand for mental health treatment. Implicit in each of these disparate activities are potentially incommensurable logics (Mol, 2008) that specify particular understandings of the problem's nature and how it might reasonably be addressed.

This chapter begins from the premise that student mental health is a contested epistemic object (Danziger, 2003), constituted by a tangle of intersecting and diverging lines of discourse. Such discourses are located within a heterogeneous *situation* (Clarke, 2005) involving countless individual and collective actors, non-human actants (including texts and documents), and sociocultural and political elements. The co-location of multiple interests and discourses sets the stage for tensions: students (and educators, counsellors, or other professionals concerned with student wellbeing) may feel pulled in different directions by conflicting accountabilities, expectations, norms, and values.

Constructing mental health

Mental health is a relatively new addition to the *psy* canon (Rose, 1998). Like related notions of madness (e.g., Foucault, 1965) or psychiatric diagnosis (e.g., Brinkmann, 2016), mental health knowledge and practices can be understood as socially constructed, historically contingent, and subject to prevailing power relations. Although scientific and psychiatric professionals have considerable power to shape common sense about the nature of mental health problems, knowledge is not created in an exclusively top-down fashion; it emerges through the intertwining activities of a complex *circulatory system* (Latour, 1999) involving technologies and procedures, communities of practice and scholarship, alliances and benefactors, and representations in public forums such as media. If "the meaning of a word is its use in the language" (Wittgenstein, 1963, p. 20), then any attempt to understand the meaning of mental health must go beyond official definitions to include heterogeneous representations in sites ranging from university policies to social media "clickbait" to students' self-descriptions.

Of course, discursive constructions of mental health matter little apart from their uptake in people's "doings, sayings, and relatings" (Mudry, 2016, p. 5) – their production of thinkable *ways of being a person* (Hacking, 2007) in a given situation. Certain practices are endemic within a particular culture, and come to feel natural and self-evident; others must be actively disseminated through efforts such as public education campaigns, "consciousness raising," training seminars, and so forth: "Mental Health 101," both metaphorically and (sometimes) literally speaking.

When making sense of ambiguous emotional difficulties in their lives, students are interpellated (Althusser, 1984) by one or more discourses, each of which entails affordances – that is, resources for sense-making and action – as well as constraints and blind spots. Such processes of discursive mediation can occasionally become problematic: we may experience uncomfortable tensions when hailed simultaneously by incommensurable discourses, or (conversely) become too tightly bound to the resources of a single discourse, caught up in interactive feedback loops that constitute a form of "capture" (Massumi, 2011, p. 48). Such discursive capture (Strong, 2012) or narrative "entrapment" (Shotter, 1993, p. 14) can obscure alternative responses and occasion conflict with others who operate from within different discourses.

A note on methods

Empirical data cited in this chapter come from a multisite corpus, collected for a forthcoming dissertation, that includes a) institutional mental health policies and service descriptions from eleven Canadian universities, b) widely shared online texts from websites such as *BuzzFeed* and *Huffington Post*, and c) interviews with ten young adults attending the University of Calgary (Canada) who self-identified as having experienced a mental health problem. Principles of situational analysis (Clarke, 2005) facilitated exploration of tensions and heterogeneities in the data. Throughout the chapter, I strive to track between complementary hermeneutics of suspicion and affirmation (Kearney, 2004), critiquing each discourse while appreciating the resourcefulness with which students use it to self-interpret and problem-solve.

Biomedical discourses of student mental health

The very term *mental health* is inextricable from medicalized discourse, positioning emotional suffering and idiosyncrasies as both *mental* (cognitive, internal, etc.) and *health*-related (somatic, symptom-focused, etc.; Rosenbaum & Liebert, 2015). Despite recent efforts to conceptualize mental health and mental illness on separate, intersecting continua (e.g., Keyes et al., 2012), the terms are often treated as interchangeable: "mental health problems" becomes a euphemistic reference to mental illness. With or without the formal assistance of diagnostic manuals, biomedical understandings invoke a *diagnose-and-treat* logic (Strong, Vegter, Chondros, & Job McIntosh, 2017) that prioritizes expert knowledge and authoritative "prescription" (formal or informal) of interventions.

Medical constructions abound within awareness campaigns and educational tools: for instance, a recent campaign from the Canadian Mental Health Association (www.b4stage4.ca) revolved around the hashtag *#b4stage4* ("before stage four"), comparing mental health conditions to cancer and demanding investment in prevention and screening efforts. While *parity* arguments (e.g., "the brain is an organ, just like any other"; Francolini, 2017, para. 1) may elide meaningful dissimilarities between emotional suffering and somatic disease, they are nonetheless powerful rhetorical devices that pull popular understandings of mental health in somatic, biomedical directions.[2]

"Finally getting an answer": affordances of biomedical discourse

On many postsecondary campuses, medicalized descriptions – particularly those that are formalized as diagnoses – operate as a *lingua franca* permitting communication among diverse stakeholders concerned with student distress. For students, psychiatric diagnoses unlock institutional services and accommodations that may be crucial to their success or even survival. Such access to resources constitutes a concrete incentive to interpret one's struggles in diagnostic language: as depression rather than heartbreak, anxiety disorder rather than worry or existential crisis, and so forth. In addition to pragmatic advantages, biomedical discourse confers a number of subjective affordances, to which I now turn.

Clarity and legitimacy

In her book *Putting a Name to It: Diagnosis in Contemporary Society*, Annemarie Jutel (2011) describes the sense of relief that a medical explanation can confer. The patient brings "a picture of disarray" (p. 4) to the doctor's office and emerges equipped with a narrative that can organize their pain and re-channel their frustrated efforts. In the words of one student interviewee, Hannah (all names are pseudonyms): "I felt comforted once I got that diagnosis because then it feels like I can categorize myself. Like, this isn't just random thoughts or making stuff up in my head, it's like – this is a real thing." Being diagnosed with obsessive compulsive personality disorder confirmed and legitimated Hannah's difference; it offered, in Jutel's (2011) words, "a sanctioned explanation of what makes . . . her different from everyone else" (p. 5).

Resources and control

In addition to reassurance that her problem was "a real thing," Hannah's diagnosis (this time, of depression) supplied her with actionable knowledge and an authoritative advisor (i.e., her doctor): "That's why I liked having the diagnosis. Just because, it's like – I'm working with someone who knows about it; I know about it now, and we're working through it together." Notably, shifting the problem from the realm of the everyday to that of professionalized knowledge and care can shut out friends and family who wish to help – indeed, Hannah deployed this understanding to silence her parents' expressions of worry and exclude them from this sphere of her life ("Relax, I got it under control . . . I have someone who, that's their job").

Pre-empting blame

A commonly cited effect of medicalized explanations is a neutralization of moral attributions – a shift "from badness to sickness" (Conrad & Schneider, 1992). Understanding depression as "a chemical imbalance in the brain" allowed one interviewee, Brent, to conclude: "It's just something that is different about you. And there's nothing wrong with that; it's just – something that needs to be solved with either therapy or medication or something like that." Another interviewee (Daniela) was even more direct in her rejection of characterological interpretations: "It's not that you're, like, a weak person or anything. It's literally that your brain is <u>different</u>. It's wired differently and you're gonna react differently to things."

Resisting medicalization: critiques of biomedical discourse

Medicalization has been defined as a process whereby "the jurisdiction of medicine began expanding, redefining certain areas once deemed moral, social, or legal problems (such as alcoholism, drug addiction, and obesity) as medical problems" (Clarke, Shim, Mamo, Fosket, & Fishman, 2010, p. 1). Critics such as Allen Frances (2013) argue that "the medicalization of ordinary life" can thwart appropriate agency and responsibility-taking; invite over-prescription of pharmaceuticals, with attendant risks and side effects; and foster a sense of "self-enfeeblement" (Gergen, 1994, p. 150) that perpetuates a "cycle of progressive infirmity" (Gergen, 2009, p. 49).

Student experience, with its confluence of transitions and pressures, has been subject to considerable medicalization, particularly since "the current culture . . . pressures students to find quick fixes" (Whitaker & Cooper, 2007, p. 245). Students operating "in a context that values 'the production of producers'" (Fromm, 2007, p. 38) may balk at the prospect of typical but disruptive developmental challenges and look to diagnosis and medication to restore their social, emotional, and academic status quo. There is also growing concern over the use of medications (particularly ADHD stimulants) as study aids; by 2013, "peer-reviewed journal articles started reporting that as many as a fifth, a quarter, or even a third of all college students in the United States take stimulants to help with midterms, finals, or term papers" (Hinshaw & Scheffler, 2014, p. xxii). Many students have become, to borrow Nikolas Rose's (2003) evocative phrase, "neurochemical selves" (p. 46) who attribute their emotional discomforts – sadness, fears, stresses – to chemical imbalances in the brain. Frances (2013) challenges such a shift, asserting that "the difficulties people have in meeting society's expectations should not all be labelled as mental disorders. Thirty percent of college students cannot suddenly have developed ADHD" (p. 186).

From agents to patients

According to Art Frank (1995), seeking care within a medical framework entails a "narrative surrender" (p. 6) whereby the person – now a *patient* – relinquishes storytelling authority to medical professionals. Evidence of this power differential can be found in university mental health centre descriptions. One website invites students to "drop in to Health Services to meet with a nurse who will assess your mental health needs and guide you to the appropriate resources" (Concordia University, n.d., "At Health Services," para. 1). Beyond choosing to "drop in," students are positioned as passive repositories of "needs" awaiting expert assessment and guidance. Another description indicates that "after the intake appointment, our team of counselling staff will make a counselling plan based on their professional opinion and in light of the student's goals and concerns" (York University, n.d.-a, "After the Intake," para. 1). Once their goals and concerns have been transformed into relevant information, students themselves become implicated (but absent) actors (Clarke, 2005) within the planning process.

Eclipsing alternative responses

At many Canadian universities, mental health strategies call for care to be "integrated" or "coordinated" across multiple services (e.g., counselling, medical, psychiatric) in order to avoid "silos" and duplication. Such integration is predicated on the assumption that services provided by each profession are fungible and commensurable – that is, that they operate from a shared underlying logic of student distress. Practices, theories, and values that deviate from dominant norms risk being marginalized or eclipsed.

In many "harmonized" arrangements, doctors and nurses are positioned as obligatory access points for mental health services, including counselling. At one university, this policy is justified in the following way:

> A number of mental health challenges have a physical basis that needs to be explored or treated before a specialized referral can be made. Meeting initially with a physician or nurse allows for a diagnosis and treatment of any underlying physical causes of mental health issues.
> (University of Toronto, 2015, "FAQs," para. 5)

This arrangement gives precedence to medical modes of responding over emotional, relational, spiritual, or political forms of problem-solving. Whatever understanding a student has attributed to their concern – homesickness, heartbreak, an abusive relationship, and so forth – it must pass through the medical gaze before encountering any alternative professional framework (if it ever does). "Harmonizing" care, in many cases, entails a degree of homogenizing care.

Unifying under a biomedical framework offers institutions a sense of control over the messy chaos of student lives in the form of evidence-based practices and, in some cases, a centralized database of problematic students. "One door" approaches, it is promised, "will simplify the pathway to care, will reduce fractured care and will provide *ongoing monitoring* [italics mine]" (University of Toronto, 2015, "What will be different"). While "monitoring" is often part of medical care, it simultaneously invokes a sense of unpredictable threat – positioning students as *risky* in ways that must be tracked and managed.

Surveillance medicine and the self-monitoring subject

Even as biomedical rationalities privatize student distress (within individual brains/minds/bodies), they simultaneously position mental health as a public health concern to be managed via the active cooperation of a self-monitoring student body. Consider the following excerpt from a blog post profiling a student leader and mental health advocate:

> In summer 2015, [she] hit rock bottom. When she realized her life was at risk however, she called the Here 24/7 telephone hotline and sought immediate medical attention. After checking into Grand River Hospital, [she] was diagnosed with clinical depression and began necessary treatment for the condition.
> (Hammermueller, 2016, p. 2)

Consistent with what Armstrong (1995) has called surveillance medicine, anecdotes such as this valorize a subject position that involves continuous self-inspection for emotional "risk factors" and proactive self-selection for diagnosis and treatment when problems arise. In case students do not spontaneously identify their experiences as medical concerns, online screening tools invite them to channel the clinical gaze via their smartphones and laptops ("answer a questionnaire and see if you may be struggling with common mental health problems").

Dilemmas of biomedical discourse

In an analysis of the Danish television show *Mad or Normal*, Brinkmann (2016) identifies three sites of paradox in diagnostic culture: one concerning the alleged equivalence of psychiatric and somatic illness, a second concerning the status of psychiatric patients as "normal" and yet "special," and a third concerning the transient versus enduring nature of disorder. Conceptual paradoxes such as these yield practical dilemmas for students navigating mental health difficulties.

Dilemmas of chronicity

As Brinkmann (2016) points out, psychiatric diagnoses are – at their most basic – labels for clusters of manifest symptoms. Nonetheless, current popular belief holds that mental disorders often persist in the absence of symptoms, akin to a chronic disease that must be "managed" to forestall relapse (in one interviewee's words: "it gets better – but at the same time, it's always gonna be something that could pop up at any moment"). This poses self-interpretive challenges to students who were diagnosed in the past but have been symptom-free for months, even years. When I asked Hannah whether she considers herself someone who *has* or *had* depression, she equivocated for some time before venturing: "I would lean towards. . . . I have it, but I'm asymptomatic? . . . I feel like I wouldn't say I had it until I was able to be happy off the medication."

Hannah's logic is sound enough ("Well – they're antidepressants. So . . . if I'm taking antidepressants, [then] I'm still depressed, but the medication's doing its job"). However, it provides her with no resources to decide when to stop taking the medication (if ever): "I kind of leave that up to what my doctors think. . . . If they think I'm coming to a point where I'm stable enough to get off them, then I'll follow that path." The threat of relapse is ongoing and omnipresent, effectively undermining

Hannah's licence to judge her own level of stability or wellness. Since she was experiencing no objectionable side effects at the time of the interview, Hannah found this arrangement acceptable; for other students, managing ostensible risk in perpetuity (irrespective of subjective wellness) might be a source of ongoing tension.

Dilemmas of authority

Despite increasingly collaborative rhetoric that urges patients to be "active participants" in the medical encounter, doctors (and authoritative diagnostic texts) typically retain final say on diagnosis and treatment (Jutel, 2011). How, then, do students navigate unexpected or discrepant elements of a diagnostic encounter? Daniela described one such experience:

> Eventually, the last medical student I [saw], he was like "I think you have Attention Deficit Disorder." And I'm like, "<u>what</u>? Like, I'm d<u>epressed</u>." . . . And he sent me home with all these tests, and I did them all. . . . And he was like, "yeah, you have ADHD!" . . . I was like, "okay, <u>fine</u> but, like – I don't get distracted by shiny things! I'm <u>not</u> that person." They're like, "just trust us for a little bit."

She acquiesced and, despite struggling at first ("I was on very high dosages of everything, and just – things weren't clicking"), ultimately came to accept the diagnosis as true: that she was indeed the person shown to her in the mirror of medical expertise (cf. De Vos, 2013).

Another interviewee, Mayumi, recalled consulting her family doctor in high school, expecting to be diagnosed with depression; she was surprised by her doctor's lackadaisical response. Despite more recently wondering if she might have bipolar disorder, she had not sought a diagnostic assessment. As she explained:

> I think it always goes back to, going to my doctor, and her being like, "well, you can take medicine or you don't have to take medicine; it's kind of your [choice]." And my doctor's <u>far</u> . . . and I don't wanna go there to have her say that, when I can just cope with it myself.

While some might consider this doctor negligent (i.e., failing to take Mayumi's mental health needs seriously), the exchange may have opened up a new possibility for Mayumi: the notion that there is no single, compulsory way to name and treat emotional concerns. Rather than persisting in her search for an authoritative answer (e.g., by seeking a second opinion), Mayumi learned to manage her emotional ups and downs via her own resourcefulness and the support of family and friends.

Therapeutic discourses of student mental health

Alongside biomedical discourse, the twentieth century witnessed a proliferation of therapeutic discourse focused on managing emotions, optimizing wellness, and enhancing skills and capacities. Rather than a mere absence of symptoms, therapeutic discourse idealizes *flourishing* (i.e., "feeling good about a life in which you are functioning well"; University of Calgary, n.d., "What is flourishing?"). Guided by positive psychology, self-help sensibilities, and countless manifestations of therapy culture (Furedi, 2004), students are called to capitalize on the many self-improvement opportunities that are extended to them. Therapeutic discourse articulates a split model of responsibility: the self is held blameless for its flaws (which are attributed to past traumas, family dynamics, etc.) but highly responsible for its future self-transformation (Illouz, 2008) through diverse *technologies of the self* (Foucault, 1988).

"I didn't have the language to understand": affordances of therapeutic discourse

Therapeutic and psychological narratives have taken hold in myriad cultural sites, where they have been endlessly extended, diversified, and reinvented. Unlike medical discourse, therapeutic narratives are richly textured and emotionally compelling – making them appealing resources for self-interpretation during ambiguous emotional struggle.

Self-understandings

For my interviewees, therapeutic explanations served as a salve for the intense distress of incomprehensibility that had characterized their pain. As Daniela recounted:

> My stepdad would get really frustrated, because all I'd do is just, like, cry. And he's like, "Why aren't you answering, like, why are you like this? Say something, why – " and I was like, "I just – I don't know what to tell you; I'm sorry." And I'd just be, like, crying all the time.

Working with a therapist allowed Daniela to "hash out" a narrative to understand and articulate her suffering, one that offered a platform from which to take action.

Illouz (2008) has argued that "the narrative of self-help is fundamentally sustained by a narrative of suffering" (p. 173). The further we venture into therapeutic self-understandings in an effort to optimize the conduct of our lives, the more psychic injuries and shortcomings we will discover. Daniela recalled:

> I was talking to my therapist and was able to sort of understand why my parents did the things they did . . . eventually I started developing a much broader understanding of what I thought I had wrong with me in the first place.

From a starting point of assuming that she was "depressed," this student came to identify a list of additional needs: address an anxiety disorder, improve self-worth, transform family relationships. Therapeutic expertise is welcomed as the technology by which her full, true self becomes knowable. As De Vos (2013) observes, "the *look, that's what you are* imposes the meta-position, resulting in an *oh really, is that the way I am?*" (p. 67). Psychology, he claims, invites us to look upon ourselves from a distance – as psychologists.

Language to express and relate

For some students, therapeutic language itself served as a technology with which to *speak* where this had previously been unthinkable. For interviewee Geoffrey, whose mental health problems intensified following a series of assaults, working with a counsellor involved gradually assimilating new ways of expressing his feelings and experiences:

> We also worked on, just, methods of language. . . . So, just working on a more factual – er, I shouldn't even say factual. But just a language that makes you feel comfortable, and makes you feel like you can explain some of the more intimate details of your life.

Geoffrey's repair – from "factual [language]" to "language that makes you feel comfortable" – suggests an understanding that there may be multiple valid ways of narrating an emotional experience. Nonetheless, for him, therapeutic language unlocked ways of speaking that offered grounds not only for self-compassion but, importantly, for telling his story to others who could respond with love and support.

Strategies for self-management

In addition to facilitating a shared understanding of their distress, therapeutic discourse furnished my interviewees with a number of symbolic "tools" for managing their unruly emotions. As Charlotte remarked, "there's a lot of behind the scenes things you have to do." Strategies were near-exclusively *individual*, even in the context of relational concerns such as family conflict (e.g., "I learned how to communicate with people and be like, hey – this way that you're treating me is not okay"). Communication, within therapeutic discourse, has been rationalized: transformed into a set of skills that can be mastered individually, divorced from the particularities of specific relationships (Illouz, 2008).

Critiques of therapeutic discourse

According to Nikolas Rose (1998), "contemporary individuals are incited to live as if making a *project* of themselves: they are to *work* on their emotional world . . . to develop a 'style' of living that will maximize the worth of their existence to themselves" (p. 157). My student interviewees seemed quite willing to "make projects of themselves" – after all, who would not wish to be happier, healthier, and more productive? However, a growing body of scholarship has critiqued the many ways in which therapeutic ideals reproduce neoliberal economic philosophies and extend their insidious consequences for subjectivity. Like neoliberalism, which positions individuals as ultimately responsible for their own success or failure, wellness culture urges students to focus on transforming their *individual* bodies, brains, and psyches via the broad subject positions of consumer and (self-)entrepreneur (May, 2012). Popular psychotherapeutic notions such as mindfulness (Barker, 2014) and resilience (Bracke, 2016) construct students as self-governing "docile bodies" (Foucault, 1977/1995, p. 135) whose distress poses little threat to dominant power relations. Aubrecht (2012) writes that such vocabularies

> operate as insurance for the university against critique that the social organization of everyday life and distribution of resources within the university contribute to suffering and to the appearance and experience of uncertainty (represented as depression and anxiety) in students' lives.
>
> (p. 72)

Economic logics

The neoliberalization of postsecondary institutions involves a turn to market logics and corporate management styles, including preoccupations with efficiency, productivity, and competitiveness (Parker, 2014). Student mental health is arguably valuable to the extent that it confers instrumental advantages (e.g., cost savings or enhanced recruitment); according to one school's mental health strategy, "stakeholders can be helped to endorse wellness as a goal, *by linking it to tangible benefits* [italics mine]" (Fitzpatrick & Di Genova, 2014, p. 6). Such benefits include "more productive undergraduate and graduate students who complete excellent work in a timely way" (presumably draining fewer resources). For students, we read, "wellness leads to increased *opportunities to realize potential* [italics mine] with concrete benefits such as improved employability" (p. 6). The document constructs a particular type of valued student: healthy, high-achieving, independent, self-optimizing – or, in other words, "comfortable, confident and capable of performing" (University of Toronto, 2014, p. 2).

Shaping the emotional self

To be a "good" student in the twenty-first century, one must not only maintain good grades but develop a panoply of "soft" skills in a particular emotional style: the ideal student is expressive, enterprising, and entitled (that is, confident and assertive; Martin & McLellan, 2013). By valorizing the emotional habits of the social stratum that has consumed the most psychological advice – that is, the middle class – norms of emotional intelligence come to constitute "a new axis of social classification" (Illouz, 2008, p. 205) clothed in meritocratic language. As one university administrator enthused:

> There are other traits we hope students have when they graduate. Are they resilient? Do they feel empowered? Can they empower others? By adopting a holistic view on what success means, we start to realise that we need to approach things differently. GPA is great, but so is an A+ in empathy.
> (Latimer, 2016, "Wellness is a big tent," para. 2)

Although metaphoric, this claim concretizes a tacit sense that there are indeed measurable norms associated with emotional competencies – and that failure to learn and express this set of competencies carries a real risk of being left behind (Boler, 1999).

Dilemmas of therapeutic discourse

Dilemmas of normativity

Both medicalized and therapeutic discourses orient to mental health problems as treatable (or surmountable) and therefore temporary. Students who are unable to overcome emotional impairments occupy a precarious position within the university community, with their membership "represented as contingent on the success of institutional programs and services designed to help them be more like 'most students'" (Aubrecht, 2012, p. 75). One interviewee, Geoffrey, encountered a similar line of thinking:

> Even though there's so many people sup<u>port</u>ing mental health, there's still also this desti<u>na</u>tion – they're like, "well, Geoffrey, why are you depressed? You've been depressed for 8 months!" Y'know, like, "why aren't you better?"

The expectation that students' storylines will mirror the "'Look, I Overcame' narrative" (James, as cited in Bracke, 2016, p. 67) permits the university to plan for only minor disruptions to standardized timelines, grading schemes, and so forth. A student's failure to bounce back from hardship comes to signal "a lack of learning or common sense, and a symptom of an inherently inferior subject position" (Aubrecht, 2012, p. 80). Geoffrey rejected this interpretation, imagining a different mentality in which

> you're not <u>ill</u> or <u>not</u> ill, you're just a person. Y'know? You're a person experiencing emotions and feelings each day. And sometimes it can be overwhelming, or sometimes it can be great, right? And – it shouldn't be dictated by <u>bus</u>iness.

Claiming one's right to be "just a person . . . experiencing emotions and feelings each day" offers a position from which to resist corporate imperatives of productive wellness. However, this value may sit uneasily alongside the (understandable) desire to mitigate difficult feelings via therapeutic technologies, or to shape one's emotional expressions into socially acceptable forms. Although certain self-help texts extoll the complementarity of self-transformation and self-acceptance, alliances of these two values are often tenuous, requiring frequent re-accomplishment.

Recognition discourses of student mental health

Within the final form of discourse I will explore, mental health becomes an axis of social identification (akin to gender, race/ethnicity, sexual orientation, and so forth), with associated meanings to be collectively resisted, redefined, and reclaimed. In many cases, resisting stigma involves valorizing those who experience mental health challenges: not only are such people *not* lazy, damaged, frightening, or self-indulgent, but they are (perhaps exceptionally) brave, intuitive, creative, and so forth. Within this logic, the definitive response to students experiencing distress should not be treatment or therapy, but *recognition*.

Hacking's (2007) work on *looping effects of human kinds* is relevant here. The "making up" of certain kinds of people relies upon intersections of knowledge, experts, and institutions. Expert classifications tend to generate stereotypes, to which persons thus classified inevitably respond. One possible response is to embrace the classification as a valued identity – for instance, many individuals diagnosed with Asperger's disorder join a worldwide online community of "Aspies" (Giles, 2014) within which they continue to "enhance and adjust what is true of them" (Hacking, 2007, p. 289): championing new terms (e.g., *neurodiversity* rather than disorder) and highlighting special strengths alongside particular (ostensibly shared) challenges. Often leveraging the same neurobiological expertise that pathologizes them as individuals (Ortega & Choudhury, 2011), such movements work "not only to upgrade self-conceptions and raise consciousness, but also to change the knowledge of the powerful about the oppressed" (Hacking, 2007, p. 290).

"I wanna be proud of who I am": *affordances of recognition discourse*

Recognition discourse offers powerful resources for advocacy. In my interview with Charlotte, she described her frustration with a friend's parents who refused to recognize their daughter's mental health disability and were "just telling her that she's lazy . . . it's like, 'oh, you're just not getting your stuff together. You're just not trying.'" She recalled this friend's father asking, "What kind of person fails two classes in a row?" to which she promptly retorted: "Somebody that needs support and isn't getting it." Charlotte explicitly rejected the implication that her friend was a morally deficient *kind of person* (cf. Hacking, 2007), and located the problem instead in a social–institutional failure to extend necessary accommodations. Within this logic, accessing accommodations became not only appropriate but essential, justifying drastic measures such as forging the parents' signatures on the required paperwork.

Another interviewee, Mayumi, hesitated when asked whether she self-identified as someone with depression, but ultimately agreed that she did. She clarified:

> I think I kind of need that label to . . . explain why I feel sad for no reason, or feel this need to not wanna get out of bed every so often. Um – to just say that is kind of easier? And as mental health is getting more attention and becoming more normalized, I think it's easier to say that I need a mental health day. I need a day to just like, watch Netflix all day [laugh].

Seen one way, Mayumi could be accused of taking advantage of a mental health label in order to shirk her duties (one can imagine the retort, "wouldn't we *all* like to watch Netflix all day!"). Alternatively, she can be heard as asserting a commitment to self-compassion. Mayumi's characterization of depression as an "easier" explanation suggests a pragmatic stance towards its truth value: she does not insist that the label represents the ultimate truth about her and her feelings, but is nonetheless comfortable occasionally claiming the social licence that it affords. The classic notion of the *sick role* (Parsons, 1964) becomes (to an extent) intentionally taken on – in a way that is understood not as malingering, but as a valid strategy for taking a (temporary) break from life's pressures.

Far from being ashamed of their mental health problems, many interviewees expressed appreciative understandings of their selves and difficulties. Several attributed their struggles to being exceptional in some way; for instance, being particularly considerate, being a critical thinker, or caring about global human rights issues. Their eventual success at overcoming the problem was also taken as a mark of character. As one interviewee, Carl, explained: "I like that this happened to me. It proves something. Proves that I could endure this type of pain." Overall, interviewees connected mental health problems with their identities in ways that thickened preferred storylines (White & Epston, 1990), reassured them of the adequacy of their best efforts, and fostered pride in the young adults they had become.

Critiques of recognition discourse

The proliferation of online communities has arguably fostered a "madness for identity" (Charland, 2004, p. 335), wherein psychiatric diagnoses are increasingly embraced as mediators of self-understanding (Brinkmann, 2016). Such practices may organize and stabilize a sense of self in relation to struggles that might otherwise be situated and transient. Similar concerns have begun to find expression in popular media, albeit grounded in a more essentialist focus on the blurring between "genuine" clinical depression and "wannabe depressives" (Bine, 2013, p. 3). Aesthetic cultures of "beautiful suffering" flourish in online spaces such as Tumblr, with the potential to romanticize depression, glorify self-pity, and enable young people to feed off one another's strong emotions (Bine, 2013; see also Yeomans, 2014).

Us vs. them

In 2015, *Huffington Post* published a photo series entitled "My Anxious Heart" that purportedly "nails what it feels like to have an anxiety disorder" (Holmes, 2015). The dramatic photographs are described as communicative tools that can help "open a dialogue between those who suffer from [anxiety] and those who have never understood it" (para. 3). Juxtapositions of "we who suffer" versus "they who misunderstand" – also hearable in online articles such as "31 Secrets of People Who Live With Anxiety" or "15 Things Anyone Who Loves A Woman With Anxiety Should Know" – are grounded in categorical logics (Cromby, Harper, & Reavey, 2013) that sharply separate mental disorders from other human pains. While conferring unique status upon sufferers' distress, such dichotomies construct a gulf between sufferers and those who might try to relate to them on the basis of common experience (e.g., of periods of intense worry). In this sense, recognition discourse may inadvertently amplify the loneliness of traversing a mental health problem.

Problem-saturated descriptions

Consistent with concerns about the glamorization of suffering, many popular articles about mental health concerns proffer intensely bleak, totalizing representations. For instance, a *BuzzFeed* post entitled "Here's What No One Tells You About Having Both Depression And Anxiety" (Borges, 2015) delivers a list of unremittingly hopeless predicaments that suggest a subjectivity of paralysis (e.g., #1, "It's freaking out at the idea of getting anything less than a stellar score on a test, but not having the energy to study"; #19, "It's sitting awake at 3 a.m. worrying about a future you're not even sure you want to have"). Such articles are accompanied by graphics that evoke darkness, isolation, and anguish. Perhaps as a rhetorical strategy to pre-empt or counter minimizations of their pain, young people with mental health problems often articulate their experience as pervasively negative, unremitting, and problem-saturated (White & Epston, 1990).

Appearance vs. reality

Alongside the us/them dichotomy described above, recognition discourse often establishes a contrast between outer appearance and inner reality. A widely shared article from *ESPN.com*, "Split Image" (Fagan, 2015), warned of this discrepancy: "On Instagram, Madison Holleran's life looked ideal: Star athlete, bright student, beloved friend. But the photos hid the reality of someone struggling to go on." The figure of the successful student hiding crippling mental health problems accomplishes at least two discursive effects. First, it establishes risk as omnipresent: even seemingly thriving students may, in reality, be at risk of suicide. Second, it foregrounds the subjective realm as the ultimate arbiter of wellness. If a student does not *feel* well, then they are not well, regardless of any evidence to the contrary. Such a construction may collide with psychiatric diagnostic criteria, which may require functional impairment above and beyond emotional distress.

Taken together, these discursive arrangements interpellate students with mental health problems as a distinctive *kind of person* (Hacking, 2007) with the right to describe their intense suffering and have these descriptions believed and taken seriously by those around them. In many circumstances, this arrangement fosters compassion and loving support. At the same time, self-interpretations that are so thoroughly defended against challenge (e.g., from confused friends who point to a student's active social life and many accomplishments) carry the potential for capture within the implications of a single (and, in this case, problem-saturated) discourse.

Dilemmas of recognition discourse

Dilemmas of accountability

While "recognizing" and "celebrating" students' mental health identifications may seem unproblematic, tensions arise when students' self-declared (and professionally ratified) limitations collide with academic standards. How many concessions may be extended without compromising the integrity of a grading system (and, by extension, of the university)? What constitutes fair treatment for students with mental health concerns, and what prevents students from using mental health language to excuse a lack of effort? Although I have heard student service providers struggle with questions of accountability in off-the-record conversations, such dilemmas are a relative *site of silence* (Clarke, 2005) in institutional texts.

An exception can be found in a list of "Frequently Asked Questions by Faculty About Students With Mental Health Disabilities" (York University, n.d.-b): "Why does a student wait until the last minute to ask for help, especially if the course work is outlined in the syllabus?" The language used to articulate this question ("wait until the last minute") seems to anticipate faculty frustration with student behaviour that is perceived as exasperating and irresponsible. However, the answer proffers a different narrative, wherein students are "fiercely independent" and "do not want to ask for help unless they feel they need it." It simultaneously invites faculty into a stance of compassion toward students who may "feel undeserving of help." No possibility is articulated that students with mental health disabilities could occasionally be unfocused, disorganized, indifferent, and so forth – in other words, that they could be subject to the same foibles as other students. While it is certainly plausible that illness interferes with students' "best intentions" and "true abilities," such assumptions unintentionally construct students with mental health concerns as *less human* than other students, who may benefit from the freedom to fail. Faculty are cautioned not to penalize students "for their absences and/or deferred work, if it is disability related," but are provided no discursive platform from which to expect a student to do better *in spite of* a disability.

Dilemmas of performativity

Popular culture and media, by modelling dramatic forms (and norms) of emotionality, may occasion amplified feelings of suffering (Illouz, 2008). One interviewee, Chris, talked a great deal about how her experience of depression may have been shaped by popular culture (she specifically cited the *Twilight* series of melodramatic young adult vampire novels/films). As she explained:

> I think I might've had this idea of, y'know, if you're sad and brooding all the time it's somewhat poetic and romantic, because you're really feeling. I just felt like, this is what depression is: you're sad and you're brooding and you're drinking and you're crying and you're feeling all these things. And so it was like, I'm edgy or cool or something because I'm feeling all these deep emotions. But I look at it now and I'm like – what was I doing? Like, just engaging in self-destructive behaviour.

Although Chris's confusion and pain (having been slandered and shunned by a family member) was legitimate, she retrospectively understood her response as performative: "I didn't know what to do, so I just picked the dramatic and stereotypical forms of anger, aggression, sadness, [and] loneliness, and played them out." She ultimately came to reject this mode of suffering as "pandering" and "manipulative," as well as detrimental to her education and health.

Another interviewee, Geoffrey, reflected on his subjectivity at the height of his mental health struggles:

> I just actually felt like something's wrong with me, almost . . . But then, there's also a benefit to that. Because you're like, "oh, well, it makes me different" – and, y'know, that's, always this desire, especially when you're [young], to stand out. Right? So maybe I found that was beneficial. I don't know, uh, maybe.

Geoffrey's uncertainty here suggests a tension; he is less willing than Chris to paint his younger self's distress as inauthentic, yet he speculates that his dramatic feelings *could* have flourished within a youthful sense that being "crazy" meant being special. He was not (at that moment) equipped with a framework by which to articulate his feelings as both legitimate *and* occasioned by discursive positioning, which left him uncertain as to how to resolve this dilemma.

Discussion

Each of the forms of mental health discourse described above – biomedical, therapeutic, and recognition-based – offers a particular complement of resources that can be invaluable for navigating ambiguous and distressing circumstances. At the same time, students may find themselves bumping up against the limitations of a given discourse: recognizing, or perhaps merely suspecting, that there may be other ways of being and responding that lie beyond what the discourse makes thinkable. In other cases, they are interpellated by multiple discourses and feel caught betwixt "different 'goods,' reflecting not only different values but also involving different ways of ordering reality" (Mol, Moser, & Pols, 2010, p. 13).

Students, as well as administrators, may be tempted to seek an authoritative resolution to mental health tensions. What is the *right* way of balancing accountability against compassion? But while synthesis and compromise may grant certainty, they also shut down conversation. There is something uniquely generative about tensions: they signal spaces where reality is not yet foreclosed and new possibilities may yet be imagined. They signal that we remain compelled by both accountability *and* compassion. They permit options of discursive flexibility, "narrative braiding" (Cobb, 2013), or using the implications of one discourse to resist those of another when it becomes odious or too dominant.

This chapter represents one small effort to chart meaning-making around student mental health, and the situation is ripe for analytic exploration along different axes. Rather than the three forms of discourse highlighted in this chapter, I could have considered how students took up the five "languages of suffering" identified by Brinkmann (2014): diagnostic, religious, existential, moral, or political. One interviewee, Anthony, associated his depression with a failure to live virtuously; another, Sabrina, understood depression as an existential signal ("I wasn't really doing anything that aligned with the values I claimed to have. . . . Whenever I've been depressed it's like, 'you need to change something; you're not going in the right direction'"). Such descriptions can sensitize us to multiplicity among the "theories of change" (Duncan & Miller, 2000) that structure students' responses to emotional distress.

Finally, more research is needed to "turn up the volume on lesser but still present discourses, lesser but still present participants, the quiet, the silent, and the silenced" (Clarke, 2005, p. 175). In this case, "lesser but still present discourses" include political, collective, and critical positions. We find stirrings of acknowledgment: for instance, one text appreciatively notes a small cadre of educators who teach "critical/structural/Mad positive aspects of mental health" (Ryerson Mental Health Advisory Committee, 2013, p. 3) and declares its commitment "not only to medical conceptions of illness and health but Indigenous conceptions of social, spiritual and community well-being, critical notions of Madness and disability and cultural interpretations of wellness" (p. 3). Nonetheless, the same document laments a "lack of consistency in message and content" (p. 4) among its mental health programs and services; such tensions between pluralism and standardization are likely to persist.

For policymakers, managers, educators, and helpers in a "best practice" era, multiplicity may feel unpalatably messy and overwhelming. A manageable starting point may be to practice getting curious about local responses to student distress. At the very least, we should not attempt to pave over controversies by insisting upon a unified canon of mental health knowledge; the situation *is* heterogeneous, whether we acknowledge it or not, and students recognize this. Attempts to impose a single, unified narrative only push their dilemmas "underground," rendering them unspeakable. We can better serve students by engaging with complexities, becoming comfortable with provisional answers, and co-creating "ways of going on together" (Gergen, 2009, p. 9) through this churning discursive flux.

Notes

1 Thanks to Dr Tom Strong for feedback on an earlier draft of this chapter.
2 When medical terminology is deployed in a novel fashion – such as the suggestion that a student may be mentally "injured" rather than mentally ill (University of Toronto, 2014, p. 2) – it seems possible that such language may be taken up in both metaphoric and, occasionally, literal ways.

References

Althusser, L. (1984). Ideology and ideological state apparatuses (notes towards an investigation). In L. Althusser (Ed.), *Essays on ideology* (pp. 1–60). London, UK: Verso.

Armstrong, D. (1995). The rise of surveillance medicine. *Sociology of Health & Illness*, *17*, 393–404.

Aubrecht, K. (2012). The new vocabulary of resilience and the governance of university student life. *Studies in Social Justice*, *6*(1), 67–83.

Barker, K. K. (2014). Mindfulness meditation: Do-it-yourself medicalization of every moment. *Social Science & Medicine*, *106*, 168–176.

Bine, A. (2013, October 28). Social media is redefining 'depression.' *The Atlantic*. Retrieved from www.theatlantic.com/health/archive/2013/10/social-media-is-redefining-depression/280818/

Boler, M. (1999). *Feeling power: Emotions and education*. New York, NY: Routledge.

Borges, A. (2015, October 15). Here's what no one tells you about having both depression and anxiety. *BuzzFeed*. Retrieved from www.buzzfeed.com/annaborges/20-feelings-that-sum-up-having-both-depression-and-anxiety.

Bracke, S. (2016). Bouncing back: Vulnerability and resistance in times of resilience. In J. Butler, Z. Gambetti, & L. Sabsay (Eds.), *Vulnerability in resistance* (pp. 52–75). Durham, NC: Duke University Press.

Brinkmann, S. (2014). Languages of suffering. *Theory & Psychology*, *24*(5), 630–648.

Brinkmann, S. (2016). *Diagnostic cultures: A cultural approach to the pathologization of modern life*. London, UK: Routledge.

Charland, L. C. (2004). A madness for identity: Psychiatric labels, consumer autonomy, and the perils of the Internet. *Philosophy, Psychiatry, & Psychology*, *11*(4), 335–349.

Clarke, A. E. (2005). *Situational analysis: Grounded theory after the postmodern turn*. Thousand Oaks, CA: Sage.

Clarke, A. E., Shim, J. K., Mamo, L., Fosket, J. R., & Fishman, J. R. (2010). Biomedicalization: A theoretical and substantive introduction. In A. E. Clarke, L. Mamo, J. R., Fosket, J. Fishman & J. K. Shim (Eds.), *Biomedicalization: Technoscience, health, and illness in the US* (pp. 1–44). Durham, NC: Duke University Press.

Cobb, S. (2013). Narrative 'braiding' and the role of public officials in transforming the public's conflicts. *Narrative and Conflict: Explorations of Theory and Practice*, *1*(1), 4–30.

Concordia University. (n.d.). Mental health services. Retrieved from https://web.archive.org/web/20160821170008/www.concordia.ca:80/students/health/mental-health.html.

Conrad, P., & Schneider, J. W. (1992). *Deviance and medicalization: From badness to sickness* (Exp. ed.). Philadelphia, PA: Temple University Press.

Cromby, J., Harper, D., & Reavey, P. (2013). *Psychology, mental health and distress*. New York, NY: Palgrave Macmillan.

Danziger, K. (2003). Where history, theory, and philosophy meet: The biography of psychological objects. In D. B. Hill & M. J. Kral (Eds.), *About psychology: Essays at the crossroads of history, theory, and philosophy* (pp. 19–34). Albany, NY: State University of New York Press.

De Vos, J. (2013). *Psychologization and the subject of late modernity*. New York, NY: Palgrave MacMillan.

Duncan, B. L., & Miller, S. D. (2000). The client's theory of change: Consulting the client in the integrative process. *Journal of Psychotherapy Integration*, *10*(2), 169–187.

Fagan, K. (2015, May 7). Split image. *espnW*. Retrieved from www.espn.com/espn/feature/story/_/id/12833146/instagram-account-university-pennsylvania-runner-showed-only-part-story.

Fitzpatrick, M., & Di Genova, L. (2014). *Report of the mental health working group*. Retrieved from www.mcgill.ca/studentservices/files/studentservices/mhwg_executive_summary_and_recommendations_0.pdf.

Foucault, M. (1965). *Madness and civilization: A history of insanity in the age of reason*. Trans. R. Howard. New York, NY: Vintage Books.

Foucault, M. (1988). Technologies of the self. In L. H. Martin, H. Gutman, & P. H. Hutton (Eds.), *Technologies of the self*. London, England: Tavistock.

Foucault, M. (1995). *Discipline and punish: The birth of the prison*. Trans. A. Sheridan (2nd ed.). New York, NY: Vintage Books. (Original work published 1977)

Frances, A. (2013). *Saving normal: An insider's revolt against out-of-control psychiatric diagnosis, DSM-5, Big Pharma, and the medicalization of ordinary life*. New York, NY: Harper Collins Publishers.

Francolini, J. (2017, August 22). Brain health: The promise of science & social change. Retrieved from http://patrickjkennedy.net/572-2/

Frank, A. W. (1995). *The wounded storyteller: Body, illness, and ethics*. Chicago, IL: University of Chicago Press.

Fromm, M. G. (2007). The escalating use of medications by college students: What are they telling us, what are we telling them? *Journal of College Student Psychotherapy*, *21*(3/4), 27–44.

Furedi, F. (2004). *Therapy culture: Cultivating vulnerability in an uncertain age*. New York, NY: Routledge.

Gergen, K. J. (1994). *Realities and relationships: Soundings in social construction*. Cambridge, MA: Harvard University Press.

Gergen, K. J. (2009). *An invitation to social construction* (2nd ed.). London, England: Sage.

Giles, D. C. (2014). 'DSM-V is taking away our identity': The reaction of the online community to the proposed changes in the diagnosis of Asperger's disorder. *Health*, *18*(2), 179–195.

Hacking, I. (2007). Kinds of people: Moving targets. *Proceedings of the British Academy, 151,* 285–318.

Hammermueller, R. I. (2016, January 19). EngSoc president leaves mental health legacy on campus. Retrieved from https://uwaterloo.ca/student-success/blog/post/engsoc-president-leaves-mental-health-legacy-campus.

Hinshaw, S. P., & Scheffler, R. M. (2014). *ADHD explosion: Myths, medication, money, and today's push for performance.* Oxford, England: Oxford University Press.

Holmes, L. (2015, May 18). This stunning photo series nails what it feels like to have an anxiety disorder. *Huffington Post.* Retrieved from www.huffingtonpost.ca/entry/anxiety-photos-katie-crawford_n_7292548.

Illouz, E. (2008). *Saving the modern soul: Therapy, emotions, and the culture of self-help.* Berkeley, CA: University of California Press.

Jutel, A. G. (2011). *Putting a name to it: Diagnosis in contemporary society.* Baltimore, MD: Johns Hopkins University Press.

Kearney, R. (2004). *On Paul Ricoeur: The owl of Minerva.* Aldershot, UK: Ashgate.

Keyes, C. L. M., Eisenberg, D., Perry, G. S., Dube, S. R., Kroenke, K., & Dhingra, S. S. (2012). The relationship of level of positive mental health with current mental disorders in predicting suicidal behaviour and academic impairment in college students. *Journal of American College Health, 60*(2), 126–133.

Latimer, J. (2016, September 6). *Concordia's holistic approach.* Retrieved from www.concordia.ca/cunews/main/stories/2016/09/06/campus-wellness-support-services-reshaping-how-health-care-is-delivered.html.

Latour, B. (1999). *Pandora's hope: Essays on the reality of science studies.* Cambridge, MA: Harvard University Press.

Lunau, K. (2012, September 5). Campus crisis: The broken generation. *Maclean's.* Retrieved from www.macleans.ca/news/canada/the-broken-generation/

Martin, J., & McLellan, A. (2013). *The education of selves: How psychology transformed students.* Oxford, England: Oxford University Press.

Massumi, B. (2011). *Semblance and event: Activist philosophy and the occurrent arts.* Cambridge, MA: MIT Press.

May, T. (2012). *Friendship in an age of economics: Resisting the forces of neoliberalism.* Lanham, MD: Lexington Books.

Mental Health Commission of Canada. (2012). *Changing directions, changing lives: The mental health strategy for Canada.* Calgary, Canada: Author.

Mol, A. (2008). *The logic of care: Health and the problem of patient choice.* New York, NY: Routledge.

Mol, A., Moser, I., & Pols, J. (2010). Care: Putting practice into theory. In A. Mol, I. Moser, & J. Pols (Eds.), *Care in practice: On tinkering in clinics, homes and farms* (pp. 7–25). Bielefeld, Germany: transcript.

Mudry, T. E. (2016). *Behaviour is in the practice: Examining excessive behaviours using a practice framework* (Doctoral dissertation). Available from ProQuest Dissertations and Theses database. (No. 10630418)

Ortega, F., & Choudhury, S. (2011). "Wired up differently": Autism, adolescence and the politics of neurological identities. *Subjectivity, 4*(3), 323–345.

Parker, I. (2014). Managing neoliberalism and the strong state in higher education: Psychology today. *Qualitative Research in Psychology, 11*(3), 250–264.

Parsons, T. (1964). *The social system* (1st Free Press Pbk. ed.). New York, NY: The Free Press.

Rose, N. (1998). *Inventing ourselves: Psychology, power, and personhood.* Cambridge, UK: Cambridge University Press.
Rose, N. (2003). Neurochemical selves. *Society, 41*(1), 46–59.
Rosenbaum, P. J., & Liebert, H. (2015). Reframing the conversation on college student mental health. *Journal of College Student Psychotherapy, 29*(3), 179–196.
Ryerson Mental Health Advisory Committee. (2013). *Ryerson Mental Health Advisory Committee Report.* Retrieved from www.ryerson.ca/content/dam/mentalhealth/Ryerson%20Mental%20Health%20Advisory%20Committee%20Report.pdf.
Shotter, J. (1993). *Conversational realities: Constructing life through language.* London, UK: Sage.
Strong, T. (2012). Conversation and its therapeutic possibilities. In A. Lock & T. Strong (Eds.), *Discursive perspectives in therapeutic practice* (pp. 308–321). Oxford, UK: Oxford University Press.
Strong, T., Vegter, V., Chondros, K., & Job McIntosh, C. (2017). Medicalizing developments in counsellor education? Counselling and counselling psychology students' views. *Canadian Journal of Counselling and Psychotherapy, 51*(2), 161–186.
University of Calgary. (n.d.). *UFlourish week.* Retrieved from https://web.archive.org/web/20170830024345/www.ucalgary.ca/wellnesscentre/uflourish-week.
University of Toronto. (2014). *Report of the Provostial Advisory Committee on Student Mental Health.* Retrieved from http://mentalhealth.utoronto.ca/sites/default/files/Report%20on%20Student%20Mental%20Health%202014.pdf.
University of Toronto. (2015). *Where did CAPS go?* Retrieved from https://web.archive.org/web/20160430045003/www.studentlife.utoronto.ca/hwc/where-did-caps-go.
Whitaker, L. C., & Cooper, S. E. (2007). The big picture and what can be done to improve it. *Journal of College Student Psychotherapy, 21*(3/4), 243–257.
White, M., & Epston, D. (1990). *Narrative means to therapeutic ends.* New York, NY: W. W. Norton.
Wittgenstein, L. (1963). *Philosophical investigations.* Trans. G. E. M. Anscombe (2nd ed.). Oxford, UK: Blackwell.
Yeomans, E. (2014, December 18). Can Tumblr help young people with mental illnesses? *Live Mag UK.* Retrieved from www.livemaguk.com/mental-health-tumblr/
York University. (n.d.-a). *Accessing counselling services.* Retrieved from https://web.archive.org/web/20160810131520/http://pcs.info.yorku.ca/accessing-counselling-services/
York University. (n.d.-b). *Frequently asked questions by faculty about students with mental health disabilities.* Retrieved from http://mhds.info.yorku.ca/faculty-resources/faq/

Chapter 5

Counseling for university students

*Giulia Savarese, Oreste Fasano,
Nadia Pecoraro, Monica Mollo,
Luna Carpinelli and Pierpaolo Cavallo*

Premise

Some of the major studies on stress and transition processes will be discussed in the first part of this chapter, and in the second part we will present the results of research conducted at the "Counseling Center of the Athenaeum Michele Cesaro"[1] of the University of Salerno, which provides psychological reception, hearing and support to students experiencing discomfort (Savarese & Iannaccone, 2013).

Stallman (2010) estimated the prevalence of stress and anxiety as well as mental health problems in university students. He found that 67% of them show more or less severe clinical symptoms related to anxiety, distress and depression. During these years, meeting with the students and their discomfort has allowed us to verify what Stallman found and to trace the profile of the candidate seeking help (Savarese et al., 2016), as well as to focus on risk and resource factors.

By age, the young university student is in a delicate phase of his/her life cycle: not only does the university course fall on the educational and training path that the student has to face, but it also coincides with a process of identity transition (Zittoun, 2006). This is a dimension closely linked to the construction of the professional role and also to the transition from the teenage condition to the more mature one of student and young adult.

In this phase of change, students are required to reorganize their social role and, more generally, their own ego, by redefining old and new patterns (Perret-Clermont & Iannaccone, 2005). The student has to deal with critical situations related to the overcoming of different development tasks, and appropriate cognitive, emotional, affective, strategic–behavioral and relational skills are needed (Savarese et al., 2016)

The university experience can be a stressful life phase. Some students, in fact, say they feel overwhelmed by this new condition, and this can very easily affect their psycho–physical health. The students we meet at the Counseling Center show the first symptoms of discomfort: irritability, sleep problems, headaches, loss of appetite, dizziness; fatigue linked to the preparation for imminent examinations, conditioned by the rhythms imposed by the school institution, but also by personal and social expectations, social retreat and risk behaviors. In some cases, the symptomology describes a much more structured discomfort, which has become a real disorder, often with a remote anamnesis, which therefore requires more structured psychotherapy pathways or medical–psychiatric interventions.

In our clinical experience, the majority of students with dysfunctional and maladaptive or psychopathological behaviors saw broadly reduced expressive symptoms of discomfort and increased coping and self-esteem skills by the end of the help path (Gustems-Carnicer, and Calderón, 2013; 2014).

Introduction

Identity transition with the university student

The university course coincides with a student's transition phase, in which he/she is called upon to respond to numerous development tasks (Cassidy & Trew, 2004).

There are two elements of particular importance for the process of identity redefinition: transitions and micro-transitions. The analysis of micro-transition processes (sudden change of role, position, and environmental situations) is particularly interesting in the study of identities because they necessarily involve "psychological changes" and consequent transformation of the representation that people have of themselves, of context and role. Meeting the university context represents a phase of the students' life cycle, a time of transition, during which they are required not only to redefine new life experiences and relational contexts but also to re-elaborate the idea of their own present and future plans (Salvatore et al., 2003; Sestito, Sica, & Ragozini, 2011). It is therefore a psycho-social phenomenon and is often accompanied by high anxiety levels, low self-esteem and social anxiety (Tilleczek, Ferguson, & Campbell, 2011).

Zittoun (2004, 2006, 2007a, 2007b, 2014) ontogenetically defines '*transition*' as a '*mobile*' period, which allows for an exploration of possible paths and personal changes through a trial and error attempt. From a structural and dynamic point of view, transition is triggered by a *breaking* element defined by an event or change or by something unexpected that requires a new and sustainable adaptation between the person and his/her current environment, through a process of elaboration tied to the construction of meaning. Transition designates the post-break processes of rebalancing and of restoring of one's sense of continuity and integrity.[2]

Transition therefore contains a *problem/rupture* phase but also commitment to resolving the problem, and resolution. This process implies that people can continue to carry out their actions, perhaps attributing the causes of failures to the outside rather than the *locus of internal control* (Zittoun, 2006).

Ruptures therefore require a repositioning process: in other words, they may prompt new acquisitions, correspondences and personal redefinitions; so, they set themselves as interesting and productive for the emergence of psychological changes.

In this sense, transition is an opportunity for development, that is, a new symbolic formation that provides a better adaptation to a given social and material situation, protecting one's own sense of self (Zittoun & Perret-Clermont, 2001). It can, however, become evolutionary if the person is able to leave the previously occupied position and, based on his/her skills and knowledge, create ways of thinking and acting to help re-establish a new regularity by passing through uncertainty.

During the university course, students are required to carry out a *cultural integration* between their systems of meaning and the new university codes, in order to build the sense of their training pathway (Iannaccone, Ghodbane, & Rosciano, 2005) and self within that context. Access to university life and academic life itself is not just a matter of adapting to a new social environment; it has more to do with a process of *identity repositioning*, cultural transfer and building of new meanings (Zittoun, 2006; Gomes, Dazzani, &Marsico, 2017).

> Access to university should be able to be globally defined (and observed) in terms of psycho-social transition processes, a real 'entry' into a culture that would raise, among other things, identity problems, since every transition and transition process redefines the relationship between self and others.
> (Iannaccone et al., 2005, p. 39)

Coulon (1997) explains how abandoning studies is often the result of a lack of synthesis between university demands and the students' ability to adapt and accommodate new academic codes, use its various resources and assimilate its routines. In fact, meeting with the university context always requires the implementation of strategies for the search for *anchor points* and *sense* (Bruner, 1986, 1990).

The meeting with the training setting therefore requires not only acquiring new knowledge and skills but also attributing new meanings to reality, mediating them with the pre-constituted ones and thus activating a new positioning towards reality itself.

In many cases, new demands from university contexts can be assimilated to old patterns (Bell, Wieling, &Watson, 2005) through circumvention strategies (Josephs & Valsiner, 1998) in order to remove conflict and tension generated by opposite meanings. For example, one student may say that it is important to pass all examinations scheduled for the semester but, failing to do so, he/she may find excuses of various nature. In other cases, however, it is possible to activate a real rupture with the old systems of self and world significance: a state of tension, disorientation and fear is activated, which can momentarily ignite culturally located coping strategies (books, songs, films and others) (Gomes, & Teixeira2016; Martsin, Chang, & Obst, 2016). For example, in the face of anxiety, a student can perform a *ritual* (i.e., spending an hour a day watching TV series or staying at the personal computer). These strategies can only be functional if they are momentary and anchored to the articulation processes, but are always non-functional if they are excessively present in the person's life. Students with proper self-esteem (not low nor too high) and with the perception of peer network support are probably more disoriented in the moment of dismay following the rupture process.

With regard to clinical symptoms, sometimes associated with anxiety and stress, we believe that, except in cases where a psychopathological picture with an early history is present, an alteration of the symptom may be a momentary expression related to the functioning of the personality. The research we conducted has indeed shown that the students no longer had clinical symptoms (Savarese et al., 2013, 2014) following the counseling pathway.

University students and stress

Stress is considered to be a physiological reaction of an organism (APA, 2013). In other words, stress is the physical and psychological reaction of a person to a perceived or real question of change. In fact, stress is a natural phenomenon; it is part of every individual's life, and its main function is to help us deal with difficult situations. In this sense, within the person's tolerable limits, it can also be considered in positive terms because it strengthens reaction times, thus improving performance. The problem arises when one is excessively overloaded without experiencing the limit of possibilities (organism and psycho-physical balance), and in relation to the stage of the life we are living: the body might come to talk in our place through excessive stress symptoms.[3]

It can be divided between *eustress* and *distress*. By *eustress* we mean positive stress, able to keep the mental tension necessary to begin the adaptive response in the subject; we talk of distress, on the contrary, for negative stress, when the individual becomes unable to react to stress stimuli (Pancheri, 1980).

It is also necessary to distinguish between the so-called *stress factors* (stress-causing situations) related to the context and the *behavioral responses to stress* (physical and/or psychological reactions to these situations) related to the person: the way we react to an event is extremely individual and very much depends on the meaning we attribute to a specific situation and how it adheres to previous situations in our lives. For example, in the case of a student, a bad exam can reactivate the sense of inadequacy experienced in previous school grades, perhaps in specific disciplines or with particular teachers.

When the demands of the life context are perceived by people as excessive compared to their ability to deal with them (*coping skills*), we self-define as "stressed", experiencing a negative emotional response. Attention is therefore focused on the assessment of stress that depends on the stimulus, the type of response and the subjective interpretation of the stimulus–environment relationship; perception is thus a result of interpretations of the meaning of the stimulus in itself and of the individual's resources to deal with it.

Access to university is a process of *psycho-social transition* into a new culture, and since each transition is a change process, students have to perform two tasks: 1) redefine themselves on the identity plan; 2) redesign their network of relationships.

Facing the university course can be a stressful experience, but attending university for many years in the hope of achieving one's training and professional goals can also be particularly frustrating and emotionally stressful.

The enrollment phase is a delicate moment for all students: it coincides with a change of life and everyday habits, often determined by the cadence of courses and examinations, which also have an impact on social and personal life (think of the possibility to cultivate hobbies). In fact, the process of integration into the new university environment is a progressive and complex adaptation to a new social and cultural context.

The student has to gradually build *new social meanings*, which are defined and negotiated within learning communities, embedded in a broad social and cultural network (Cole, 1996; Bruner, 1990).

Many students leave their family home, begin to experience new autonomy, begin to live in new contexts, physically separate from their dear ones, try to establish a new network of social contacts, deal with spending by counting on a predetermined budget and begin a new study path. Social relationships mutate: there is often a shift in the group of friends, new crews are born, some friends end their evolutionary course; furthermore, in some cases, as for away-from-home students, you are living on your own. It is clear how this adaptation phase requires the student to reorganize a social network of support.

Not too rarely, university enrollment manifests itself with a *soft* impact: the student trying to face these demands with the available resources; in other cases, the impact is *harder*: after a first phase of adaptation, the issues arise at the first exam session. There are old fears, bad self-reflection, memory of old school failures; this increases the sense of fear and frustration in the students. It is a clash with this reality that activates the questioning of one's own formation and identity project. In fact, we often happen to encounter students who, after failing some exams, repeatedly ask themselves "Is this the right path for me? Am I capable? What do I want to do as a grownup?"

Students seeking help are often in a stall phase, blocked on a failed or never completed exam: in many cases, it is necessary to modify their own study strategies by adapting them ad hoc; in others, the stalemate conceals dismay, a total loss of "sense frames".

Sometimes youngsters drop out of university: students stuck just a few exams from the end or on their thesis, frightened by an uncertain professional future but also by the evolutionary leap that will further put them to the test, often breaking painstakingly built equilibriums (Manzi, Vignoles, & Regalia, 2010) to cope with uncertainty in later steps in their life course trajectory (Corte's, 2016).

In the face of this change, fortunately, not all students have high levels of stress or react with clinical symptoms; in some cases, even events that can lead to stress are not necessarily negative, or even something expected and desired can be perceived as and turn out to be stressful. It is then wondered why a stimulus is perceived as dangerous by one student and not by another, and also how different strategies ever activate in some and not in others.

In general, literature highlights how stress in university students is associated with depression, anxiety, low self-esteem (Berrío, Mazo, 2011; Aselton, 2012; Beiter et al., 2015), low social support and inappropriate coping strategies (Lyrakos, 2012; Clinciu, 2013; Carnicer & Calderon, 2014). Stress is more present in the early years of enrollment (Serlachius, Hamer, &Wardle, 2007; Elias, Ping, &Chong Abdullah, 2011); among the stress factors are few social relationships (Lyrakos, 2012; Thawabieh & Qaisy, 2012) and being female (Baker, 2003; Serlachius et al., 2007).

In our studies conducted at the Counseling Center, there was a correlation between low self-esteem, dysfunctional self-centered and outward coping strategies and clinical symptoms in university students (Savarese et al., 2013, 2014, 2015, 2016) and female gender. In all, dysfunctional anxiety was present. Studies on university students' performance show that the best results are obtained by those who feel contained anxiety and are able to control it (Andrews &Wilding, 2004). These people achieve results even better than those who do not experience any form of anxiety, as they have an optimum level of "activation" over the task. But when the exam anxiety takes on excessive dimensions, it can become a big obstacle for the student: it is experienced as a negative emotional state, accompanied by nervousness and worry, linked to a high body activation and capable of affecting behaviors and performance. In fact, strong anxiety can inhibit intellectual performance and impede concentration and memory, greatly worsening the student's academic performance.[4]

Studies of anxiety are consistent with the fact that the response to anxiety from examination is not unambiguous but rather caused by several coexisting factors at the same time. It also has to be considered that students who experience anxiety during a test are those who feel they are also evaluated in their intelligence and personal skills (generalization mechanism) rather than on cultural preparation and, therefore, tend to make their self-esteem dependent on others and, in this specific case, on the teacher's grade.

When there is excessive insecurity linked to low self-esteem, the thought of possibly failing a test becomes unbearable, since it is mistakenly linked to personal value. The exam is loaded with different meanings (attributions), so the exam stops being just an exam and becomes a test to show something to someone (family, friends, teachers or oneself). Tremendous importance is given to performance and outcome, to which the students often inevitably accompany feelings of shame, self-devaluation and reactive depression, even impotence. The risk is that anxiety becomes anguish, if not panic, when it is fed by the feeling of having to risk it all every time (self-esteem, confidence, approval, love) and risk losing it.

Finally, some studies focused on students' *burn-out*. The conclusions of these studies have highlighted motivational drops, distress and increased risk of burn-out in university students, particularly in the field of study of *helping professions* (Timmins &Kaliszer, 2002; Schaufeli, Martinez, Pinto, Salanova, & Bakker, 2002; Schaufeli, Salanova, González-Romá, & Bakker, 2002; Deary, Watson, & Hogston, 2003; Barboza & Beresin, 2007). These students present typical symptoms of stress and overload. Especially when stress is manifested for long periods, the risk is that the battery is exhausted and inevitably the student's motivation falls; there are uncontrollable emotional reactions and the student feels disoriented and impoverished. He/she is no longer able to do anything and may even have the feeling of losing the joy of living. However, even though burn-out is caused by excess stress, this does not mean that a stressful situation will necessarily lead to burn-out. Among the major causes of a student's burn-out, Markus Anker (2010) identified the new university system, characterized by studying times that have become much shorter and more intense, able to put the student at a disadvantage. Another factor of stress is adaptation to a new environment, which is a challenge especially for foreign students. Many students with poor performance are in fact highly motivated but unable to overcome the obstacles of anxiety and insecurity: they would be willing to study hard in exchange for even modest grades, but struggle to achieve results and progressively begin to suffer psychological and cultural "paralysis".

It is also worth considering that oftentimes young people have few obligations toward their families, as what is asked of them is mainly the commitment to succeed at school/university, which therefore becomes a unique and totalizing task (Schaufeli, Martinez et al., 2002; Schaufeli, Salanova et al., 2002).

In Italy, there are no studies directly centered on burn-out in university students, but there are some which, looking for the causes of university drop-out, have found a strong *distress*frame. The main causes of this distress are: excessive demand for commitment, emotional problems and disappointment of expectations (Dante, Valoppi, & Palese, 2009).

The research

Objectives

1 Highlight a possible relationship between: coping strategies with stress, detected by CISS scale, and:

   a some explanatory variables (gender, age, higher level of education, select faculty, year of enrollment, live near the university campus);
   b level of self-esteem;
   c Global Severity Index (GSI).

2 Detect a possible change, as a result of a university psychological counseling path, both to the stress and coping indexes rather than to the global unease, as well as to the self-esteem.

Participants

Participants were 122 students who asked to undertake a psychological support path at the Counseling Center of the University of Salerno.

A descriptive analysis was carried out to analyze the socio-nominal characteristics of the sample. The general participants were 67.2% females and 32.8% males, with an average age of 25.41 years (DS = 4.15).

Forty percent attended a higher education degree with humanistic specialization, the remaining 60% a technical/scientific one.

As far as the chosen faculty is concerned, 30.1% attended study courses in the humanistic area, 38.9% in the technical/scientific area, 31% in the area of helping professions.

Sixty-five percent of students were on par with the pre-set study course, while 35.0% were late on their pre-set sequence years.

Tools and procedures

The following tests were administered to the students who requested psychological support, during pre and post phases (six months follow-up):

1   An ad-hoc socio-nominal card with the sections: sex, age, level of education, faculty chosen, enrolment year and attendance.

    a   *CISS (Coping Inventory for Stressful Situations* (Parker & Endler, 1992): this is a scale to measure multidimensional aspects of coping. CISS is divided into three scales, each consisting of 16 items: *Maneuver (T)*: describes efforts to solve a problem by restructuring it cognitively or trying to alter the situation. The fundamental accent is on the task or on the planning and on the attempts of problem solving; *Emotion (E)*: describes the emotional reactions that are oriented towards the self, with the aim of reducing stress; *Avoidance (A)*: describes cognitive activities and changes aimed at avoiding stressful situations. It involves two sub-scales: *Distraction (D)*: avoiding the stressful situation by distracting with other situations or tasks (orientation towards the task); and *Social Diversion (SD)*: avoiding stressful situations through social diversion (orientation toward the person).
    b   *Rosenberg Self-Esteem Scale* (Rosenberg, 1965): it is a scale that measures the level of personal self-esteem; high scores indicate greater self-esteem.
    c   *SCL90-R* (Derogatis, 1983): it is a scale for self-assessment of general psychopathology that considers a broad spectrum of psychological and psychopathological symptoms, measuring both internalizing (depression, somatization, anxiety) and externalizing symptoms (aggression, hostility, impulsiveness). For the purpose of our data analysis, in this study, only the "specific index" criterion denominated *"Global Severity Index" (GSI)* is discussed, which evaluates the intensity of the level of psychic discomfort complained of by the subject, and some indexes that denote manifestations of stress such as: *somatization (SOM), depression (DEP), anxiety (ANX)* and *phobic anxiety (PHOB)*.

Analysis of the results

For each test, the scores[5] of the whole sample were analyzed.

To verify a relationship between the illustrative variables defined by the socio-nominal card and the scores obtained at the CISS test, a variance analysis (ANOVA) was conducted. To find out the relationship between the scores provided for each test, a correlational analysis (r-Pearson) was performed. Finally, in order to verify the score modifications between administration in pre- and post-counseling intervention, a T-Student test for paired samples was applied.

The results indicate that:

1. Regarding **stressful anxiety events** (detected by Scl-90R), it is noted that the highest clinical score is *depression* (X = 64.91; ds = 9.57.01), followed by *anxiety* (X = 63.53; ds = 11.034), *phobic anxiety* (X = 59.12; ds = 12.18) and *somatization* (X = 56.82; ds = 11.70). All averages fall within a range of *moderate to high* clinical discomfort; furthermore, a lower self-esteem correlates with higher *levels of depression* (R = −0.310; p = 0.001; df = 122) and *phobic anxiety* (R = −0.182; p = 0.047); df = 122).
2. Scores in the **CISS scales** show, in comparison with the *cut-offs* considered by the instrument, a higher than average score in the *Emotion* scale (X = 60.45; ds = 9.42), a lower score than the average in the *Maneuver* scale (X = 41.49, ds = 10.44) and average scores in the scales of *Avoidance* (X = 50.58; ds = 7.02), *Distraction* (X = 50.15; ds = 9.23) and *Social Diversion* (X = 46.11; ds = 11.64). The *Emotion* scale positively correlates with *Avoidance* (R = 0.382; p = 0.00; df = 122); the *Avoidance* scale positively correlates with *Distraction*(R = 0.665; p = 0.00; df = 122) and *Social Diversion*, its sub-scales (R = −0.565; p = 0.02; df = 122).
3. The crossing of the **CISS data with the illustrative variables** shows that the *Maneuver* scale negatively correlates with *age* (R = −022, p = 0.015, df = 122): the more students grow, the less they seem to have coping strategies; on the other hand, the *Emotion* scale has a significant relationship with being a student at or away from home (F = 6.31, p = 0.013, df = 122). Away-from-home students have a score that falls in the upper range of the average (X = 62.42, ds = 10.38); at-home students have a slightly higher average score on this scale (X = 57.09, ds = 8.45). There is no significant relationship between the CISS scales and other illustrative variables (p > 0.5).
4. Regarding the relationship between stress, coping and self-esteem: a positive correlation is found between the *Maneuver* and *Self-esteem* scales (R = 0.220, p = 0.016, df = 122); that is, those with higher self-esteem also have a greater coping ability in stressful situations. There is a negative correlation between the *Emotion* and *Self-esteem* scales (R = 0.219; p = 0.016; df = 122). Lower self-esteem corresponds with a greater folding on self. Students generally score an average falling within the *low self-esteem* range (X = 14.22, ds = 5.40).

5   As far as the **relationship between CISS and GSI** is concerned, it is noted that, the greater the *Maneuver*, the lower *GSI-general discomfort* (R = −0.339; p = 0.00; df = 122). On the other hand, a positive relationship exists between *Emotion* scale and GSI (R = 0.438; p = 0.00; df = 122). Students generally score an average score that falls within the *moderate to intense* range (X = 63.95, ds = 10.23).

Considering the average scores obtained in the scales of **CISS, GSI** and **Rosenberg** before (pre) and after (post) the counseling path, the T-Student for paired samples shows that:

- In the CISS scales, there is an increase in the average range of scores in the post phase of the *Maneuver* scale (X = 48.82, ds = 11.79). The difference is statistically significant (t = −8.54, gdl = 117, p = 00);
- In the *Emotion* scale, on the other hand, in the post there is a decrease in *mean* values (X = 51, ds = 10.25), and this data is statistically significant (t = −7.53, gdl = 117, p = 00);
- In the *Avoidance* scale, compared with the pre, a slight increase in mean has to be noted (X = 51.17, ds = 7.6), which is statistically significant data (p > 0.5);
- As to the *Distraction* scale, in the post there is a slight increase in the average (X = 52.43, ds = 9.49). The difference is statistically significant (t = −2.70, gdl = 118, p = 008);
- The *Social Diversion* Scale presents an average score increase (X = 50.41, ds = 10.33) in the post and is statistically significant (t = −6.30, gdl = 118, p = 00).

We can say, therefore, that in the **post-intervention of psychological counseling**, there have been more ways of dealing with perceived stress. At **Rosenberg's test** on self-esteem, a higher score was observed in post-intervention because it went from the initial *low self-esteem* of pre-intervention to the *average self-esteem* range (t = 9.35, gdl = 116, p = 00). Also, for the GSI value, there was a lowering of mean scores from *High* to *Medium* severity of clinical symptomatology (X = 54.43; ds = 11.30), and this decrease was statistically significant (t = 9.35, gdl = 116, p = 00).

Conclusions

The existing literature and our clinical practice suggest that, following the psychological counseling intervention, not only does perceived stress reduce but so do the clinical symptoms of the user; individual and relational resources (e.g., self-regulation, resilience, coping) activate, which mediate the relationship between the person and his/her difficulty; the individual psychological tools for problem solving, self-esteem and *personal wellness* enhancement, as well as a positive assessment of one's quality of life, restart; finally, ways to deal with distress structure or restructure.

Notes

1 The Counseling Center of the University "Michele Cesaro has been active at the university since 2011 and has welcomed from the opening of about 550 consultancy applications for students enrolled in various degrees at the same university. Counseling generally runs out of five rounds of talk time and a sixth follow-up. In other cases, it may be a process that is more or less short, through which the student becomes aware of his or her difficulties and can reformulate an appropriate application that is directed towards psychotherapy or psychiatric pathways.
2 The concept of crisis and resolution has been proposed by Erikson to discuss key points in life trajectories: according to him, a crisis designates "a necessary turning-point, a crucial moment in development, when having to choose the ways to distribute the additional resources of recovery of growth and differentiation" (Erikson, 1968, p. 11).
3 When we experience intense emotion in our body, there are a number of biochemical reactions, and, specifically, when we perceive ourselves under pressure, our body reacts as if we were facing an attack. Basically, our metabolism speeds up, our heart rate increases and blood pressure as well as triglyceride and cholesterol levels in the blood rise, while sexual hormones decrease. If the stressful situation lasts for a long time, it can become chronic at the expenses of our body: we can accuse a series of disorders of being caused by stress-induced hormonal changes. Among the most commonly referred disorders are: chronic fatigue, tachycardia, chest tightness, digestive problems, hair loss, menstrual irregularities and blockage of ovulation, irritable bowel, constipation, muscle pain and so on. Stress can also have a negative effect on the immune system because when we are stressed we are more vulnerable to infections, illnesses and the development of autoimmune diseases. Unfortunately, when a person is very stressed, he/she often does not listen to the signals of malaise that the body continues to send, considering them unnecessary. Although these symptoms do not constitute a true illness, they are in fact the signal that our body and our mind are worn out under the burden of a stress overload. It is therefore important, if we are to prevent more serious illnesses in the future, to take these alarm bells seriously, adjusting our lifestyle (Chetta et al., 2003).
4 According to Yerkes and Dodson's law (1908), up to a certain individual tolerance threshold, an increase in stress may result in increased productivity. Basically, between the *activation and performance level* there is an inverted U-shaped reversal relationship: this implies that increased attention, memory, muscle tension and other functions (such as increased heart rate) that result in anxiety are considered as useful energy charge for overcoming the test. The problem occurs when the level of anxiety exceeds the levels of positive excitability, which is propaedeutic for activation, to reach levels that can affect performance. In this case, anxiety is experienced as negative interference and frequent symptoms are excessive sweating, migraine, tachycardia, nausea, hyperventilation and feeling unable to remember. This state means that even performing very basic reasoning or remembering data that until recently was clear becomes a very difficult task and is in some cases impossible. In practice, with low arousal levels, we get rather "poor" performance (for example when we are bored and unmotivated or when we are too self-confident), but even when activation levels are too high, our performance decreases! When arousal starts to rise too much, then "healthy" stress becomes real anxiety that can lead us to judgment errors and to make wrong decisions. There is, therefore, an "optimum" activation level that maximizes our performance.
5 In the case of SCL-90R and CISS scales, these are T scores.

References

American Psychiatric Association. (2013). *Diagnostic and statistical manual of mental disorders (DSM-5®)*. American Psychiatric Washington, DC.
Andrews, B., & Wilding, J. M. (2004). The relation of depression and anxiety to life-stress and achievement in students. *British Journal of Psychology*, 95(4), 509–521.
Anker, M. (2010). *Rapporto di ricerca sul burn-out degli studenti svizzeri*. www.swissinfo.ch/ita/quando-lo-studio-ti-brucia/
Aselton, P. (2012). Sources of stress and coping in American college students who have been diagnosed with depression. *Journal of Child and Adolescent Psychiatric Nursing*, 25(3), 119–123.
Baker, S. R. (2003). A prospective longitudinal investigation of social problem solving appraisals on adjustment to university, stress, health, and academic motivation and performance, *Personality and Individual Differences*, 35, 569–591.
Barboza, J. I. R. A., & Beresin, R. (2007). Burn-out syndrome in nursing undergraduate students. *Einstein (São Paulo)*, 5(3), 225–230.
Beiter, R., Nash, R., McCrady, M., Rhoades, D., Linscomb, M., Clarahan, M., & Sammut, S. (2015).The prevalence and correlates of depression, anxiety, and stress in a sample of college students. *Journal of Affective Disorders*, 173, 90–96.
Bell, N. J., Wieling, E., & Watson, W. (2005). *Identity development during the first two university.*
Berrio, G. N., & Mazo, Z. R. (2011). Academic stress. *Revista de Psicología de la Universidad de Antioquia*, 3, 65–82.
Bruner, J. (1986). *Actual minds, possible words*. Cambridge, MA: Harvard University Press.
Bruner, J. (1990). *Acts of meaning*. Cambridge, MA: Harvard University Press.
Cassidy, C., & Trew, K. (2004). Identity change in Northern Ireland: A longitudinal study of students' transition to university. *Journal of Social Issues*, 60, 523–540.
Chetta, G., Bedetti, S., & Pisano, S. (2003). *Oltre lo stress*. Roma: Ed. e-motion.
Clinciu, A. I. (2013). Adaptation and stress for the first year university students. *Social and Behavioral Sciences*, 78, 718–722.
Cole, M. (1996). *Cultural psychology*. Cambridge, MA: Harvard University Press.
Cortés, M. (2016). A dialogical self: Trajectory equifinality model for higher education persistence/abandoning of study. In T. Sato, N. Mori, & J. Valsiner (Eds.), *Making of the future. The trajectory equifinality approach in cultural psychology*. Charlotte, NC: Information Age Publishing.
Coulon, A. (1997). *Le métier d'étudiant: l'entrée dans la vie universitaire*. Paris: PUF.
Dante, A., Valoppi, G., & Palese, A. (2009). Fattori di successo e di insuccesso accademico degli studenti infermieri: revisione narrativa della letteratura. *International Nursing Perspectives*, 9(2), 45–52.
Deary, I. J., Watson, R., & Hogston, R. (2003). A longitudinal cohort study of burnout and attrition in nursing students. *Journal of Advanced Nursing*, 43(1), 71–81.
Derogatis, L. (1983). The SCL-90R manual-II: Administration, scoring and procedures. *Baltimore: Clinical Psychometric Research*. Towson, MD: NCS.
Elias, H., Ping, W. S., &Chong Abdullah, M. (2011). Stress and academic achievement among undergraduate students in Universiti Putra Malaysia. *Procedia – Social and Behavioral Sciences*, 29, 646–655.
Erikson, E. H. (1968). *Youth and crisis*. New York/London: W.W. Norton & Company.
Gomes, A. R., & Teixeira, P. M. (2016). Stress, cognitive appraisal and psychological health: testing instruments for health professionals. Stress and Health, 32(2), 167–172.

Gomes, R., Dazzani, V., & Marsico, G. (2017). The role of "responsiveness" within the self in transitions to university. *Culture &Psychology*, *23*(3) 1–14.

Gustems-Carnicer, J., & Calderón, C. (2013). Coping strategies and psychological well-being among teacher education students. *European Journal of Psychology Education*, *28*, 1127–1140.

Gustems Carnicer, J., & Calderón, C. (2014). Empatía y estrategias de afrontamiento como predictores del bienestar en estudiantes universitarios españoles. *Electronic Journal of Research in Educational Psychology*, *12*(32).

Iannaccone, A., Ghodbane, I., & Rosciano, R. (2005). La "Ricerca del Significato" nel contesto universitario: il mestiere di studente. In T. Mannarini, A. Perucca, & S. Salvatore (Eds.), *Quale psicologia per la scuola del futuro* (pp. 37–57), Roma: ICA, Firera Publishing Group.

Josephs, I. E., & Valsiner, J. (1998). How does auto-dialogue work? Miracles of meaning maintenance and circumvention strategies. *Social Psychology Quarterly*, *61*, 68–83.

Lyrakos, D. G. (2012). The impact of stress, social support, self-efficacy and coping on university students, a multicultural European study. *Psychology*, *3*(02), 143.

Manzi, C., Vignoles, V. L., & Regalia, C. (2010). Accommodating a new identity: Possible selves, identity change and well-being across two life-transitions. *European Journal of Social Psychology*, *40*, 970–984.

Martsin, M., Chang, I., & Obst, P. (2016). Using culture to manage the transition into university: Conceptualising the dynamics of withdrawal and engagement. *Culture & Psychology*, *22*(2), 276–295.

Pancheri, P. (1980). *Stress, emozioni, malattia*. Milano: Mondadori.

Parker, J. D., & Endler, N. S. (1992). Coping with coping assessment: A critical review. *European Journal of Personality*, *6*(5), 321–344.

Perret-Clermont, A. N., & Iannaccone, A. (2005). Le tensioni delle trasmissioni culturali: c'è spazio per il pensiero nei luoghi istituzionali dove si apprende? In *Quale psicologia per la scuola del futuro?* (Vol. 1, No. 3, pp. 59–70). Carlo Amore.

Rosenberg, M. (1965). *Society and the adolescent self-image*. Retrieved from psycnet.apa.org.

Salvatore, S., Freda, M. F., Ligorio, B., Iannaccone, A., Rubino, F., Scotto di Carlo, M., Bastianoni, P., & Gentile, M. (2003). Socioconstructivism and theory of the unconscious. A gaze over a research horizon. *European Journal of School Psychology*, *1*(1), 9–36.

Savarese, G., Carpinelli, L., Fasano, O., Mollo, M., Pecoraro, N., & Cavallo, P. (2015). Stress and anxiety for the university students. *SM Journal of Psychiatry & Mental Health*, *1*, 1.

Savarese, G., Carpinelli, L., Fasano, O., Mollo, M., Pecoraro, N., & Iannaccone, A (2013). Study on the correlation between self-esteem, coping and clinical symptoms in a group of young adults: A brief report, *European Scientific Journal*, October, 1–6.

Savarese, G., Carpinelli, L., Fasano, O., Mollo, M., Pecoraro, N., & Iannaccone, A. (2014). La ricerca del benessere individuale nei percorsi di counseling psicologico universitario. In R. Felaco & L. Clarizia (a cura di), *Atti del Convegno I LUOGHI DEL BENESSERE, Edizione Ordine Psicologi della Campania*, Napoli.

Savarese, G., Fasano, O., Pecoraro, N., Mollo, M., Carpinelli, L., & Iannaccone, A. (2016). *Giovane, studente, in difficoltà:identikit dell'utente dei centri di counseling universitari*. Rivista italiana di counseling, ISSN 2284–4252, http://rivistaitalianadicounseling.it/giovane-studente-difficolta-identikit-dellutente-dei-centri-counseling-universitari/ http://rivistaitalianadicounseling.it/giovane-studente-difficolta-identikit-dellutente-dei-centri-counseling-universitari/, Volume 3, Numero 1, EAN977–2284425008–60305.

Savarese, G., & Iannaccone, A. (Eds.). (2013). *Counseling in action.* Roma: Aracne Libri.
Schaufeli, W. B., Martinez, I. M., Pinto, A. M., Salanova, M., & Bakker, A. B. (2002). Burn-out and engagement in university students: A cross-national study. *Journal of Cross-Cultural Psychology, 33*(5), 464–481.
Schaufeli, W. B., Salanova, M., González-Romá, V., & Bakker, A. B. (2002). The measurement of engagement and burn-out: A two sample confirmatory factor analytic approach. *Journal of Happiness Studies, 3*(1), 71–92.
Serlachius, A., Hamer, M., &Wardle, J. (2007). Stress and weight change in university students in the United Kingdom. *Physiology & Behavior, 92*, 548–553.
Sestito, L. A., Sica, L. S., & Ragozini, G. (2011). I primi anni dell'università: processi di definizione dell'identità tra confusione e consolidamento. *Giornale di Psicologia dello Sviluppo, 99*, 20–33.
Stallman, H. M. (2010). Psychological distress in university students: A comparison with general population data. *Australian Psychologist, 45*(4), 249–257.
Thawabieh, A. M., & Qaisy, L. M. (2012). Assessing stress among university students. *American International Journal of Contemporary Research, 2*(2), 110–116.
Tilleczek, K., Ferguson, M., & Campbell, V. (2011). Youth transitions through school: Intersections of poverty, mental health and engagement. *Policy Paper Prepared for a Youth Policy Framework, Ontario Ministry of Children and Youth Services.* Toronto, ON: Ministry of Children and Youth Services.
Timmins, F., & Kaliszer, M. (2002). Aspects of nurse education programmes that frequently cause stress to nursing students—Fact-finding sample survey. *Nurse Education Today, 22*(3), 203–211.
Yerkes, R. M., & Dodson, J. D. (1908). The relation of strength of stimulus to rapidity of habit formation. *Journal of Comparative Neurology, 18*(5), 459–482.
Zittoun, T. (2004). Symbolic competencies for developmental transitions: The case of the choice of first names. *Culture & Psychology, 10*, 131–161.
Zittoun, T. (2006). *Transitions: Development through symbolic resources.* Charlotte, NC: Information Age Publishing.
Zittoun, T. (2007a). Dynamics of interiority: Ruptures and transitions in the self development. In L. M. Simão & J. Valsiner (Eds.), *Otherness in question: Labyrinths of the self* (pp. 187–214). Charlotte, NC: Information Age Publishing.
Zittoun, T. (2007b). The role of symbolic resources in human lives. In J. Valsiner & A. Rosa (Eds.), *The Cambridge handbook of sociocultural psychology* (pp. 343–361). Cambridge, MA: Cambridge University Press.
Zittoun, T. (2014). Transitions as dynamic processes—A commentary. *Learning, Culture and Social Interaction, 3*(3), 232–236.
Zittoun, T., & Perret-Clermont, A. N. (2001). Contributions à une psychologie de la transition. In *Congrès international de la Société suisse pour la recherche en éducation (SSRE), Société suisse pour la formation des enseignantes et des enseignants (SSFE)* (pp. 1–11). Société Suisse pour la recherche en éducation (SSRE).

Chapter 6

The discomfort of writing in academia

Noomi Matthiesen and Charlotte Wegener

Introduction: the joy and discomfort of writing

On the exact same day as we embarked on writing this chapter, we received the agenda for the next teachers' meeting at our department. Thomas, the head of our Study Board, reported on a discussion at a recent examiners' meeting. The discussion at the meeting had been sparked by one experienced examiner's observation that psychology theses in general are well structured and well communicated. However, they also tend to be quite boring. Most theses follow the exact same template, and few students take risks, the experienced examiner had argued. Thomas asked in the meeting agenda whether we recognized any of this in our own practice and suggested we discuss it. He also summed up some conditions in academia that these past (and boring) theses might reflect. Among the main points discussed by the examiners were a strong performance and zero-error culture, defensive and goal-oriented study programmes and a shortage of time for supervision, writing up and completing the master's programme generally. This can be illustrated by the author Doris Lessing, who writes in the preface of *The Golden Notebook*:

> Like every other writer I get letters all the time from young people who are about to write their theses and essays about my books. . . . They . . . ask for a thousand details of total irrelevance, but which they have been taught to consider important, amounting to a dossier, like an immigration department's.
> These requests I answer as follows: 'Dear Student. You are mad.'
> (Lessing, 1962/2013, p. 16)

We recognize this, indeed, as writing advisors/teachers and as researchers for whom writing makes up a large part of our practice. In this chapter, we look into some of the dynamics of writing in academia that are more or less identical for students and their teachers. Undergraduates and faculty share fundamental conditions in this regard (Johnson, 2017). We are all part of a strong performance culture, we are all measured on goal-oriented parameters and we are all expected to write well in various genres: papers for high-ranked journals, funding applications, reports and, not least, to be visible on social media. These conditions may trigger discomfort, even fear. At the same time, writing is a potentially creative and joyful activity through which we can investigate new material, process ideas and propose things we claim to know. An unhappy relationship with writing has many undesirable outcomes ranging from past, boring texts to stress, delay and even dropout. We have observed an inclination (in research and in practice) to try to minimize discomfort; here, however, we suggest another path. We want to embrace the discomfort of writing and claim it to be a productive force. Assisting students in developing effective writing routines and behaviours can be relevant at times, but writing is ultimately an activity that spans order and disorder and moves between the known and unknown (Johnson, 2017). Our premise is this: writing from the power of discomfort and even *into* discomfort, instead of trying to escape it, can take the writing beyond fear – and make it more interesting. We want our students to linger in the discomfort, to practise experimenting and meandering; we want to infuse them with the courage to pause. We draw on Tyson Lewis's (2011) understanding of Agamben's work on potentiality and studying and argue that, while students today are pressured to effectively actualize a product, writing can be a playful (at times uncomfortable) practice of surrendering to bewilderment, lingering, meandering and dwelling in potentiality. We also want them to experience the sheer joy of putting fingers to keyboard and producing something new in the world.

In her book on writing, *Big Magic: Creative Living Beyond Fear*, Elizabeth Gilbert (2015) insists convincingly on the joy, pleasure and lightness of writing. Listen to the kind of conversation she would have with aspiring young writers:

> 'Do you love writing?' I ask.
> Of course they do. *Duh.*
> Then I ask: 'Do you believe that writing loves you in return?'
> They look at me like I should be institutionalized.
> 'Of course not,' they say. Most of them report that writing is totally indifferent to them. And if they do happen to feel a reciprocal relationship with their creativity, it is usually a deeply sick relationship. In many cases, these young writers claim the writing flat-out hates them. Writing messes with their heads. Writing torments them and hides from them. Writing punishes them. Writing destroys them. Writing kicks their asses, ten ways to Sunday.
>
> (Gilbert, 2015, p. 204)

Whether writing loves us back may seem like an odd question. We can read it as a statement of the nature of the world, quite a spiritual one. Or we can read it as a metaphor for our relationship with work, no matter the nature of this work. It is either an ontological or an epistemological question. Or we can do both. We have signed up for a study programme or a job that requires writing. Nobody promised writing would come easy. There is no law, however, that writing should torment us. Writing is *work* that needs to be done. It is part of the contract – for students and their teachers. It is potentially much more fun than cleaning bathrooms all day, and it is definitely less complicated than performing brain surgery for twenty hours in a row.

Writing, like most work, can be tedious and perplexing; it can progress slowly or regress. There are plenty of sources of discomfort in the process, but our point here is that this is not *erroneous*. The error occurs when discomfort turns into, or is mistaken for, fear. Fear is restrictive, even lethal.

This chapter interrogates discomfort as built in to the practice of writing in higher education. Writing is ultimately an existential endeavour that entails discomfort as a productive force, yet the structure of the educational system may restrict this force and instead instil a discomfort that is saturated with fear and thus risks impeding the coming-to-be of the subject. The goal of the chapter is to legitimize a certain kind of discomfort, a discomfort connected to passion and joy, a discomfort that is inevitable in genuine learning experiences – a productive discomfort through which the subject comes into being. So, how do we teach our students and (so as to become better role models and perhaps even happier researchers) ourselves to go beyond fear, even when discomfort strikes hard? How do we convince our students that writing loves them? What can we do to assist them into a reciprocal relationship with their creativity? A healthy one? One that does not just involve discomfort, but embraces it?

First, we need to understand the dynamics of discomfort, to which we devote the first part of this chapter. Second, we suggest a way of thinking about students' writing that helps us and them to embrace discomfort.

The nature of discomfort

Higher education students write essays and papers as a part of their studies. For many, it is a tense process involving joy, pain, triumph and impatience. These writing processes are supposed to lead to new insights and learning. However, the quest for new insights and the emotional fluctuations inherent in writing processes become problematic when performance and time pressure take over. In the introduction, we addressed external factors such as zero-error culture, defensive and goal-oriented study programmes and a shortage of time. We also addressed internal factors (if this is the right term) resulting in a sick love/hate relationship with writing itself. Dividing this pressure as deriving from either internal or external factors, however, is unproductive and even impossible – this pressure is real to the student, no matter its source. The cultural landscape of higher education today is complex, and the logics of the economic market reign in conflicting ways. On the one hand, students are positioned as consumers, and teaching becomes a product (Biesta, 2011). On the other hand, students are positioned as raw material ready to be moulded into whatever the mass society needs (2011). Education is simultaneously an entertainment industry and a manufacturing business. Effectiveness and outcome have become central driving forces; at the same time, student satisfaction is a weighty parameter of success. In this increased culture of double performativity, we are all infused with a drive for risk-free and frictionless learning processes. As teachers, we are supposed to create the most effective educational environment possible. There is an increased focus on alleviating suffering in education and enhancing student wellbeing; discomfort is considered 'wrong' and should be minimized. For instance, Mintz (2008) shows how mathematics teachers go to great lengths to alleviate the suffering of students when tackling difficult maths problems. And the agony of learning in general, and of writing in particular, *does* reduce the productivity of education. Discomfort results in flight from practice, resort to procrastination and displacement of one's attention to Facebook, Twitter or Snapchat. But, as Mintz and others (e.g. Jones, 2010) have argued, struggle, suffering and discomfort are conditions of learning processes. We will now take a close look at this dynamic of fleeing from and lingering in discomfort when it comes to writing.

The blank page

The experience of being confronted with a blank page holding endless possibilities of paths to walk, ways to progress, can in itself be a disconcerting experience. It is full of uncertainty and unease and, for some, full of excitement and freedom. Where to start? How to proceed? Which words will open up the journey and allow for progression? Which will close down the journey and make enthusiasm congeal?

> Where is the way? There is no way to be found. A white sheet of paper is full of ways . . . we will go over the same way ten times, a hundred times.
> (Jabès, cited in Derrida, 1978, p. 69)

Writing papers and essays in higher education is an exercise in learning, a question of producing new insights, and consequently the destination, the end point of the writing excursion, is not defined beforehand, making the process even more uncertain. Below, we will describe two paradoxes ingrained in the practice of writing higher education theses and essays. We argue that these paradoxes, and the impossibility of transcending them, inevitably create discomfort. It can be a productive discomfort, though. It can be a condition of coming-to-be and appearing as a unique individual, risk filled and vulnerable, yet ultimately the essence of education.

The paradox of learning to write

Writing is tradition. It is long-established practices with rules and criteria that determine quality and excellence in each research tradition. There are rules about structure and notions of what constitutes relevant content. There are guidelines that delineate the benefits of meta-communication at the beginning of a section to communicate what will be done, and meta-communication at the end of the section to summarize the main point of the argument. There are rules for what constitutes a full and valid argument. There are rules for the content of a methods section, for referencing and concluding. These rules vary depending on the particular genre of writing and the particular research field and subject. The rules are embedded in the particular tradition of the field, and some of these rules may be quite explicit. Others are tacit, even inexplicable, i.e. the rules are difficult to grasp with words and thus difficult to teach.

Being a good writer does not make one a good writing teacher. Through observations and recordings of supervisory sessions complemented by interviews, Paré (2010) found that supervisor feedback is often ambiguous, enigmatic and difficult to understand. He notes that supervisors' ability to write well does not necessarily qualify them to impart the art of good writing. As language is often learned as a by-product of participation in particular activities – academic language being no exception – good academic writers may not be able to explain the reason for their advice. They may be unable or unaware of the need to explain why 'they suggest or demand that something be phrased a certain way, expect a particular tone or style, insist that a specific reference be inserted, or favour one way of organising and presenting data over another' (Paré, 2010, p. 109). A good writing teacher knows that instruction and guidance in academic writing cannot be reduced to mere instrumental techniques and genre requirements. Teaching academic writing *is* partly about providing relevant technique and assisting the decoding of genre. But writing is also identity work. Paré (2010) found that supervisors in his study spoke with authority about what should be done to make students' writing move forward. The advice was potentially useful but often unelaborated and thus difficult for the students to understand and translate into a better product. What students need to understand – and what supervisors could be better at explaining – is that supervisory feedback is part of an enculturation process. Through writing and feedback, the student learns more about the community they are entering. Since the supervisor is a member of that community, he or she is one of the main resources on which students can draw when becoming scholars.

As with many other practices, knowing how to be in the world in a way that is considered appropriate and good is essentially an embodied knowledge. Dreyfus (1991) exemplifies this by pointing out that the distance at which it is appropriate to stand from one's conversational partner varies from culture to culture, from tradition to tradition. We all know what the appropriate distance is, we feel it, yet we would be hard put to describe it in words. We only feel it when it is wrong.

The same can be said about certain aspects of writing. There are aspects that are quite difficult to describe, yet, as teachers, we have no trouble judging whether the writing is of high quality. We feel it. We know it. This means that, rather than being told how to do writing well, much of this learning must be done by engaging in the practice, i.e. it requires reading not just for content but also for style, vocabulary and structure, and it requires drafting, giving and receiving feedback and rewriting.

Writing is thus a skill that must be trained. This process of discovering what is appropriate and good through engaging in practice leads to clumsiness, muddle and mistakes. This may in itself be a discomforting experience, but in an educational practice governed by performance requirements, constant assessments and grading as well as satisfaction surveys, there is not much room for trying out one's own voice and creativity and writing some potentially bad texts (often called 'mistakes'). So, in addition to the strenuous experience of learning the know-how that is tacit and embodied without clear directions, there is the constant pressure to perform and the overhanging judgement of whether or not one has lived up to these inarticulable standards. Likewise, as teachers, we are reluctant to encourage our students to experiment, because we risk leading them astray with no time to finalize the text properly.

However, good student writing is not merely about following certain rules (both explicit and implicit) in order to produce a product that is recognized by the tradition as an (adequate) academic paper or essay. Writing must produce something unique, something distinct that is in and of itself an independent substance – otherwise, it would simply be copying. The practice of writing thus embodies a particular paradox, i.e. the paradox of the student simultaneously doing as tradition prescribes (immersed in the thoughts of others and established traditions) and yet coming to be as an independent and unique subject released from the rules that bind him or her. Kant termed this 'the paradox of learning' (Oettingen, 2008). The educational philosopher Gert Biesta (2014) distinguishes between three aspects of schooling: qualification, socialization and subjectification. The first two, qualification and socialization, are about learning particular skills and being introduced to established traditions and practices. The last aspect, subjectification, has to do with coming-to-be as a unique individual. The three aspects are intertwined and mutually constitutive – the latter contingent on and determined by the first two.

Samuel Beckett makes a similar distinction, in which life is considered as consisting mainly of habits, unreflectively engaged in through interaction in tradition-bound practices. Habits are activities into which we are socialized. They evolve from engagement in tradition and in the established norms of social being and thinking. But, for Beckett, there are times *between* the continuity of periods of habit that have a particular significance. These times between the periods of habit 'represent the perilous zones in the life of the individual, dangerous, precarious, painful, mysterious and fertile, when for a moment the boredom of living is replaced by the suffering of being' (Beckett, cited in Wood, 2009, p. 41). He too thus argues that, while living is on the whole characterized by tediously, almost mindlessly, doing as others do, there are moments when the individual steps up and comes into being. These moments are risk filled and strenuous, and thus consequently entail discomfort. They are risk filled because they involve being open to judgement and the possibility of failure. More importantly, however, these are spaces of vitality and individuality – fertile soil from which creation can grow.

In this sense, writing is a practice that demands both the habitual submissiveness to tradition and the unique coming-to-be. It is thus fundamentally an existential endeavour. The existential nature of writing is captured by Jacques Derrida in his essay collection *Writing and Difference* (1978). Here he argues that, although the subject is producing the book (or the thesis or essay), the process of coming-to-be also means that the written word is producing the subject. We come into being through writing. Derrida writes: 'Little by little the book will finish me' (p. 65). Leaning on Derrida, it becomes reasonable, with Gilbert (2015), to ask our students (and ourselves) if they (we) love writing, but equally if writing loves them (us) back. We will return to love soon and, as we all know, love can be quite discomforting, so love is no cure for the struggle. But it is a cure for boredom and indifference.

The paradox of writing itself

In writing, one must struggle with capturing the complexity of that aspect of life with which the text deals, while being confined by the constriction of words. Iris Murdoch captures this by writing, 'You may know a truth, but if it is at all complicated you have to be an artist not to utter it as a lie' (cited in Nussbaum, 1990, p. 3). In Derrida's essay on the work of the Jewish poet Jabès, he writes: 'Is not to write, once more, to confuse ontology and grammar? The grammar in which are inscribed all the dislocations of dead syntax' (Derrida, 1978, p. 78). The paradox of writing has to do with the set rules of language confining expression, setting boundaries for it, yet making expression possible. When writing, we are grappling with, grasping and conveying truths, truths about the lived world, that in essence are ungraspable. Derrida further writes: 'Between the too warm flesh of the literal event and the cold skin of the concept runs meaning' (p. 75). Grasping the complexity of actual events and truths of human lives with words is a reduction of the lived experience. Yet, when the right words settle into text, we have created something new in the world, something that did not exist beforehand, a new textual truth to be experienced – by ourselves and others. It is not just a weak and imperfect reflection of life; it is also an utterance with a life of its own. We handle the words, and it handles us. Is it healthy? Can this mutually constitutive practice become more loving, more passionate, so as to make the discomfort productive?

Through an increased mastery of language and an insistence on a passionate relationship with language, we can approach this complexity with less fear and teach our students to do so too. Samuel Beckett exemplifies this in *Worstward Ho* (1983), where he expands our understanding of the notions of 'better' and 'worse,' showing masterfully, through the upheaval of the simple dichotomy between best and worst, that there are a multitude of values that we assign to difference, and simultaneously displaying the limits of grammar:

> Less best. No. Naught best. Best worse. No. Not best worse. Naught not best worse. Less best worse. No. Least. Least best worst. Least never to be naught. Never to naught be brought. Never by naught be nulled. Unnullable least.

> Say that best worst. With leastening words say least best worse. For want of worser worst.
>
> (Beckett, in Ngai, 2005, p. 248)

And, while grammar is in a sense too impoverished to capture and portray the truth of the lived-in world, it is simultaneously too broad and imprecise. Consequently, Jabès writes:

> How can I say what I know
> with words whose signification
> is multiple?
>
> (Jabès, cited in Derrida, 1978, p. 73)

Here, it is not the impoverished nature of words that is lamented, but rather their multiplicity, their imprecision and the abundance of meaning possible when we start placing them side by side. The English novelist A.S. Byatt captures this wonderfully in the words of her protagonist, Phineas, in *The Biographer's Tale* as he describes his dropping out from university:

> It was a sunny day and the windows were very dirty. I was looking out of the windows, and I thought, I'm not going to go on with this any more. Just like that. It was May 8th 1994. I know that, because my mother had been buried the week before, and I'd missed the seminar on Frankenstein. I don't think my mother's death has anything to do with my decision, though as I set it down, I see it might be construed that way. . . . I went on looking at that filthy window above his head, and I thought, I must have things. I know a dirty window is an ancient, well-worn trope for intellectual dissatisfaction and scholarly blindness. The thing is, that the thing was also there. A real, very dirty window, shutting out the sun. A *thing*.
>
> (Byatt, 2001, p. 1)

Phineas is putting things to paper, discovering new connections or causal links. Or maybe he just puts independent facts to paper, insidiously realizing that he is losing control as the text proceeds? A dirty window is a thing that turns into a metaphor for his feeling of detachment from life, and the sequence of events makes them look like cause and effect, maybe even *makes* them cause and effect. However, Phineas cannot get undisturbed access to things (to life): as soon as he sets down his experiences and thoughts in writing, he discovers that the thing is not so much the name of an object but rather a particular subject–object relation (Brown, 2001). He cannot just say what happened. He cannot leave himself out of the equation. Causal links and connections emerge as soon as incidents are randomly or purposely placed side by side. Language does that, and so do our minds (Wegener, 2014). We produce and are produced. We cannot escape it. But we can pause and stay right there and see what is happening.

(Im)potentiality

We have thus far argued that writing is both limited and made possible by the constraints of grammar and the unruliness of associative links made possible every time words are placed in a row. It is an existential endeavour of coming-to-be that requires immersion in tradition and the production of individual uniqueness through words. We have argued that this is a laborious process that is risk filled and consequently inherently uncomfortable. This is potentially either a productive or an unproductive discomfort. A healthy or sick love relationship. However, this coming-to-be cannot merely be understood as actualization, i.e. producing a product, taking a stand, becoming *some*-thing. Inspired by Agamben, Lewis (2011) argues that coming-to-be must instead be understood to be more substantially about (im)potential, i.e. the space for dwelling and *not* actualizing. He argues that studying is such a playful dwelling. Building on this, we will argue that writing can be understood as a playful dwelling – giving in to confusion and bewilderment and continuously experimenting with different paths one could take. Let us explain:

The relationship between potentiality and actualization: potential is the possibility for something to be actualized. (Im)potentiality is not its opposite, but rather has to do with the being-able to abstain from doing. Byung-Chul Han (2015) suggests broadening this distinction by differentiating between the terms positive potency, negative potency and impotence. Positive potency has to do with actualizing, while negative potency is the *active* not-to. Impotence is instead the inability to act, i.e. the opposite of positive potency. Negative potency, our ability not to be, is a pre-requisite for the actualized coming-to-be as a unique subject. While the ethos of the neo-liberal subject is to maximize actualization (be all you can be!), both Lewis (2011) and Han (2015) argue for a more sensitive approach to potentiality that creates space for dwelling in the potential, rather than forcefully actualizing – space in which one can get lost, explore alternatives, linger in indecision and eventually choose both what to actualize and what *not* to actualize. What makes us human, according to Lewis (2011), is precisely the capacity to not be, to remain in potentiality, i.e. to not actualize.

Like Lewis, Han (2015) argues for the active choice not to act, i.e. to suspend action, but nuances this by critiquing Agamben. In Herman Melville's short story *Bartleby the Scrivener: A Story of Wall-Street*, the copyist Bartleby starts gradually to cease acting, notoriously using the phrase 'I would prefer not to.' Byung-Chul Han critiques Agamben for idealizing Bartleby. Agamben shows that Bartleby maintains infinite potentiality and thereby complete freedom – the freedom to be anything he chooses. However, the story ends with Bartleby's death by starvation, because he preferred not to eat. There are a multitude of interpretations of this story, but Han (2015) points out that it illustrates that in order to be, in order to exist, one must act. We cannot merely exist in potentiality or (im)potentiality.

Choosing what not to be, what not to actualize, entails the choice to actualize something else. Yet Han also insists that:

> although delaying does not represent a positive deed, it proves necessary if action is not to sink to the level of laboring. Today we live in a world that is very poor in interruption; 'betweens' and 'between-times' are lacking. Acceleration is abolishing all intervals.
>
> (Han, 2015, p. 22)

The term 'laboring' here is drawn from Hannah Arendt's *The Human Condition* (1958), where the concept of labour is used to denote everyday rhythms and the meeting of everyday needs that are repetitive, e.g. eating breakfast or emptying the dishwasher. The term is similar to Beckett's understanding of habits described above. Han is thus arguing that, in order to come into being as an individual, to rise above merely following habits, routines and traditions, it is necessary to delay, to stay in potentiality – to not, at least for a while, actualize. It is this delaying that can be captured in Lewis's exposition of the notion of studying.

Studying as dwelling in potentiality: Lewis (2011) argues that, in a performance society, which he terms a 'learning society,' education is 'obsessed with the measure of what someone *can do* in order to fulfil a particular role within the economy' (p. 588). He argues that in neo-liberal education there is a hubris which insists on students maximizing their activity, pulling themselves together 'through a self-initiated entrepreneurialism' (p. 589). This focus on potential, the focus on what a child or a student can *become*, and thus what s/he can actualize, results in a narrow interest in productivity. In the performance society, students are thus denied access to the (im)potential – the space of not-being, not actualizing. Students are put under the pressure of a relentless demand for actualization. While this demand is rooted in a discourse of positive potential, it is also rooted in the needs of the market or the nation state. The notion of studying is instead a space where the student stays in potentiality and does not actualize.

Studying, according to Lewis (2011), is a scholarly dwelling in potentiality, where all possibilities are held open. It is a practice where the student is caught up in the ideas of others, and is struck by these in a way that can be likened to shock. Unable to completely grasp the new notions, yet unable to let go, the student 'stumbles along on a quest for new clues . . . without clear direction, without clear methodology, without an end in sight' (Lewis, 2011, p. 292). Derrida, too, believed that it was bad for readers to be fearful or to be in a hurry to be determined, i.e. it is bad to push actualization rather than dwell in (im)potentiality. Instead, he likewise argued for the keeping-open of possibilities (Wood, 2009).

In the performance educational system, studying becomes a burden, something that needs to be overcome, and an obstacle to achieving the end goal. As Lewis (2011) writes:

> Thus, there is a rush to meet national standards through testing ('we have to meet standards *now* so that you can become productive workers!') or there is a rush to close the gap between education and political praxis ('we have to act *now* in order to change the world!') or there is the rush to finish the dissertation ('the only good dissertation is a done dissertation!'). In these perspectives, studying is an obstacle, an irritant, an infuriating reality whose only utility is its instrumental value for reaching another end.
>
> (p. 592)

He further writes, 'if the lesson of learning is to become a self-regulating entrepreneur then the lesson of study is to become nothing at all but rather remain within a pure capacity to be or not to be' (p. 587). Thus, studying is, in this sense, about impotence, i.e. the inability to bring into actualization. The endless possibilities are not necessarily held open through power held in negative potency, but may rather be held open by a submissiveness to the overwhelming and endless ocean of thoughts, ideas and knowledge. Yet it is precisely this inability to act that the student must simultaneously surrender to and struggle with. This dialectical dynamic of surrender and struggle is the foundation of the learning that allows the subject to come into being. It is the condition for solving the insoluble paradox of learning.

Writing as studying: Lewis (2011) argues that studying can be likened to play: 'I would propose that study is precisely when we *play with learning*, decoupling learning from instrumental economic usages in relation to entrepreneurship, and thus find within learning an impotent opening to freedom' (p. 595). We propose developing the practice of writing as a playful space of studying – a space for experimenting and taking wrong turns, a space that requires time to be bewildered, time to be stuck, time to create a wrong path and to go back and try a different course. What is missing in the production society and an education that pushes for actualization is precisely this space for both negative potency (deliberately suspending action) and impotency (submissively giving way to confusion and overwhelming endlessness). To pause, to hesitate and to linger in confusion and not-being is to halt actualization. It is to slow down, perhaps even grind to a halt, but does not necessarily mean that one should stop writing – writing *can* be playfully exploring the labyrinth in confusion and bewilderment. In a world of performance and achievement, this playful meandering is irreversibly interwoven with discomfort. To write is in essence to perform and to actualize, to produce and to be judged by the reader. It is thus a condition of writing as a practice in its entirety, not merely the writing of papers for a higher education course. But the short timeframe, the condition of learning and producing at the same time, the concrete evaluation through a grade, all enhance this discomfort and also limit the possibility of lingering – i.e. it reduces the possibilities of becoming.

The academic culture of higher education is thus not conducive to this playful, meandering writing that we have argued for here, i.e. the kind of writing that adheres to the labour of studying, that lingers and delays, pauses, so as to actively choose what to actualize as well as what not to actualize, i.e. come into being by thinking otherwise and doing otherwise. The kind of writing that insists on struggling with the complexity of the world, wrestling with the limits of grammar, stepping into the 'dangerous, precarious, painful, mysterious and fertile, when for a moment the boredom of living is replaced by the suffering of being' (Beckett, cited in Wood, 2009, p. 41).

Concluding remarks

The rush and hurriedness of the performance culture creates a discomfort that is counterproductive for writing that is existential in essence. What we suggest here is not to rush to production to try to minimize it, but to dwell, and that this not-being and not-doing can create a space in which we can meet discomfort with curiosity. We are being weighed and measured on our text production, on the quality of our texts, their impact, and also on the quantity of our output. Efficiency and productivity are at a premium. One of the most rebellious things to do in academia and in society in general may be to do nothing (not even meditate to become more relaxed – and, eventually, more productive).

One problem noted by writing researchers is precisely that many writing advice manuals address writing as if it were a straightforward and linear production process (Lee & Kamler, 2008). Epistemologically, many of these books favour behaviour over process and reject rhetorical invention (Johnson, 2017). That is, students are encouraged to finish thinking, then plan for the writing, stick to the plan and primarily to write *a lot* as this is the safe way to a finished text. However, writing as coming-into-being is not linear and does not evolve only through hurried activity towards a nearby deadline. Because writing processes are never mere reproduction, like other creative processes they are at times chaotic. Most of us know this intuitively, yet we stick to the notion that we must plan first and then write, or we try to avoid chaos by planning harder or strictly following our own plans and the rules of our discipline. Pausing to build a passionate and healthy relationship with writing is an alternative strategy. Writing must be considered to be itself an act of learning and becoming, not just 'writing up' findings in an acceptable format, on time. 'I write in order to learn something that I did not know before I wrote it', writes Richardson (2003, p. 501). Here, she is referring to the idea that we are not just writing to pass on knowledge. We are writing in order to think, learn and become. Through writing, she says, we can actually achieve new insights, insights that we could not attain solely by reading, thinking and talking with others. Pablo Llambías, the former head of the Danish Writers' Academy

(Forfatterskolen), even claims that we can write texts that are smarter than ourselves (cited in Wegener, 2016). This means: writing teaches *us*.

Paraphrasing Doris Lessing, we may say to our students: 'Dear student, you are not mad. You've been told to go about writing by taking control, asking experts to tell you the truth, and to perform quickly and smoothly. Here is what you also need to do: take your time to spot a filthy window and ponder its tangible and metaphorical qualities, feel what it is like to not-(yet)-know, and not-(yet)-do, and know that discomfort, but not fear, is fine. Discomfort is part of a creative, mutual and healthy relationship with writing.'

References

Arendt, H. (1958/1998). *The human condition*. Chicago & London: University of Chicago Press.
Beckett, S. (1983). *Worstward Ho*. New York: Grove Press.
Biesta, G. (2011). *Learning democracy in school and society: Education, lifelong learning and the politics of citizenship*. Rotterdam: Sense Publishers.
Biesta, B. J. J. (2014). *The beautiful risk of education*. Boulder, CO: Paradigm Publishers.
Brown, B. (2001). Thing theory. *Critical Inquiry, 28*(1), 1–22.
Byatt, A. S. (2001). *The biographer's tale*. New York: Vintage Books.
Derrida, J. (1978). *Writing and difference*. Chicago: University of Chicago Press.
Dreyfus, H. (1991). *Being-in-the-world: A commentary on Heidegger's being and time, division 1*. Massachusetts: Massachusetts Institute of Technology.
Gilbert, E. (2015). *Big magic. Creative living beyond fear*. London: Bloomsbury.
Han, B. C. (2015). *The burnout society*. Stanford: Stanford University Press.
Johnson, K. (2017). Writing by the book, writing beyond the book. *Composition Studies, 45*(2), 55–72.
Jones, M. J. (2010). When teachers must let education hurt: Rousseau and Nietzsche on compassion and the educational value of suffering. *Journal of Philosophy and Education, 44*(1), 45–60.
Lee, A., & Kamler, B. (2008). Bringing pedagogy to doctoral publishing. *Teaching in Higher Education, 13*(5), 511–523.
Lessing, D. (1962/2007). *The golden notebook*. London: HarperCollins Publishers.
Lewis, T. E. (2011). Rethinking the learning society: Giorgio Agamben on studying, stupidity, and impotence. *Studies in Philosophy and Education, 30*, 589–599.
Mintz, A. (2008). *The labor of learning: A study of the role of pain in learning*. Proquest Digital Dissertations, AAT 8721152 (New York, Columbia University).
Ngai, S. (2005). *Ugly feelings*. Cambridge, MA/London: Harvard University Press.
Nussbaum, M. (1990). *Love's knowledge: Essays on philosophy and literature*. Oxford: Oxford University Press.
Oettingen, A. von. (2008). Pædagogiske antinomier og permanente problemer – bidrag til en moderne pædagogik. *Res Cogitans, 1*(5), 1–22.
Paré, A. (2010). Making sense of supervision: Deciphering feedback. In P. Thomson & M. Walker (Eds.), *The Routledge doctoral student's companion: Getting to grips with research in education and the social sciences* (pp. 107–115). London: Routledge.
Richardson, L. (2003). Writing: A method of inquiry. In N. K. Denzin & Y. S. Lincoln (Eds.), *Collecting and interpreting qualitative materials* (2nd ed., pp. 499–541). Thousand Oaks, CA: Sage.

Wegener, C. (2014). Writing with Phineas. How a fictional character from A. S. Byatt helped me turn my ethnographic data into a research text. *Cultural Studies <=> Critical Methodologies*, *14*(4), 351–360.

Wegener, C. (2016). *Skriv med glæde. En guide til akademisk skrivning.* Copenhagen: Samfundslitteratur.

Wood, S. (2009). *Derrida's writing and difference: A reader's guide.* London & New York: Continuum International Publishing Group.

Chapter 7

In deep water
University students' challenges in the processes of self-formation, survival or flight

Casper Feilberg

Introduction

As a second semester project supervisor, I encountered the following narrative during the first face-to-face meeting with a student project group:

> 'When you want to make the most of your high grade point average, you go for the most prestigious line of study such as anthropology, psychology or medicine', Cathrine said. John, Anne and Cathrine, the three first year students, were trying to make me understand the topic proposed for their project. 'You don't spend your grade point average in pursuit of a career as a school teacher or a farmer', John continued. 'But I know of a guy, a good friend, who did just that: he didn't go for the prestigious careers – and it is types like him that we want to interview, to understand why'. The three ambitious students gave each other a meaningful look. The topic was as clear as daylight to them. I, the supervisor, on the other hand, struggled to follow their line of thinking. Since when had it become a law of nature that you had to spend you grade point average for a study that is as prestigious as possible? What experiences and educational background had formed these students? From later discussions I learned that all three students had a high grade point average from upper secondary school, that they were performance oriented, and they all experienced times of doubt with regard to their choice of line of study, viz. psychology, during the first year.

Looking back and reflecting on the fore-understandings of the students, and of me as a lecturer of psychology, I realize that I expected students to choose a line of study in the light of their heartfelt interest, so that an appetite and a wondering curiosity for the field of work and understandings within psychology guided students towards the study of psychology. The students, on the other hand, came with another assumption that they took for granted: that high grades signify success within an educational 'career'.

Compared with many other lines of study, the studies of psychology in Denmark enjoy a high grade point average for admission, highly motivated students and a high percentage of completion. And, in accordance with the Danish welfare state, students do not pay tuition fee at all; furthermore, they are financially supported by society on a monthly basis with State Educational Grants (SU). What discontent and problems can students face in an educational context like this?

The motivation of upper secondary school students is an important place to start. The introductory case highlights some important recent tendencies in a Danish higher learning context (e.g. Møldrup, 2017): some students feel pressed by 'society', 'family' and 'friends' to make 'the best of' the vast possibilities that are open to them (voiced by John in this case), by choosing a study with a high grade admission level. This is never clear-cut. My point is that these students *primarily* base their choice of line of study on the grade admission level (Willerslev, 2017). I believe this line of acting and reasoning is based on the assumption that a line of study with a high grade point average for admission in itself marks a goal worthwhile of pursuit and is a mark of success: among politicians, careers advisors, parents and secondary school students, as the case of John, Anne and Cathrine illustrates.

These tendencies affect the study environment of high-grade line of studies such as anthropology, medicine and psychology, and their consequences are currently debated within Danish higher learning (e.g. Willerslev, 2017; Brinkmann, 2016; Kyllingsbæk, Jensen & de Neergaard, 2018). What we see here, I believe, is a clash between strategic career students and an institution which promotes immersion, a wondering interest and involvement with the topics. Following Willerslev (2017) and Brinkmann (2016), I fear that these strategic students are misguided and end up pursuing an educational path in which they are not personally engaged. And as we saw in the case of John, Anne and Cathrine, they experienced a returning pang of doubt with respect to their choice of study, to a degree that affected their motivation and involvement.

Let us return to the project group of John, Anne and Cathrine and their project work. As their supervisor, I challenged their preunderstandings, encouraged them to follow their interests and supported the development of their academic and empirical inquiry into their subject to the best of my ability. Their work progressed slowly and with difficulty; they had many disagreements, I later learned, but they did not address them during our meetings in the beginning, and I did not detect their tension, although I did experience that their involvement in the project was underwhelming. Their performance at the oral exam surprised me, because it stood out from my six other project group exams that semester. During the oral defense of the project report, the students showed a lack of an academic approach; no self-reflective and critical perspectives on their own inquiry with respect to their methodic choices, theoretical interpretations, and empirical findings. I also play a role in this, of course. But what made their exam stand out in my memory was what I experienced as a clash between their self-image as accomplished students and their performance during the exam, which expressed the opposite. They appeared very confident and convinced by their presentations and oral defense. They seemed little prepared for discussions concerning e.g. the weaknesses of the project report; the students seemed, to me, convinced that the goal of the project exam was to impress the examiners, rather than discussing their subject and their way of inquiring into it and understanding it theoretically. All of this points to what I theoretically will describe as the absence of a change in their habitus; they seemed surprisingly unaffected by their first year of study. This can of course point to problems in my supervision, in the teaching within the different modules of the first year, a lack of social and intellectual integration in the institution, a lack of motivation and involvement in the process of culturing a mind of their own (Tinto, 1993; Feilberg, 2014).

In this context, I wish to pursue the last perspective. As an educational institution, we can do much pedagogically in regard to optimizing the flow and the design of students' educational practices and their content, but they have to do the work themselves (Kemp, 2010). Subject motivation and involvement in social and academic activities are therefore also an important part of the story. No involvement, no new habitus (Feilberg, 2014). I have elsewhere made the argument that the university as an educational institution has only succeeded if the students who leave the institution are fundamentally different from the students who entered five years earlier. This change in personality, knowledge, perception etc. can – I argue – be termed as an embodiment of a professional and academic habitus of the psychology student (cf. Bourdieu, 1990), a process that involves processes of formation, personal involvement as well as both collective and individual activities (Feilberg, 2014, pp. 88-89; Gadamer, 2004).

In the case of John, Anne and Cathrine and their exam, what stands out to me is their lack of a wondering attitude and a deep subject involvement, which for me is fundamental to the university as an institution and the core of being a researcher. As Willerslev (2017) points out, a core value of the university is a culture of wondering and exploration that challenges what we know. To become a part of this culture, Willerslev argues along the lines of Gadamer (2004), supervisors and students alike must be willing to put themselves and their preunderstandings at risk; and this process of realization can very well be difficult and even painful to the learning subject (Willerslev, 2017, p. 121). This analytical identification of a lack of involvement in the project work might also shed light on John, Anne and Cathrine's reoccurring experience of doubt with regard to their choice of line of study.

If a primary motivation for your choice of study rests on it being a high grade point average study, how resilient are you when faced by the hard and sometimes painful processes of studying, learning and evolving? No wonder you may experience the pang of doubt even though you are a high grade student in psychology. Strategic career students and their focus on earning high grades by fulfilling the learning goals of the study program are prone to experience doubt more often and even dropout (Tinto, 1993). But as Willerslev (2017) points out, this tendency is not one that the individual student can be held responsible for; a problematic new grading scale (7-point grading scale), educational reforms that highlight narrow learning goals and a culture that generally despises errors lead students with the best of intentions to follow these markers of success.

I concur with Willerslev's perspective on the structural backdrop that informs the self-understanding of the career students. But I also argue, as a lecturer, supervisor and educational researcher, that education must be about more than passing an exam or maximizing a grade output. One could object and ask what normative values are a person like me guided by, and what right do I have to expose students to those values? Is science not about being objective, value-free and unbiased? I respect the choices and priorities of every student, and of course, examination must follow the rules set by the university, the ministerial regulations and the study program to make sure that a fair and professional evaluation takes place. But as a lecturer and a supervisor, I argue and encourage students to involve themselves and grapple with questions of science and profession themselves, just as I exercise a normative and pedagogical approach to education.

To reflect these positions, the chapter will firstly introduce an existential-phenomenological perspective on higher learning pedagogy and ideals, secondly three empirical cases will be presented and discussed and finally, I will discuss and conclude on the findings.

The need of reflected normative ideals, theory and empirical research

According to Biesta (2010) and Kemp (2004) discussions within educational practices that go beyond managing education as a technique, and beyond emancipatory criticism of practice that does not propose concrete consequences and informed actions, must include a normative perspective: a vision and ideals that can guide a concrete practice as a student and a lecturer. It is simply not meaningful to discuss educational practices in a supposedly non-normative or value-free way. Or to discuss educational practices in an endlessly critical and emancipatory way that does not inform concrete action (Kemp, 2004). Of course, as a part of academia, normative positions, understandings and ideologies cannot live as personal, unreflected fore-understandings, practices and motives. On the contrary, as Biesta, Habermas and Kemp have argued, we – every student and every lecturer – need to reflect on what ideals and values we act out within higher learning (Biesta, 2010; Habermas, 1986; Kemp, 2004). And we must reflect upon this *theoretically*, so that our actions and habits can be analyzed and interpreted in the light of collective and systematic conceptions. And so that it may be criticized, supported or revised in the light of empirical research. This is key in any *pedagogically* reflected practice (Kemp, 2004). There is a plurality of theoretical perspectives within the debate on the ideals or visions of higher learning and the idea of the university in society, each highlighting different and overlapping perspectives with respect to the other traditions. Students experience styles of institutionalized and personalized ideals and values during lectures, supervision, in the organization of the study and the chosen curriculum etc., as part of their everyday educational life. From a Bildung perspective, it is up to each student – inspired by or opposed to the positions presented – to make up their own mind and standpoint.

An existential–phenomenological perspective on formal education and Bildung

Existential phenomenology offers rich discussions of education and Bildung[1] (e.g. Gadamer, 2004; Ricoeur, 1988; Kemp, 2010). Inspired by this tradition, I argue for the need of a double perspective on students' educational practices at the university:

- a formal educational perspective that focuses on learning and examines the qualifications, skills and knowledge of the course modules, as described in the study program, *and*
- a Bildung perspective that addresses the processes of formation and of the ideals of the university or the profession; none of which can be conjured up by command or directly examined.

The distinction between the formal educational perspective and the Bildung perspective is theoretical and inspired by Peter Kemp (2010, pp. 27, 151–152). The distinction between formal education and Bildung makes it possible to introduce normative, value-laden and personal perspectives into the discussion of higher learning. The Bildung tradition is especially strong within continental philosophy. The concept of Bildung has historically been applied to bring focus on to the dimensions and aspects that current educational tendencies shove into the background (Gustavsson, 1998; Gustavsson, 2014, p. 109). Bildung is in this chapter understood as culturing through 'wild' processes of formation (Bildung processes): these can be identified in the light of values and 'ideals' such as the embodiment of an academic and professional habitus and traits such as a sense of psychological phenomenon, autonomy and independence (Gadamer, 2004, pp. 8–17; Feilberg, 2014, pp. 3–4, 246–275). Inspired by Bourdieu's sociological concept of habitus, which signifies systems of durable dispositions that organize practices and representation (1990, p. 53), the habitus of the academic and psychological profession is understood as a theoretical description of the varied but stable dispositions and traits which characterize the collective psychological profession. In my conceptualization of the academic and professional habitus (Feilberg, 2014), I highlight a sense and a psychological understanding of aesthetic meaning and lived phenomena on the one hand, and a habitual readiness to explain and interpret in the light of a scientific theory and method on the other. A cultured member of the psychological profession has embodied his/her own independent and reflected variation of the dispositions and traits of the academic and psychological habitus: this is what the education of psychology in a Bildung perspective can aim to support their students to embody as much as possible of.

It is also possible to identify a range of ideals of the university. According to Habermas (1986), for instance, the function of the university and its role in modern society, for researchers and students alike, centers around what he terms 'corporative truth seeking', in the sense that researchers and students alike seek better ways of understanding the phenomena and subjects of research, and that this practice is dependent upon openness in the form of public arguments and communication. Corporative truth seeking through openness is an ideal that goes beyond mere competition and performance-optimizing strategies; it denotes a common and shared ideal, which I include in a Bildung perspective.

The theoretical inspirations of this article stem from Bourdieu, Habermas and others, but the ontology is existential phenomenology through and through. We are as a bodily existence already always in a historical, social, cultural and natural (biological) world, according to Merleau-Ponty (2012). Existential phenomenology does not understand human beings as fundamentally characterized by a first-person perspective, a minimal self or our consciousness. Instead, we are thrown into a situation (Geworfenheit); from this facticity, we can either experience being as a differentiated person *or* decentered and undifferentiated as 'das Man' (Heidegger, 1927; Gadamer, 2004; Feilberg, Norlyk & Keller, 2018). Existential phenomenology stresses both our individual existence and collective existence: this perspective both highlights the importance of the individually reflected choices of each student and each lecturer, as well as the collective existence and social responsibility that flow from our common lifeworld (Merleau-Ponty, 2012; Keller, 2015). Still, both the individual existence and the collective existence 'stand out' from a being that is more anonymous. According to Feilberg, Norlyk & Keller:

> Varieties of the anonymous, pre-personal being that Heidegger associated with *das Man* . . . and Merleau-Ponty with our bodily existence, are at play in trivial as well as creative forms of social relations, roles, and positions. This is the case, for instance, in dramatic and mythical shapes of social relations such as those of 'winner and looser' or 'us and them'.
> (Feilberg, Norlyk & Keller, 2018, p. 219, emphasis in original)

First-year students, for instance, are very tuned into the expectations of peers and lecturers; it is important to feel capable and accepted academically and socially. In the background of these experiences, 'mythical shapes' of succeeding or failing unfold anonymously.

Let us look into the background of this specific phenomenon of succeeding and failing in our present time. Being a young person today is – as Giddens (1991) has pointed out – very much characterized by constructing our own narrative of self, and this creates anxiety. Anxiety is a part of the being of a young person, because the personal project of one's identity is very much at the center of all social and cultural practices in our present Western culture. Who am I and what should I become? The concept of anxiety in this context points to the existential–phenomenological (Heidegger, 1927) observation that the experience of anxiety is characterized by – not a fear of something *in particular*, but precisely – an undifferentiated (general) and existential uncertainty. In this context, an undifferentiated uncertainty of 'everything and nothing', of who I am or should become as a person. As a decentered existence, we thus fluctuate between having a firm grip of ourselves and experiencing that everything is up in the air. According to Merleau-Ponty (2012), this dramatic aspect of our bodily existence is social through and through; just as we can be unclear about who our next of kin really are, we can similarly be unclear as to who we are ourselves. According to existential phenomenology, these experiences are an expression of the existential condition of our bodily existence: that we as a personal existence and a social existence are imbued by our anonymous being, which put our personal project on a shaky ground. We find it difficult, for instance, to navigate between expectations of ourselves and those of others (family, peers, lecturers, professional ideals etc.), because in the immediate experiences it is not clear whether they stem from oneself or from others. The case of John, Anne and Cathrine can be interpreted and understood in the light of this intermixture and confusion of expectations, spiced with a great deal of fear of losing, making errors or being on the wrong side of social expectations. But due to our anonymous being, we only arrive at distinctions between self and others through a secondary reflection and differentiation process, which can be understood as Bildung. In other words, due to the fundamentally social and anonymous characteristics of our existence, (psychology) students such as John, Anne and Cathrine are more than ever challenged by the project of personal existence: who am I, unlike you?

If living with uncertainty, insecurity, being in deep water, caught in uncontrollable processes and going through painful processes at times is part of being a university student from an Bildung perspective (Gustavsson, 2014, p. 111; Kemp, 2010; Feilberg, 2014, 2017), then it is important to describe the meaning behind this, to make it understandable. This process would, at an analytical level, include identifying the ideals[2] or values at play in the specific instance. Likewise, it is important to describe the typical pitfalls that follow these processes. Now, according to a Bildung perspective, it is a combination of these three aspects (understanding the meaning of the processes as they are lived, explicating the ideals and values at play and identifying the possible pitfalls) that is the key to making it possible for students to self-reflectively navigate, select and deselect involvement, according to their motivation and priorities; and to put them in a position where they can support each other and reflect on the processual aspects of student life, in a dialogue with peers, supervisors and lecturers.

To illustrate and describe the empirical background of these theoretical understandings, three qualitative cases will now be presented and discussed.

Andrea – from a grade-maximizing strategy to preparing herself for her professional life

The case of Andrea can shed light on the motive of a grade-maximizing student and the possible Bildung processes that such a student can undergo. This case derives from a two-year qualitative field work of the education of psychology, Aalborg University (Feilberg, 2014, pp. 497–508). Andrea is an ambitious student; when I meet her, she is nevertheless about to skip a grade maximizing strategy that she has been linked to for three years of her study. She is now in the seventh semester. But as a bachelor's student, she spends a major part of her study adhering to a grade-optimizing strategy: telling the examiners what she thinks will impress them. During oral examinations, she thus takes on viewpoints, far from her personal understandings, only to show off her academic competencies. She actively avoids personal involvement in the subjects of her projects: instead she seeks a position of 'suitable distance'. Andrea sums it up in the following way: 'my motivation has been to study what I believed would give a good outcome and apply it in a way that I believed would secure a good outcome' (Feilberg, 2014, p. 498).

But while working as a trainee psychologist, she discovers that she does not know her own standpoints as a psychologist, and she cannot remember the rote learned concepts. From then on, she chooses actively to 'prepare herself' for the profession of psychology by examining and taking up subjects of personal interest and conflict. These projects are 'harder to navigate' emotionally, as she no longer is detached and uninvolved. However, she now develops theoretically underpinned standpoints *of her own* (Feilberg, 2014). Now, Andrea is, in other words, actively seeking a mind of her own.

The case of Andrea can be said to illustrate the importance of the choice of subject being guided by personal interest, to promote what can be interpreted as processes of formation and exemplarity. By studying a problem field intensively over time, she is able to develop her own position within the current traditional understandings and thus develop a grip of her own habitus as a future psychologist. This process of 'making up her own mind' is much harder and more 'frustrating', according to Andrea. During the last two years of study, she has 'matured' and has improved at 'experiencing the paradox . . . because there are opposites in the real world'. She has learned that *lived experiences* are more complex than *theories*, and she has improved at containing the paradoxes of real life.

The case of Andrea also illustrates that Bildung processes are not limited to a module or semester; they can take years, just as they are not confined to the professional self or the personal self, but move across both the private, personal and professional person.

Group drama connected with supervision: the circular processes of scientific inquiry

The 'circular processes' of scientific inquiry

The emotional drama of project work and scientific inquiry does not only follow first semester students, as the following case highlights. The case describes Agnete and her project group and supervision, which I had the opportunity to observe and follow (Feilberg, 2014, pp. 471–483). Agnete and her project group consist of five students, and they are in the second semester of psychology. I will highlight a situation from their supervision with the experienced supervisor Berit.

134 Casper Feilberg

The group suddenly experiences emotional drama and being in deep water during supervision when the supervisor asks them to rewrite their introduction and rethink their research question, two weeks prior to deadline. They experience this as if they are about to fail as a group. Berit senses this and explains that returning to and rethinking fundamental questions is central to the scientific process: she describes it as 'circular processes' and underlines that these are a natural part of scientific inquiry and writing. The students are nevertheless shocked and Berit must give them a break to talk it over and calm down. During this break, several of the students express despair, saying 'I want to just die', 'let us ignore what Berit says, and hope for a merciful censor' and 'I want to drop out'. But one student is able to cope and begins urging them to think and ask questions. During the break and the restarted meeting, the group is able to cope with the emotional drama (container–contained, Bion, 1962), and in the light of this, they are able to begin to reflect and actually understand the criticism that their supervisor raises. Finally, they are able to regain emotional balance and act on what Berit is trying to communicate to them. This case illustrates the emotional drama that scientific inquiry entails: to be able to develop one's understanding, even though you seek a safe ground. It also highlights the dramatic emotional life that can be a part of learning and formation processes.

First semester students in deep water

I will now describe a recent observation of a first semester project group during the problem-based learning (PBL) group exam. These first semester students have the above case of Agnete as a part of their curriculum of the PBL module. I was recently the censor of a group of six students during their oral PBL project exam. During this exam, a group member reflects on the work process of the group in the following way: 'when we read the case of Agnete, we thought: we will never experience such dramatic emotional reactions to supervision and criticism. Fast forward two months, and we find ourselves in exactly the same panic situation after supervision. The "mean" circular processes and all': the rest of the group members laugh and nod knowingly. In the group's description of their processes during project work – a mandatory appendix of every project report at psychology – they highlight the 'great frustration' that some group members experienced during and after supervision. These students expressed frustration as they felt their supervisor, Erik, did not guide or 'help' them enough; the group coped with this situation by collectively reflecting on the supervising and thus helping the frustrated students to build an understanding and an 'overview' of the supervision session. Finally, the group stresses their general experiences of frustrations and 'a feeling of wanting to give up' during this, their first project work, but also their collective support and interdependence with respect to 'cheering up each other' and holding on to a 'belief in prevailing' and meeting the project deadline (quoting the project description of the project group). This group had truly found themselves in deep water but had found a constructive way to firm ground and a more secure position and understanding.

This case illustrates, in my point of view, that it is possible to prepare students for difficult processes with case examples that thematize the exemplary difficulties that students experience during the project work, in addition to supervisor attention, theoretical literature and seminar exercises.

Discussion

This section describes the exemplary motives and social dynamics that influence high grade studies, critically examining the consequences and highlighting the need of a theoretically underpinned understanding of what it entails to be a university student, in a way that reorganizes their world and what projects they orient themselves towards.

Stress, fear of failing or emotional drama

Recent study environment surveys in Denmark report an alarming level of stress perceived among upper secondary school students as well as among university students (EVA, 2017, 2015, p. 29). One can object that we do not yet have historical and reliable data to support the widespread assumption that students' level of stress is significantly higher than, for example, ten years ago, nor that this level of stress is strongly linked to their educational practices and experiences. Furedi (2003) has for instance convincingly shown in an Anglo-American context that – among other disciplines – therapy and psychology have influenced our very core understanding of what it means to be a self and how we have expressed and understood our emotional life and vulnerabilities in recent years in Western society. Following Furedi (2003), students' self-reported perception of stress can very well be influenced by changes in our cultural habits and expressions with respect to our emotional life. Kids, students and lecturers express their feelings to a higher degree. Terms such as stress and depression are part of everyday language. Therefore, it is important to include, for instance, clinical psychological research and non-self-rated inquiry into stress surveys among students.

Adding to this, I argue for the importance of developing a deeper understanding of the processes connected to studying and undergoing processes of formation as a student, especially of the emotional dramas and experiences of being in deep water and overwhelmed by uncertainty and anxiety. The transformative aha-experiences and the wild processes of formation that students may experience, are in this tradition understood as an integral part of Bildung (Gustavsson, 2014, p. 111; Kemp, 2010). Existence must to some extent be at stake to make these 'wild' and transformative processes of formation possible, and this is in itself dramatic and important to support as a higher learning educator (Feilberg, 2017).In this chapter, I have thus presented qualitative case studies as a means to help us understand more about the background of these tendencies with respect to the study of psychology at Aalborg University, a high grade point average study. Through the application of qualitative analysis as well as theoretical and conceptual interpretation, I suggest a differentiation between experiences of 'stress' and emotional drama as springing from either a) a performance orientation that focusses on social markers and educational accomplishments in themselves, or b) processes of formation, confrontation with the complexity of the field of study or the praxis of the profession. This distinction can help lecturers, students and organizers differentiate between 'stress' and doubt as a result of competition, comparison and an strategic career approach on the one hand, and the frustration and painful but important Bildung processes that are a part of higher learning and research as the above cases have illustrated, on the other hand.

This distinction also supports intervention with respect to these matters. In the first case (a), the markers must be discussed collectively and openly in the light of questions such as: 'what is the idea of the university?' In the latter case (b), Bildung processes, the uncertainties of scientific processes and of life, must be contained and addressed individually, as a project group and collectively as a semester. The semester organizers, lecturers and supervisors can play an important role in addressing and discussing the dilemmas and values that occupy the lifeworld of the students.

Conclusion

This chapter looks into psychology students' emotional dramas and experiences of being in deep water, of experiencing doubt and meaninglessness. The chapter, on the one hand, puts a critical focus on the grade-optimizing strategy and current tendencies of lackluster involvement that follow this approach to studying. On the other hand, the chapter critically examines the emotional pain that can arise from the dramatic, transformative aha-experiences and the uncontrolled processes of formation that several educational researchers see as a natural part of Bildung in educational contexts.

The chapter thus tries to develop an understanding of the dramatic and uncertain nature of life as a student. This is reflected in the light of an existential–phenomenological distinction between a) the educational perspective that focuses on the courses, exams and learning outcomes described in the study program, and b) the Bildung perspective with its focus on the 'wild' processes of formation that can be understood in the light of the ideals of the university or a profession such as the psychological profession. The ideals of self-reflection, self-understanding and corporative truth seeking are all ideals that we can strive for a whole life and yet never master. Yet they can unite us as students and lecturers and practicing professionals, as a shared goal and a specific habit in practice.

The ideal of corporative truth seeking (Habermas) relies on autonomous and responsible persons who seek a mind of their own and who pursue their projects in cooperation and discussions with others; existential phenomenology thus both highlights the importance of each person taking up their own personal existence and, at the same time, the fundamentally social existence that is undermined by and very much directed toward the shared beliefs and tendencies of the current time.

Deep water and anxiety are a part of being a person today, and it is something we should address, contain and reflect on at all levels of personal and educational life.

Notes

1 The German Bildung is difficult to translate (formation, culture do not cover its meaning) (Gustavsson, 2014; Biesta, 2002).
2 The ideals or meaning behind these Bildung processes can, according to this author, theoretically be interpreted as part of the development of autonomy and responsibility (Mündigkeit) among students (Habermas, 1971, 1986), or as part of the embodiment of traits of the academic and psychological habitus.

References

Biesta, G. (2002). Bildung and Modernity: The future of bildung in a world of difference. *Studies in Philosophy and Education*, *21*, 343–351.
Bion, W. R. (1962). *Learning From Experience*. London: Heinemann.
Bourdieu, P. (1990). *The logic of practice*. Stanford: Stanford University Press.
Bourdieu, P. (2000). *Pascalian meditations*. Cambridge: Polity Press.
Brinkmann, S. (2016). *Ståsteder: 10 gamle ideer til en ny verden*. København: Gyldendal.
EVA (2015). *Studenterservicer. Universiteternes tilbud til en bredere studentergruppe*. Danmarks Evalueringsinstitut, www.eva.dk.
EVA (2017). *Mange studerende oplever at stå i en udsat situation ved studiestart*. Notat af d. 28. august 2017. Danmarks Evalueringsinstitut, www.eva.dk.
Feilberg, C. (2014). *Dannelsen af en psykologisk og videnskabelig habitus hos psykologistuderende*. PhD thesis. Academic Books.
Feilberg, C. (2017). Skjulte kræfter og processer i vejledningsrummet. Dannelsesperspektiver på projektarbejde og projektvejleder-rollen ved universiteterne. *Psyke & Logos*, *38* (2), 134–158.
Feilberg, C., Norlyk, A., & Keller, K. D. (2018). Studying the Intentionality of Human Being: Through the Elementary Meaning of Lived Experience. *Journal of Phenomenological Psychology*, *49*(2), 214–246.
Furedi, F. (2003). *Therapy culture: Cultivating vulnerability in an uncertain age*. London: Routledge.
Gadamer, H. G (2004). *Truth and method* (Online edition 2nd, rev. ed., Continuum impacts). London: Continuum.
Giddens, A. (1991). *Modernity and self-identity: Self and society in the late modern age*. Cambridge: Polity.
Gustavsson, B. (1998). *Dannelse i vor tid*. Århus: Klim.
Gustavsson, B. (2014). Bildung and the road from a classical into a global and postcolonial concept. *Confero: Essays on Education*, *2*(1), 109–131.
Habermas, J. (1971). *Knowledge and human interests. Appendix: Knowledge and human interests: A general perspective* (pp. 301–350). Trans. Shapiro. Beacon Press: Boston.
Habermas, J. (1986). Die Idee der Universität – Lernprozesse. *Zeitschrift für Pädagogik*, Jg. 32 (1986), H. 5, 703–718.

Heidegger, M. (1927). *Sein und Zeit*. Tubingen: Max Niemeyer Verlag.
Keller, K. D. (2015). Autenticitet. I A. D. Sørensen, & K. D. Keller (red.), *Psykoterapi og eksistentiel fænomenologi* (s. 153–185). Aalborg: Aalborg Universitetsforlag.
Kemp, P. (2004). The citizen of the world as a figure in a critical vision. *Nordisk Pedagogik*, *24*(1), 11–18.
Kemp, P. (2010). *Citizen of the world: The cosmopolitan ideal for the twenty-first century* (Contemporary Studies in Philosophy and the Human Sciences). New York: Humanity Books.
Kyllingsbæk, S., Jensen, T. B. & de Neergaard, A. (2018). Debatindlæg: Tre KU-ansatte: De psykologistuderende er for unge, for velstillede, og der er for mange kvinder. *Politiken*. d. 26.07.2018.
Merleau-Ponty, M. (2012). *Phenomenology of perception*. Trans. Donald A. Landes. London: Routledge.
Møldrup, A. L. (2017). Gymnasieelevers tanker om uddannelse og fremtiden. Cand. Psych thesis. Aalborg Universitet.
Ricœur, P. (1988). *Time and narrative*. Chicago: University of Chicago Press.
Tinto, V. (1993). *Leaving college—Rethinking the causes and cures of student attrition* (2nd ed.). Chicago and London: Chicago University Press.
Willerslev, R. (2017). *Tænk vildt. Det er guddommeligt at fejle*. København: People's Press.

Chapter 8

Corporal punishment in extracurricular sports activities (*bukatsu*) represents an aspect of Japanese culture

Yasuhiro Omi

Many parents in economically developed countries are interested in how their elementary or secondary school-aged children spend time after school and during long vacations. Moreover, there has been a marked increase in children's extracurricular activities in Western countries (Dunn, Kinney, & Hofferth, 2003; Hofferth & Sandberg, 2001; Kremer-Sadik, Izquierdo, & Fatigante, 2010). These activities, however, have not only positive but also negative consequences on children. In Europe, it has been critically indicated that children are overworked and over-busy. Kremer-Sadik et al. (2010), for example, reported parents' concerns in Rome, Italy, including that extracurricular activities impede on their children's time and compromise their well-being.

Extracurricular activities for children are common in Japan as well, and many children seem to be busy. Therefore, parental engagement and effort could be pushing Japanese parents to similar conclusions as parents in Rome. Moreover, other factors, including the unique system supporting extracurricular activities in Japan known as *bukatsu*,[1] might be making Japanese children busier.

The word "*bukatsu*" generally refers to not only school club activities but also school club organizations (Omi, 2015). Many junior and senior high school students in Japan choose one activity (*bukatsu*) from many kinds of sports, such as soccer, baseball, basketball, volleyball, tennis, badminton, table tennis, track and field, judo, and kendo, among others. They can also choose to join a brass band, a chorus, or science, art, or other clubs, but these activities are not as popular as sports.[2] Over 90% of junior high school students and over 70% of senior high school students join an extracurricular school activity (Ministry of Education, Sports, Science and Technology, Japan, 1997). Male students join sports *bukatsu* more often than females, and junior high school students do more *bukatsu* than senior high school students.

Each school decides on the number and kind of *bukatsu* activities. Moreover, a student remains a member of the *bukatsu* they chose soon after entering schools and are often required to do so, as long as they do not change their schools. *Bukatsu* is also unique in keeping children busy in comparison to other countries. In many cases, children can have few breaks from *bukatsu* all year long, and certain *bukatsu* have very long hours – seven or eight hours a day for practices or games on weekends as well as during long school vacations. Many Japanese coaches believe that children will improve only after repeated practice in *bukatsu*. Also, they believe that children will not commit acts of delinquency if they are in *bukatsu* because they will be too tired to do so. In this way, students that join *bukatsu* spend much time outside of their homes and have little time to communicate with their family members. Furthermore, in many cases, school teachers have to do unpaid coaching for *bukatsu*. Some of them do not have coaching skills for or knowledge of the activities that they coach. Also, they are not necessarily willing to do extra work for *bukatsu* (Omi, 2015). Clearly, *bukatsu* makes children, as well as their coaches and teachers, very busy. Therefore, *bukatsu* might trigger certain problems as well as poor employment conditions for teachers. This unique system of extracurricular activities has indeed caused serious problems in the past.

One of the unhappiest events related to *bukatsu* took place in December 2012. A boy that was the captain of a high school basketball team, namely a *bukatsu* captain, committed suicide over repeated corporal punishment enacted by the coach. Punishments were frequent and included 30–40 slaps during the day before practice. Surprisingly, this coach had been invited from a nearby junior high school by a teacher without the principal's permission and had coached at the junior high school in November 2014. Furthermore, even after the boy's suicide, other instances of corporal punishment of students by *bukatsu* coaches in other schools have repeatedly been reported in Japan. How could this tragedy happen? Why wasn't it followed by changes to the system and the environment?

Corporal punishment in schools has been illegal in Japan since 1941; nevertheless, such punishment has prevailed historically, particularly since the end of WWII. Certain studies have focused on the need to understand the role of corporal punishment in the Japanese sociocultural context (Miller, 2009; Fukuzawa, 2006; Le Trendre, 1994, 1999; Hill, 1996). The study discussed in this chapter explored whether contemporary undergraduate students in Japan had suffered corporal punishment from coaches and teachers in schools and communities during *bukatsu* activities, as well as in other situations during their youth. The study also addressed how they accepted and understood such punishment. The possibility of eliminating corporal punishment by coaches and teachers and eliminating their busy schedules, as well as increasing parental involvement, is discussed. Finally, cultural problems and restrictions on eliminating such punishments are explored from a theoretical perspective.

Method

Survey on corporal punishment

An onymous, not an anonymous, internet-based survey was conducted in an adolescent psychology class for undergraduate, junior and senior high school teacher trainee students during every fall term from 2013 to 2015 and during spring term in 2016. Students (N = 418; 214 men and 204 women, mean age 19.9 years)

Table 8.1 Questions on corporal punishment

1) Have you ever suffered, seen, or heard about corporal punishment from a teacher or a coach?
If you have suffered corporal punishment, please respond to the questions below about your experience. If you have only seen or heard about it, please respond to the questions below about the case that you have seen or heard. Otherwise, you don't have to respond to any more questions.
2) When did it happen?
3) Where did it happen?
4) What kind of corporal punishment was it? (*)
5) Why did you suffer it? / Why did the person(s) suffer it? (*)
6) Do you accept it?

* Exempt from analysis in this chapter

participated in the survey. Of these, 129 participated in 2013, 126 in 2014, 130 in 2015, and 33 in 2016. Participants were asked to respond to all questions in the survey. They were informed that their participation was voluntary and that their decision not to participate or how they responded to the survey would not have any effect on their grades. They were also informed that they had the right to decline to respond to any question or to withdraw from the survey at any time after deciding to participate.

The survey inquired if a participant had suffered corporal punishment from teachers or coaches. If they responded "yes", they were asked when, where, and how they had suffered punishment. They were also asked if they had accepted the punishment. If they responded "no", they were asked if they had seen or heard of friends or classmates who had received such punishment (Table 8.1). If a participant reported two or more episodes of punishment, all instances were recorded. (For example, a participant might report two episodes of corporal punishment, once being slapped by a teacher in elementary school, and the other being kicked by a coach during *bukatsu* practice at a junior high school.)

The survey method was typically problematic because of the strong social desirability effect: Participants were trainee teachers who were expected to give the "correct" responses, i.e. negative responses against corporal punishment. Also, they did not have to respond to questions other than Question 1 if they just responded "no", regardless of their real feelings. Students were not informed of the definition of corporal punishment before the survey. However, it was assumed that they had had opportunities to learn about the definition of corporal punishment in other classes, on TV, and on the internet.

Results

Of the participants, 26.3% had suffered corporal punishment before finishing high school. Some participants presented multiple episodes. Therefore, 141 episodes of corporal punishment were collected from 110 participants. The most frequent

142 Yasuhiro Omi

situation for punishment was during *bukatsu* (for sports), which consisted of 38.3% among all episodes (Table 8.2). It is also noteworthy that the most frequent situation for punishment during elementary school was at local sports clubs. The most frequent period for reporting corporal punishment was during junior high school, although it would be easier to remember any episodes that happened during senior high school, which is closer in time.

Rate of actually accepting corporal punishment was 68%; not-accepting was only 19% (Figure 8.1).[3]

Table 8.2 Situations in which students suffered corporal punishment from teachers or coaches

	Kinder garten	Elementary school	Junior high school	Senior high school	Unclear	Total
At school						
Bukatsu			20.6%	17.7%		38.3%
In class	0.7%	6.4%	7.1%	5.7%		19.9%
Recess	0.7%	5.0%	3.5%	2.8%		12.1%
Cleaning time		2.1%	2.8%			5.0%
After school			2.1%	1.4%		3.5%
Homeroom, assembly, etc.		1.4%	2.1%	1.4%		5.0%
Marching band	0.7%					0.7%
Outside of school						
Local sport		8.5%	1.4%	0.7%		10.6%
Local music				0.7%		0.7%
Cram school			0.7%	0.7%		1.4%
Unclear		1.4%	0.7%		0.7%	2.8%
Total	2.1%	24.8%	41.1%	31.2%	0.7%	100.0%

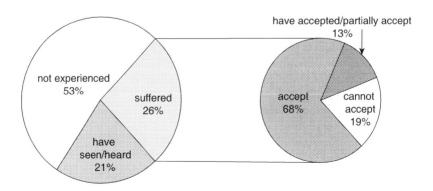

Figure 8.1 Rates of corporal punishments suffered

Discussion

The background of corporal punishment in Japan

This study suggests that corporal punishment by teachers and coaches remains a common occurrence in Japan. Nevertheless, the incidence of corporal punishment indicated in this study is expected to be much lower than the actual number of cases because of shortcomings in our method that are described below, suggesting that the problem of corporal punishment in Japan is more serious than indicated by our data. The results also show that corporal punishment tends to be given during sports coaching or teaching and that it was most common specifically during *bukatsu* activities.

Surprisingly, the majority of participants that had suffered corporal punishment from teachers or coaches accepted the punishment. The participants in this study were students training to be teachers and as such had many opportunities to learn about problems associated with corporal punishment by teachers. Moreover, the Ministry of Education, Culture, Sports, Science and Technology of Japan had notified nationwide schools and local governments about the strict prohibition of corporal punishment in schools. Furthermore, national television has repeatedly reported many incidents of problems associated with corporal punishment by teachers. Also, participants in this study, who were aspiring teachers, had studied teaching methods, educational law, and adolescent psychology, among other subjects. Nevertheless, they stated without embarrassment that they accepted the corporal punishment, instead of lying about their experience in the direction of the desirable response, which they could have easily done given the inadequate survey method used in this study, as discussed above.

It is possible that the participants that suffered corporal punishment and also knew that it is prohibited might have experienced cognitive dissonance (Festinger, 1957) and attempted to resolve the cognitive dissonance by changing their belief that corporal punishment is unacceptable. It might have been more difficult to change their belief that corporal punishment is acceptable because it is natural that they could positively accept all that they have ever experienced in their lives. Cultural forces in Japan might also have made the participants unintentionally ignore the strict prohibition of corporal punishment.

Downward collectivism and projective praise

Downward collectivism is defined as a Japanese type of collectivism that represses the individual and his or her opinions and eliminates his or her individuality,[4] even when there is no actual superior. In a downward collectivistic society, individuals might not know what to do if they are required to express an option without conforming with peers (Omi, 2012). It is suggested that *bukatsu* might lead to the development of a closed society because of *bukatsu* members' busy schedules, resulting in a lack of innovative opinions. It would be easy for a coach who is also a teacher to have absolute power over students in such a small and closed society. Additionally, as suggested by the theory of inside critique and outside praise (Hendry, 1986), Japanese people tend to derogate in-group members and admire out-group members "to get praise", which can be observed in parent–child or teacher–student relationships. For example, parents are willing to praise their friends' kids but put down their kids because they cannot directly praise them, which might be called "projective praise". A society with this implicit norm might become downward collectivistic. Such societies do not allow people to independently appraise themselves or their behavior. If a *bukatsu* is strongly affected by such norms, it might be difficult for students in the *bukatsu* to think how to play or respond by themselves, or judge what is objectively good or bad. Such a society might have a repressed atmosphere with which teenagers quickly become familiar. However, this repressed atmosphere, with hierarchical and undemocratic norms, might make them unable to doubt the justification for corporal punishment, even when the coach is absent or even after finishing *bukatsu*. Much deeper relationships would be formed during *bukatsu* than during classes among students and between students and teachers or coaches through sharing for a much longer time and making social norms stronger. The fact that a seemingly unreasonable system like *bukatsu* is still alive in schools may tell us that the system is too culturally deep-rooted to be easily changed.

If coaches' busy schedules were eliminated and they had opportunities to learn coaching skills, we would see fewer cases of corporal punishment in Japanese schools. Moreover, if student's busy schedules were removed, they would not only suffer fewer instances of corporal punishment by their coaches and teachers but also have a larger variety of rich experiences during their susceptible period. If this could be achieved, parent–child relationships would also improve because students in *bukatsu* would have more time to communicate with their parents and other family members.

Many Japanese people seem to place considerable value on being busy not only in *bukatsu* but also in many other situations outside school. For example, it is common for Japanese workers, including teachers, not to take paid vacations, and to work overtime even without being paid. Downward and repressive collectivism could also be behind the Japanese working style, although some workers might just insist that they want to show loyalty to their companies and their bosses. Will Japanese people ever break away from the idea that being busy is the most important virtue? In this sense, *bukatsu* could be a critical experience for Japanese people to unintentionally obey social norms of downward collectivism. It is concluded that Japan, compared to other countries, would have more difficulties in solving serious problems related to extracurricular school activities.

Notes

1 "*Bukatsu*" will be mainly used for extracurricular school "sports" activities in this chapter.
2 Brass band clubs as well as chorus clubs are considered to be identical to sports clubs in terms of the *bukatsu* system.

3 When two or more episodes were presented by one participant, the episode with more detail or the later episode was selected for this calculation.
4 In contrast, in American upward collectivism, each individual can choose which groups he or she will commit to, and he or she can express his or her opinion. Moreover, an individual does not have to commit to groups to which he or she is forced to become a member.

References

Dunn, J. S., Kinney, D. A., & Hofferth, S. L. (2003). Parental ideologies and children's after-school activities. *American Behavioral Scientist, 46*, 1359–1386.
Festinger, L. (1957). *A theory of cognitive dissonance*. Stanford, CA: Stanford University Press.
Fukuzawa, R. E. (2006). Classroom management, school culture and community: An ethnography of middle school discipline policies. *Hosei University Koganei Ronshu, 3*, 13–36.
Hendry, J. (1986). *Becoming Japanese*. Manchester: Manchester University Press.
Hill, B. (1996). Breaking the rules in Japanese schools: Kosoku Ihan, academic competition, and moral education. *Anthropology and Education Quarterly, 27*, 90–110.
Hofferth, S. L., & Sandberg, J. F. (2001). How American spend their time. *Journal of Marriage and the Family, 63*, 295–308.
Kremer-Sadik, T., Izquierdo, C., & Fatigante, M. (2010). Making meaning of everyday practices: Parents' attitudes toward children's extracurricular activities in the United States and in Italy. *Anthropology & Education Quarterly, 41*, 35–54.
Le Trendre, G. (1994). Guiding them on: Teaching hierarchy, and social organization in Japanese middle schools. *Journal of Japanese Studies, 20*, 37–59.
Le Trendre, G. (1999). The problem of Japan: Qualitative studies and international educational comparisons. *Educational Researcher, 28*, 38–45,
Miller, A. (2009). Taibatsu: 'Corporal punishment' in Japanese socio-cultural context. *Japan Forum, 21*, 233–254.
Ministry of Education, Sports, Science and Technology, Japan (1997). Study report on the modalities of school sport club activities (sports bukatsu).
Omi, Y. (2012). Collectivistic individualism: Transcending a traditional opposition. *Culture & Psychology, 18*, 403–416.
Omi, Y. (2015). The potential of the globalization of education in Japan: The Japanese style of school sports activities (Bukatsu). In G. Marsico, V. Dazzani, M. Ristum, & A. C. S. Bastos (Eds.), *Educational contexts and borders through a cultural lens: Looking inside, viewing outside* (pp. 255–266). Cham, Switzerland: Springer.

Chapter 9

"I see stress in many places around me, but as such, I'm over it"

Understanding psycho-cultural dimensions of university students' experiences

Pernille Hammer, Thomas Madsen and Luca Tateo

The idea

Higher education studies have been reformed worldwide and have continued to undergo transformations in the course of the last two decades, apparently producing new demands for students and teachers (Larcombe et al., 2016; Rogers, Creed, Searle, & Nicholls, 2016). It is a common topic of discussion among both students and professors that students have been reporting increasing discomfort and problems in achieving their personal and institutional goals. Growing "pressure" is reported by students themselves, and there is an increase in "stress leave requests". In addition, the authors themselves have observed in everyday practice an *over-talking* of students about how "stressful" curricula and assessment can be, and this phenomenon has also been informally observed in different national contexts by colleagues we have contacted. Such over-talking about pressure triggered the authors' curiosity and led to the study that is reported in this chapter. We think that these phenomena deserve special attention, as they can be a signal of problematic conditions related to study intensity and "catalytic conditions" of the educational institutional context, in this case the university, and its demands, which can trigger psychological discomfort and affect dropouts/retention. For these reasons, we decided to start a pilot study about students' academic experiences in the context of Aalborg University (AAU).

As with many other academic institutions, the AAU is striving to improve the study environment in an effort to be productive. Indeed, the capability of the institution to graduate students in the expected time is a productivity index, on which part of public funding is calculated. The lack of Return on (Cultural) Investments is indeed one of the main arguments that neo-liberalist and conservative approaches use to justify cutting resources to public universities (Ainley, 2016).

AAU is characterized by the problem-based learning (PBL) approach. The PBL approach adopted at AAU is a way to support the person in her construction of cognitive, affective, operative and meta-reflective tools in order to develop new knowledge, explorative life-skills and creative problem-solving. A few Danish universities rely on group-based project work. The theoretical difference between the Aalborg model PBL and PPL (problem-oriented, interdisciplinary and participant-directed project work) used at Roskilde University is whether teachers formulate the problem scenario around which the project will revolve or whether it is the students who choose the project problem themselves (Andersen & Kjeldsen, 2015, pp. 14–15). PBL is thus not just about "knowledge" in the academic sense but, most importantly, also about "skills for life". AAU, as well as other Danish universities, is also making a great effort to improve the physical study environment and students' living conditions at large (see Figure 9.1). It is thus particularly interesting to understand how students at AAU make sense of this context and of the part of their lives they spend there.

This complex and sometimes contradictory situation, in which efforts to improve the study experience are combined with an increasing report of stressful conditions, led us to the question: how do people construct a field of meaning about being a student, using the PBL approach and pressure in an academic context?

We think that developing specific understandings of these meanings can help to improve the institutional approach in working on the "discomfort" and "catalytic conditions" that can trigger "psychological suffering" as well as to support students in coping with life difficulties and developing the pleasure of studying in order to "challenges", not "problems". It seems that students' discomfort is not only related the experience of being academically put to the test and pressed to the limits of their capabilities (Holdsworth, Turner, & Scott-Young, 2017) but also, in the case of AAU, for instance, to the PBL and project work, which seem to put pressure on students and lead them to ask for sick leave, in extreme cases, or to conflict with their own workgroup mates, resulting in finally splitting up the groups just before handing in their projects. The possible problems connected to group work are even part of the curriculum on the student's first semester at AAU. Here the constitution of teamwork, the organizing of the project and student's roles, conflict management and the big responsibility for their own learning are described as a new and big challenge for students, particularly for new students (Kaae, 2013, p. 97). As one of the students in our research wisely put it once during an informal conversation: "We have never learned to fail". As authors, we have tried to approach this topic using an original methodology that is meant to stress the nuances and complexities of students' experiences, including the fundamental ambivalences of being a university student.

Some initial thoughts

The exploration of the field of meaning related to being a student is inspired by Kurt Lewin's topological psychology. Lewin's idea is that the human life space, or the psychological field, is a multidimensional space populated by several meaningful objects, each with its own specific value and meaning. These objects can be charged with positive as well as negative values, which constitute both possible directions towards achieving certain goals and barriers to those achievements. Consequently, these opposing charges generate a field of meaning populated by tension rather than balance (Tateo, 2014). Therefore, one of the starting assumptions is that any educational environment is neither homogeneous nor self-consistent. Institutional settings are characterized by the circulation of ambivalent messages and disseminated with social suggestions to promote or inhibit specific value-laden forms of development (Tateo, 2014, 2015). For instance, the whole

148 Pernille Hammer et al.

study environment is not just made for improving student's well-being but also to promote a specific value-laden meaning of how being a student ought to be. The desks and common spaces suggest some specific ideas about group-working, study/leisure organization, etc. (see Figure 9.1).

Figure 9.1 presents different examples of student environments at Aalborg University (1a and 1b), the language school of Aalborg Municipality (1c), and Roskilde University (1d) in Denmark and the library of a public middle school in Shanghai (1e). All these different settings provide social suggestions that orient meaning-making. Some environments look more informal, relaxed, leisure/like and open to

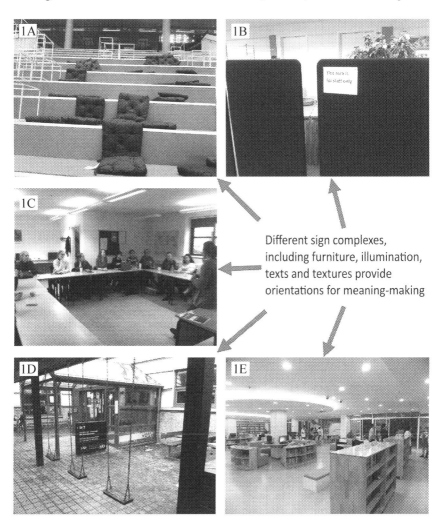

Figure 9.1 How value-laden meaning of being a student is encoded in the environment through semiotic suggestions

Photo by Tateo, 2017

group work, while others are structured in a more traditional way, providing a clear distinction between study and leisure, individuals and groups. Figures 9.1d and 9.1e are particularly interesting, as they suggest an inverse movement of *infantilization* (Bernardini, 2014) of university spaces and an *adultification* of the middle school environment. What kind of effect is thus produced on students' experience through these meaning-orientation devices? Besides the spatial setting, there are a number of semiotic devices (e.g. students' guides, manuals, informal discussions, supervision, etc.) that promote or inhibit specific directions for students' everyday life and future development. For instance, the course syllabi provide not only information about the content of the studies but also orientations about the way of studying, the usefulness of the programs and the "correct" conduct of the student.

The micro-context of academia is also related to the meso and macro systemic contexts (e.g. family values, social representations of different studies and jobs, etc.). The person is thus required to negotiate (accept, reject, being indifferent, negotiating) between all these different elements that emerge in day by day interactions and elaborate, demolish or maintain meanings.

While the environments in Figure 9.1, for instance, provide suggestions about the organization of the group/individual dimension, the pleasantness/unpleasantness of work or the kind of activities that can be done inside the university places, there are a number of other signs related to the individual or collective forms of responsibility. In the case of PBL, for instance, the tension is between individual responsibility of learning and the requirements of group work. Yet these messages are inherently ambivalent, like the balance between responsibility and agency (e.g. students are required to be autonomous but within a teaching/learning framework that is still asymmetrical). In this context, the person is required to elaborate her personal meaning and strategies to get along. We believe that these can be catalytic conditions for the emergence of a discourse about pressure and stress. We talk about "discourse" because the present study does not focus on the epidemiological aspects of stress diagnosis, but rather on the way students make meaning of their own experience, including the production of signs like "stress" and "pressure".

Under pressure

A study about stress conducted among Danish high school students suggests that a large number of young Danes feel stressed in their everyday life (Nielsen & Lagerman, 2017). In this respect, the catalytic conditions are mostly factors which in some ways are related to the future and performance, such as grades. The students expressed that their education and graduation from high school was of no use if their grades' average was not high enough. They connected a high average with success in their future working life. Thus, grades from high school are seen as of great importance. This might be related to the fact that a lot of university studies in Denmark have a limited number of available places. Consequently, candidates for popular educations are chosen on the basis of their high school grades; for this reason, acceptance into a popular field of study, such as medicine, psychology and business, often requires a substantial high school grade average.

Other researchers suggest that relationships with peers and teachers can be a stress factor as well as if the student does not feel like they can live up to the expectations of the school or teacher (Burger & Samuel, 2017). This suggests that students place a lot of value on their academic performance from high school level and internalize the notion that their academic achievements are of great importance. At the same time, unclear expectations are also a possible stressor for young students (Cavallo, Carpinelli, & Savarese, 2016; Liedberg, 2007), for which reason the above-mentioned ambivalence in messages circulating in the academic environment could also be seen as a stress factor: ambivalence is possibly understood as unclear expectations. Multiple studies conducted among university students in Denmark show that students all across the country feel stressed throughout the academic year and that there are not big differences between students in the humanities or in the natural sciences (Schiønning, 2011, Richter, 2015, Nielsen & Gunge, 2012). A survey on the well-being of students at the University of Copenhagen showed that 45% of the students who participated in the survey were stressed in their everyday lives; 76% replied that one of the biggest stressors was exams, 48.6% answered that their studies in general were a stressor and 36.1% found getting good grades to be a stressor (Balslev & Lindhart, 2017).

To sum up, the field of meaning related to being a student might be somehow ambivalent and inhibited by tension (e.g. the group/individual dimension, pleasantness/unpleasantness). Furthermore, national studies claim that students at both the high school and university level experience discomfort in their everyday lives. Hence, with this theoretical framework in mind, this study tries to interpret the signals of discomfort in order to prevent the risk of academic failure. As a preliminary step, the authors think that it is necessary to research "stress talking" as a sign of the tensions experienced by young people during higher education – i.e. acting both as a regulator of the positions of the self and related to various spheres of experience into and out of the university (self-regulation).

The study

The pilot study presented in this chapter is part of a larger research project that will have two main steps. In the first phase, the authors try to understand students' experiences and the fields of meaning attached to three social objects (being a student, PBL, stress). The methodology of this first step consists of a simple online questionnaire (see following section). The second part of the study will consist of focus groups and individual interviews with students based on the themes and issues emerging from the questionnaire. We have elaborated dilemma-situations, starting from the themes that have emerged from the questionnaires. The authors have collected and analyzed the data of the focus groups based on a dilemma in which a student is confronted with a problematic situation (without resolution) that can occur in regular activities. They asked the participants to find potential solutions to the situation in the dilemma during the focus groups – what they would say to the student and what they would do in the same situation. The analysis of the second part of the study is still in progress, so in this initial presentation only the results of the questionnaires will be discussed, and the authors will stress the emerging issues that led the interviewing activities.

Thanks to the hints emerging from the research, the authors aim to foster a "meta-reflection" about academic practices, related to creating strategies that students develop, also through supervision, to cope with pressure, explicit and systematized. This knowledge can be used in setting educational goals to implement the PBL approach and to support students in internalizing new and more effective self-regulatory strategies.

Participants

The pilot study involved bachelor students in the second (N = 24) and sixth (N = 23) semesters of the programs in Psychology and Communication at AAU.[1] The future plan is to progressively expand the number of participants of the study to also include scientific faculties and some replication of the study in Brazil, Italy and Greece. So far, 47 questionnaires have been collected,[2] and focus groups of about 20 students in their second and sixth semesters have been run. For the sake of this study, there is no interest in any kind of sampling or cross-cultural comparison, as the goal is understanding the general meaning-making process and the elements, conditions and resources students use to elaborate the meaning of their experience and how they manage the ambivalence of the educational context.

However, it is important to note that the specific context of the survey analyzed and discussed in this chapter might be slightly different from the other aforementioned countries. The survey has been carried out in Denmark, where the percentage of people with higher education is on the rise – the percentage of 15- to 69-year-olds with higher education was 30% in 2016, as opposed to 24% in 2006 (Danmarks statistik, 2016). Academic studies are paid for by the state, and students are given a state education grant applicable for up to six years of academic studies. As a result, students are often the object of an ongoing political debate on how to make university studies more effective and cost efficient. One example this is the "study progress reform" (*fremdriftsreformen* in Danish), aimed at getting students through their educations more quickly, for example by establishing a minimum of credits the students have to do in an academic year (Law 125, 2016–2017). Thus, the context for Danish academic students is one in which a normative expectation is present that students, in return for a free education and a state education grant, are expected to make the most of their education and finish it within the prescribed time in order to then be available for the labor market.

Furthermore, according to a study from 2010, Denmark is the country in Europe with the lowest percentage of young people ae living at home with their parents (Holm, 2010).[3] Moreover, according to Eurostat (2015), 42% of young Danish students are combining studying and working, both to cover the expenses of not living at home and to prepare for the labor market when they have finished their education.

Methodology

In order to grasp the complexities of the experience, the authors have tried to develop a new methodology. If you ask people about their experience, you can receive a kind of consistent and well-structured narrative about it. Yet the authors are interested in the inherent ambivalence of educational experience presented in the theoretical discussion above. In addition, students today are over-tested and over-surveyed, to the extent that going along with this "kind of stuff" has become a part of students' skills. Thus, the authors have tried to develop some *ad hoc* tools in order to go beyond the surface answers that one can receive in these types of studies. As no clinical approach to stress is implied, a very simple instrument has been designed, since the study is interested not in knowing how stressed the students are but rather in their experience of everyday academic life, in which the term "stress" seems to have some meaning.

We prepared a questionnaire for the elicitation of ambivalence: this tool is a simple online questionnaire in which students are triggered to make the ambivalences about some target concepts explicit with a simple semiotic tool. The original questionnaire is in Danish but an English translation is available, as will be the Italian and Portuguese versions. The questionnaire takes inspiration from the method used in Kullasepp (2017) to study the development of professional identity in psychology students. It is based on the concept of "horizon sign" (Tateo, 2014), a particular kind of sign that allows new emerging, but not yet semiotized, meanings to enter the person's field of meaning. Examples of these signs are "now" and "but". Horizon signs have the ability to catalyze the relationship between the self and a psychological object in the field of meaning (e.g. what it means to be a student), and thereby hopefully make the ambivalence of the student's experiences visible.

The questionnaires have been coded independently by two judges, who have identified a list of themes and a valence for each of the eight questions (each question has two sub-parts: the definition and the "but"). The judges then revised the initial themes and grouped them. The coding and revision of themes proceeded until the judges reached complete agreement on a shared version of the themes. As result of the analysis of the answers from the questionnaire, a list of themes with their related valence (positive, negative or neutral) has been obtained. The scope was to define a field of meaning for the main topics explored (being a student, PBL, stress) (see Appendix). The study is basically trying to understand what students "mean" when they talk about these things, not taking for granted that they use the terms in the same way teachers or researchers do.

Analysis

The first couple of questions were about the condition of being a university student (Question 1: As student, I am . . . but. . .). How do Psychology and Communication students talk about this? What matters the most? First, it is worth describing the content of students' answers. Table 9.1 presents the list of themes and their corresponding definitions.

"I see stress in many places around me" 153

Table 9.1 Themes about being a student

Themes of the first sub-question related to being a student

Pressure	Feeling pressured
Interest	Interested and curious about the field of study
Engagement	Engaged in the academic and/or social aspect, ambitiousness and motivation
Stressed	Stressed (e.g. about not reading everything and having too much to think about)
Happy	Happy with the field and to learn and appreciate getting into psychology
Active	Active academically and socially
Independent	Independent
Tired of school	Tired of school
Hardworking	Those who perceive themselves as hardworking, serious, conscientiously, self-disciplined, organized and determined
Okay	Okay
Journey	On a journey to become a psychologist
Busy	Really busy

Themes of the second sub-question related to being a student (but)

Happy	Feeling happy, appreciative, love and interest
Busy	Often busy
Insecure	Insecure about the future or academic abilities
Tired	Tired and exhausted
Realistic	Realistic about studies, the work load and consequences
Stressed	Stressed about exams and the way of teaching
Constrained	Constrained
Lazy	(Sometimes) Lazy, not living up to full potential (often in relation to being ambitious)
Responsibility	Responsibility follows
Undisciplined	Undisciplined, too casual and unprepared
Hanging in	Hanging in
Life outside of studies	Finding time to do other things, student job, private life, procrastination (Netflix, shopping, going out etc.), prioritizing
Motivation	Changing motivation levels (when tough), unmotivated and impatient
Individual	Also an individual (compared to being part of an institution)
Slow	Slow
Worth it	Will be worth it (feeling pressured) in the future

The second step was to consider the relationships between themes according to the elicitation of the ambivalence questionnaire. This is an interpretative action that attempts to map the field of meaning structured about the subject of the question. Indeed, if one considers the whole structure of the question (I am . . . but), one can build a graph of the relationships that gives back a structured field of meaning (Figure 9.2). In addition, the judges have grouped the themes in superordinate categories that refer to different dimensions of the experience.

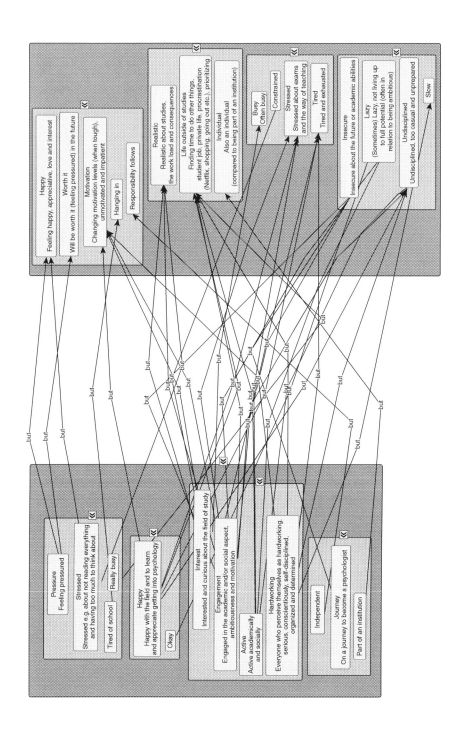

Figure 9.2 Map of the meaning field "As a student, I am … but"

Students define themselves ("As student, I am . . .") referring to four main dimensions, represented by the nested boxes in Figure 9.2. The first is about the burden and pressure of being a student (including the themes "pressure", "stress", "tired" and "busy"). The second dimension refers to affective aspects, namely positive feelings ("happy" and "okay"). The third dimension is about being an active subject (themes "interest", "engagement", "active" and "hardworking"). Finally, the last dimension is about the decency/autonomy themes ("independent", "journey" and "institution"). Yet, what meanings emerge if we look at the way student juxtapose the different dimensions? Looking at how the themes are related through the "but", one can observe that the themes only partially overlap. Indeed, there are more articulated affective and motivational dimensions (themes are "happy", "worth it", "motivation") or in the sense of ups and downs of mood during the studies (the themes are "hanging in" and "responsibility"). Secondly, there is a field of themes that refer to the inside/outside study dimension ("realistic", "life outside" and "individual"). Then, there are the themes related to pressure ("busy", "constrained", "stress" and "tired"). Finally, there are aspects related to self-confidence and self-efficacy ("insecure", "lazy", "slow" and "undisciplined").

Most important is to look at how students put the different themes in relation to each other, in order to get an image of the field of meanings about the experience of being a student. The first cluster of associations can be found between pressure and motivation (e.g. "*I am stressed but relatively happy*"; "*I am tired of school but can hang in*"; "*I am very happy for the study but exams are stressful*"). The second interesting opposition is between agency and the articulation of what is "academic" and what is "real life" (e.g. "*I am hardworking but good at finding time for other things*"; "*I am keen to follow my desire and interest, and do not stress if one may not read everything, but that rarely happens, and the bad conscience is another solid part of studying;-)*"; "*I am committed but life beyond studies is also valuable*"). Life-out-there themes are also of course related to autonomy (e.g. "*I am part of an educational institution but also an individual*"). Commitment and agency are also juxtaposed to self-confidence (e.g. "*I am very committed to my professionalism, which I take very seriously, but I may be somewhat unsure of the same professionalism*"; "*I am ambitious but also a little lazy*"). The richness of the experience is summarized by the following answer:

> I'm on an exciting journey through an academic world, that hopefully will make me a practicing psychologist[4] and really help people. But what if I reach the wall once I'm out on the other side? What if I really cannot help this person? My expectations for the challenge are both that it will be infinitely exciting and rewarding, but at the same time also anxiety-provoking, for what if I just can not help?
>
> (Respondent num. 23)

156 Pernille Hammer et al.

Formal education is by definition an intervention oriented towards an imagined future-condition. Any form of educational assessment is focused on the past–present trajectory but is actually evaluated against the future. While education is often aimed at reducing or eliminating inconsistencies and ambivalences, it seems that the respondent of the excerpt above is making explicit how a dilemmatic dimension is inherent to being a student.

The second couple of questions were about the problem-based learning approach (PBL). PBL is a differentiated family of pedagogical approaches that have been widely adopted by higher education institutions (Barrows & Tamblyn, 1980; Woods, 1987, 2006). In particular, AAU (the context of this explorative study) hosts the only UNESCO Professorial Chair in PBL. Thus, PBL seems to be a relevant part of our participants' study experience and we decided to include it into our questionnaire (Question 2: Problem-based learning is . . . but. . .). Table 9.2 presents the themes codified from the answers.

A quick glance at the themes shows that there are very different conceptions of PBL. All students interpreted the question in terms of judgements about PBL rather than describing it. This is quite typical of discourse about values: everybody agrees with them, everyone has an opinion about them, but everyone has a different view when it comes to a definition. AAU students of the first semester have a specific course about PBL as the main method of study, so they are supposed to know it. This course and the related PBL-project were mentioned by some of the students when answering the first sub-question about PBL, so the conception and opinion about PBL for these students seems to be related to their experience and recollection of this course. An example of this is participant 47, who describes PBL as "*a demanding course, despite only few ECTS points*", clearly referring to the first semester course.

Table 9.2 Themes about problem-based learning

Themes of the first sub-question related to PBL	
Great way of working	Educational, rewarding, important, fantastic, interesting, exciting or optimal way of working that gives students useful experience. Others say sometimes good
Good idea	PBL is a good idea in theory
Boring	Boring
Specific way of working	A certain way of working, (good for) group work, field work and relevant problems
Challenging	Challenging, complicated and demanding

"I see stress in many places around me"   157

Moreover, the first sub-question about PBL has fewer themes than the second. If the questionnaire had been limited to asking for the concept, it would have not captured the full articulation of students' views. Yet if we look at the relationship between themes (Figure 9.3), the picture appears more complex.

Students' ideas about PBL seem to refer to two main areas. The first one is about positive evaluation of the work method ("great way of working", "good idea", a more neutral "specific way of working"), while a second area considers PBL with a negative characterization ("boring" and "challenging"). When one observes the ways students put the different elements in relation to the field of meaning, one can see how the judgements about PBL are more articulated (*"PBL is insightful and gives many considerations for further reflection, but may sometimes seem useless and boring"*). The oppositions in the field of meanings are

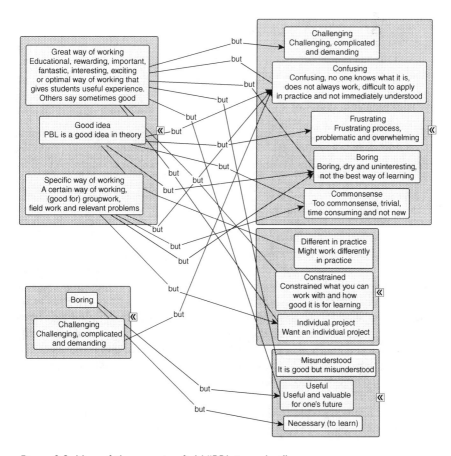

Figure 9.3 Map of the meaning field "PBL is . . . but"

generally between the themes concerning the (assumed) usefulness of PBL with those related to its ill-defined features and practices. So it can be, for instance, a *"good idea"* but *"confusing"* or *"frustrating"*:

> PBL is a great idea, which in theory has some really good possibilities, but it's hard to transfer to practice, it's as if nobody knows what PBL is in practice.
>
> (Respondent num. 3)

or

> PBL is an optimal way for me to learn – it connects theoretical knowledge with a concrete problem that you can relate to but it is a frustrating process that you cannot escape.
>
> (Respondent num. 6)

Students can also be critical towards PBL in relation to the group/individual dimension:

> PBL is a fantastic opportunity to meet other people around your common passions and interests; one can be there to support each other and cancel out each other's biases both for making the scientific work but in great deal also to make each other a little smarter as people.
>
> But now I'm only gradually starting my second project but I have some thoughts: while I can definitely stand by what I wrote above, it might be a little cool to get to write a project that was one's completely own :/
>
> (Respondent num. 33)

As we have seen in the case of Question 1, the academic institution can be inherently ambivalent (Tateo, 2015) towards the goals and values of education. Students are of course sensible to this (*"PBL is good for project work but not all supervisors practice it"*; *"PBL is a boring subject but related to the exam"*), as they are sensible to the fact that the institution is pushing for group work in a context in which "individual responsibility" for learning is highly valued as well. The practice of PBL – or the different practical instantiations (Bourdieu, 1990) rooted in the traditions of the different disciplines – leaves the respondents with the task of negotiating a meaning for PBL as a necessary condition for being student (*"PBL is boring but necessary to learn"*). Yet fortunately, students are able to engage with a negotiation of meaning:

> PBL is something that works with relevant issues, but this may go beyond one's understanding of the general theory as one tends to focus on your own little limited problem.
>
> (Respondent num. 13)

The capability of PBL to foster criticism, reflexivity and the questioning of received assumptions will be crucial in supporting students' actual development of these skills (Dolmans, De Grave, Wolfhagen, & Van Der Vleuten, 2005). As a respondent nicely put it: *"PBL sounds like a good and constructive form but may work differently in reality"*.

The third field of meaning explored in the present study is the discourse about stress in students' life. First, the authors aimed to understand what students mean when they talk about "stress" and "pressure", without taking anything for granted. Table 9.3 presents the list of themes categorized for Question 3 (Stress is ... but ...).

Table 9.3 Themes about stress

Themes of the first sub-question related to stress	
Study	Part of student life, natural and can be motivating and bound to exams
Manageable	Acceptable in short amounts of time, can drive you forward and gives a positive rush
Natural condition	Natural, inevitable and widespread in our culture and a societal problem; a condition
Discomfort	Uncomfortable, unhealthy, tough and needs to be taken seriously; a vicious circle
Academic approach	Discourse, no knowledge yet, societal problem
Pressure	A reaction to pressure, when you have too much to think about
Detect	Hard to detect yourself
Stressful	Very (...) stressful
Themes of the second sub-question related to stress (but)	
Manageable	Stress is manageable, either uncomfortable or motivational (for some), likes to be busy
No experience	Have no experience with negative stress
Bad	Can be too much and needs to be taken seriously for it not to get out of hand; how is there so much stress in a welfare state?
Study	Part of student life and caused by the way students think; busy times may not be stress; students need to change their perspective
Awareness	More awareness about stress; personal awareness is important to avoid stress; taking precautions (rest)
Necessary	Necessary
Common	Common feeling, part of everyday life, word is overused
Busy	Often because one has too much on one's mind, like to be busy – not always the same as stress
Say no	Often because you can't say no and are taking on too much work
Don't do	Stressed about what one feels like they don't do, not what one doesn't do

The themes of the first sub-question (Stress is) can be grouped in three main categories. The first refers to stress as a somehow natural or even positive condition (themes "manageable" and "natural condition"). The second dimension refers to the relationship between stress and academic life ("academic approach" and "study"). Finally, a third group of themes refers to the negative aspects of stress ("discomfort", "pressure", "detect" and "stressful") yet these are not the most frequently mentioned themes.

In the second sub-question, the themes can be grouped in a slightly different way. The first group refers to the "normality" of stress (themes "manageable", "common" and "necessary"). The second grouping refers to a dimension of agency ("awareness", "busy", "don't do" and "say no") in which the person can actively control or reject stress. Some students report "no experience" of stress, while others are concerned with the pervasive aspect of stress (theme "bad"). Finally, another theme refers to the way people interpret the academic life ("study") so that a change of perspective could help.

Considering the relationships between the themes, one can see interesting meanings about stress emerging (Figure 9.4).

Observing the relationships between themes in the students' answers, one can see how there is first a cluster showing stress as a "necessary evil" (*"Stress is part of being a student but something to be aware of, so it does not end up wrong"*, respondent num. 13; *"Stress is normal when you are a student at Aalborg University but you should be aware that it does not get chronic stress so you get sick"*, respondent num. 16). Students have resources of meaning to deal with stress, to monitor themselves:

> Stress is something that I think you struggle a lot with, at the university, especially when you want to read all the curriculum, take notes and do not miss lectures, etc. As well as having a social life on the side. But I never really get stressed at a level where it's serious. Maybe I'm too relaxed and take things as they come.
>
> (Respondent num. 42)

Agency is an important element in dealing with stress:

> Stress is something I think too many people seem to suffer from. It is as if some people live closest to life in a sickly fast lane; As if everything just has to go fast and be productive – whether it's a competitive state or whatever. But despite these thoughts, I have about stress, they are based on a very tenuous basis. I personally have very little experience with stress, as I would more or less say that I practice slow living; I do not want to hurry or hurry in the world, but rather have time to relax and look around in my life.
>
> (Respondent num. 33)

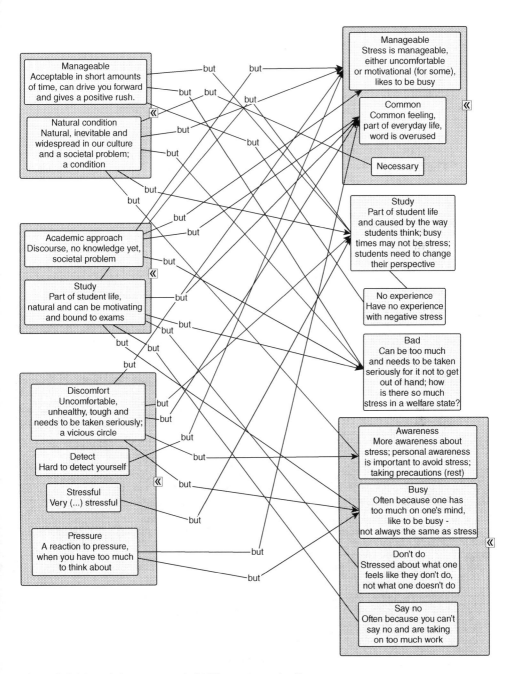

Figure 9.4 Map of the meaning field "Stress is ... but"

From students' answers, it seems that this social object (stress) conflates different meanings (e.g. pressure, expectations, responsibility, etc.) rather than a specific mental distress:

> Stress is a natural part of the study for my part, but it is probably not about what I really do, but rather about everything that I feel, that I do not reach.
> (Respondent num. 34)

On the other hand, as agency seems to be important, students' meanings call for reflection on the ambivalence between the conditions of study, the responsibility which is attributed to them and the degree of agency that students can exert. The question of agency is clearer in the answers to the last question, related to personal relationship with stress (Table 9.4). In this question, the authors have attempted to relate a personal position to the object "stress" ("I live" with, without, into, beyond, in spite of, alongside, in harmony, because of "stress") with a meaning triggered by the sign "but".

Judges have grouped the relationships with stress in three larger categories. The first refers to a quite positive attitude towards stress (themes "manageable", "busy", "motivating", "common" and "not negative"). The second dimension refers to a negative attitude (themes "fear", "ulcer" and "tough"). Finally, there is a group of themes that refers to a generic need for change, either in the attitude or the conduct (themes "sometimes", "tired", "doing too little", "awareness", "unsatisfied" and "breaks").

Table 9.4 Themes about personal relating to stress

Theme label	
Manageable	Acceptable and manageable in small quantities
Busy	Can be busy, likes to be busy
Tough	Stress is tough, takes it hard on you from time to time, gets help, feeling challenged; bad consciousness
Unsatisfied	Want to have another relation to stress
Motivating	Stress can be motivational, make one perform better and give a kick
Awareness	Important to be aware of stress and find a way to manage it
Breaks	Need breaks and look forward to vacation or a year off from studies, wants classes more spread out
Sometimes	Not stressed all the time, feel stressed but don't have (diagnosis) stress
Common	It's human, common and natural
Fear	Fearing that stress will hit you from balancing personal life and study life, worrying about stress
Tired	Can be tired from stress, can feel too busy but it is not necessarily stress
Doing too little	Worrying about doing too little and missing out, but generally feels good
Illness	Has ulcer
Not negative	Stress is not always negative

"I see stress in many places around me" 163

From the relation between themes in the field of meaning (Figure 9.5), it emerges how the issue of stress is not understood as an "emergency" by students. Despite the over-talking about stress (Brinkmann, 2014) and the growing attention to university students' psychological distress (Regehr, Glancy, & Pitts, 2013), students view stress as a part of the game ("*Despite the fact that stress can be a*

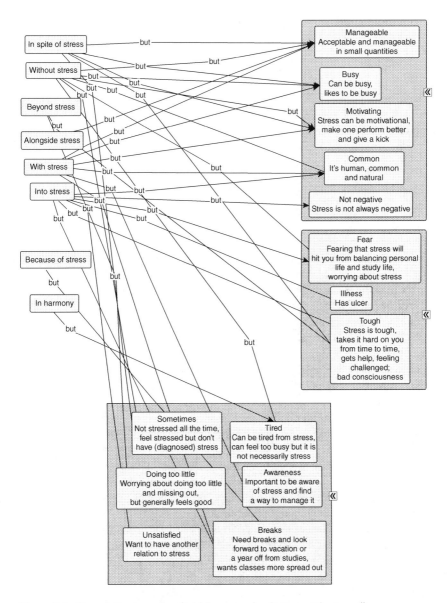

Figure 9.5 Map of the meaning field "personal relation with stress"

part of my everyday life, it still works and may be positive in the future, giving motivation to work", respondent num. 40). Of course, there are concerns ("*I live without stress but you always want to fear that it can hit one who have a full-time study and personal life to combine*", respondent num. 30).

From students' answers, a process of negotiation of meanings about stress emerges:

> I live without stress but of course there are periods when I have a lot to look to and it feels like fatigue and lack of results. However, I think it is part of a study life and it is not actual stress.
>
> (Respondent num. 39)

There is a day-by-day, acceptable component of stress in life, yet people usually get along with it. It is to some extent expected and even appreciated until a certain point.

Discussion

By using this new form of questionnaire, the authors have tried to map the field of meanings related to the experience of being a student. Questionnaires often consider the opposite polarities of answers as mutually exclusive and look for consistency in respondent's discourse. In consequence, inconsistencies are treated as mistakes or false answers. In this case, the authors assume the dilemmatic and ambivalent nature of experience, so they are interested precisely in fostering ambivalent answers. What one gets back is a more nuanced and articulated field of meanings that allows a better understanding of the complexities of the phenomenon. In the case of the question about the experience of being a university student, one can observe that students try to get along in their academic life despite the uncertainties and ups-and-downs of student life. They feel pressure, which goes together with motivation; they do not think academic life is everything but also feel somehow guilty for that. They feel committed but also continue to ask what it is worth.

Limitations and potentialities of the study

In the current pilot study, the authors were not interested in questions of "how many", so one did not need to count answers, frequency of themes, etc. The authors were interested in knowing "how" students make sense of their experience and grasp the nuances, ambivalences and complexities of the fields of meaning related to being a student. Thus, there is no quantitative knowledge about the themes that have been explored. The authors do not even think that this can be a limitation. The main limitation of this study, instead, is the fact that it tries to operationalize for the first time the inherent ambivalence of experience through a conceptual tool (the horizon sign "but") that can be useful though it needs further theoretical and empirical investigation. In addition, this study is not completely useful if not integrated with an in-depth analysis of student meaning-making processes, which will be developed through focus groups and interviews in the second part of the research project. Of course, the analysis is interpretative and can be subject to different interpretations according to different perspectives. The authors did not take into account independent variables (gender, semester), as the goal was to map meanings produced by and circulating among students. If someone were interested in these types of correlations, the instrument can gather the information anyway that allows quantitative analyses to be run. The methodology is, of course, very undeveloped and open to significant improvements, yet it can be a good point of departure. In addition, the authors are aware of the fact that the pilot study still does not capture the developmental aspects of the meaning-making process. This is an extremely relevant issue that will be addressed in the following course of study.

This pilot study shows also some interesting potentialities. First, it shows how it is necessary to take ambivalences and nuances of meaning-making into account. Second, from the analysis emerges how students can perfectly deal with these ambivalences until they have the space to maneuver and to navigate between institutional constraints and personal agency. Third, the meanings produced by students question the institutional perspective and call for further empirical studies. Indeed, the way students deal with the ambivalences of the academic context suggests that we need an exploration of how the actual practices produce ambivalence. The authors argue that students can deal with academic pressure to the extent that they have the conditions to do so.

Conclusions

If we do not understand ambivalences, we will continue to wonder how it is possible to create a better study environment but still observe students' discomfort. We have to start asking how the subjective expression of the impact of social expectations directed at students is expressed. Academic life can be complicated and full of ambivalent orientations. On the one hand, the trends toward the *commoditization* of education have led to an increase of pressure on both teachers and students for the sake of accountability and higher returns on educational investments. On the other hand, a paradoxical effect has been produced that turns basic education into a precocious environment (with less space for playing and more for academic working) and higher education into a school-like environment (providing students more tutoring, shorter piece-meal curricula and an easy study environment) (Figure 9.6).

Of course, approaches based on free exploration, playfulness and creativity have a lot of merit in opening new teaching/learning possibilities (Pike, 2002). Yet they contribute to creating particular atmospheres in the academic context that may support the process of *infantilization* (Bernardini, 2014).

166 Pernille Hammer et al.

Figure 9.6 A creative laboratory at Aalborg University
Photo by Tateo, 2017

In addition, Danish university students, as well as other Scandinavian students, can still benefit from a "privileged" position due to the (still holding on) traditional welfare system of higher education that provides social support with few equals around the world. Despite this, it seems that discomfort is growing even there.

Yet it emerges from this pilot study how Danish students can deal with academic pressure. It becomes stressful when they have to deal with the "awkwardness" of university life. In the continuation of this research project, the authors will try to explore in more detail how students make sense of the ambivalence of academic life. Yet it can already be suggested that it is worth looking in one direction: every initiative that the university undertakes is always two-faced. For instance, one of the participants, reflecting upon the meaning of her studies, writes:

> What if I reach the wall, what once I'm out on the other side? What if I really cannot help this person? My expectations for the challenge are both that it will be infinitely exciting and rewarding, but at the same time also anxiety-provoking, for what if I just cannot help?
>
> (Respondent num. 33)

Because of the inherent ambivalence of institutional settings, when the university promotes a specific value, it also implies its opposite. For instance, job market orientation and the *infantilization* of academic curricula, individual responsibility and collective work, hierarchical organization and personal agency co-exist and pressure emerges when students cannot negotiate meaning between these different expectations. One of the interesting limitations of the PBL approach, as it is currently used, is that students are not allowed to address meta-academic problems. They are required to find their own (hopefully relevant) problems and formulate research questions to which to apply academic knowledge. Yet they are not allowed to question PBL itself or to problematize it. Instead, making the ambivalences of everyday academic life explicit would help to move the reflection to a meta-level and thus improve the student capability to cope with the inherent ambivalences of any educational system. This, of course, would imply a loss of power on the institutional side and a questioning of the current managerial philosophy of higher education. On the other side, this would imply accepting that students carry more responsibilities and control over their own academic trajectories, which is what young adults should be able to achieve through university education. In this way, intellectuals and professionals in formation, as university students should be considered, would be more resilient to any form of stress and meaningless academic routine. As a student nicely put it: "*I see stress in many places around me, but as such, I'm over it*".

Notes

1 Respectively 35 students from psychology and 12 from communication.
2 Consisting of 35 female and 12 male students aged between 19 and 29 (average age 22.7).
3 For the 18–24-year-old women and men, the percentages are respectively 27.1 and 40.4, while the percentages for 25–34-year-old women and men are respectively 0.5 and 2.8 (Holm, 2010).
4 In Denmark, the term 'practicing psychologist' (*praktiserende psykolog* in Danish) refers to an individual with a master's degree in psychology, working with clients as a psychologist (e.g. in psychotherapy, coaching, etc.). Thus, the goal for many Danish psychology students is to become a practicing psychologist, as opposed to working as a researcher, a teacher, etc. The term is not the same as a psychiatrist, as psychiatrists in Denmark have a medical education.

References

Ainley, P. (2016). The Business Studies University: Turning higher education into further education. *London Review of Education*, *14*(1), 106–115.
Andersen, A. S., & Kjeldsen, T. H. (2015). Theoretical foundations of PPL at Roskilde University. In A. Andersen & S. Heilesen (Eds.), *The Roskilde Model: Problem-oriented learning and project work. Innovation and change in professional education*, vol 12. Cham, Switzerland: Springer.
Balslev, N., & Lindhart, K. (2017, September 7). Studerende bliver stressede af karakterræs. *Uniavisen*. Retrieved from https://uniavisen.dk/studerende-stressede-karakterraes/
Barrows, H. S., & Tamblyn, R. M. (1980). *Problem based learning*. New York: Springer.
Bernardini, J. (2014). The infantilization of the postmodern adult and the figure of Kidult. *Postmodern Openings*, *5*(2), 39–55. doi:10.18662/po/2014.0502.03

Bourdieu, P. (1990). *The logic of practice*. Stanford: Stanford University Press.
Brinkmann, S. (2014). Languages of suffering. *Theory & Psychology*, 24(5), 630–648.
Burger, K., & Samuel, R. (2017). The role of perceived stress and self-efficacy in young people's life satisfaction: A longitudinal study. *Journal of youth and adolescence*, 46(1), 78–90.
Cavallo, P., Carpinelli, L., & Savarese, G. (2016). Perceived stress and bruxism in university students. *BMC Research Notes*, 9(1), 514.
Danmarks Statistik (2016). *Befolkningens Uddannelse 2016*. Uddannelse og viden.
Dolmans, D. H., De Grave, W., Wolfhagen, I. H., & Van Der Vleuten, C. P. (2005). Problem-based learning: Future challenges for educational practice and research. *Medical Education*, 39(7), 732–741.
Eurostat (2015). *Regional yearbook 2015*. Retrieved on June 8 from https://ec.europa.eu/eurostat/en/web/products-statistical-books/-/KS-HA-15-001
Holdsworth, S., Turner, M., & Scott-Young, C. M. (2017). Not drowning, waving. Resilience and university: A student perspective. *Studies in Higher Education*, Published online: 13 Feb 2017. doi:10.1080/03075079.2017.1284193
Holm, H. H. (2010). Danske unge flyver først fra reden. *Danmarks Statistik*, 1 November 2010. Retrieved from www.dst.dk/da/Statistik/bagtal/2010/2010-10-29-unge-hjemmeboende.
Kaae, A. (2013). Gruppeproces og problemer. In P. B. Olsen & K. Pedersen (Eds.), *Problemorienteret projektarbejde*. Roskilde: Roskilde Universitetsforlag.
Kullasepp, K. (2017). *Psychologists' professional identity*. London: Routledge.
Larcombe, W., Finch, S., Sore, R., Murray, C. M., Kentish, S., Mulder, R. A., Lee-Stecum, P., & Larsen, L. (2016). E. Justering af fremdriftsreformen, m.v. Folketinget. *Samling 2015–2016 lovforslag*. Retrieved from www.ft.dk/samling/20151/lovforslag/L125/index.htm.
Nielsen, K. M., & Gunge, U. (2012, September 25). Studerende stresser sig syge. *Berlinske*. Retrieved from www.b.dk/nationalt/studerende-stresser-sig-syge.
Nielsen, A. M. & Lagermann, L. C. (2017). Stress i gymnasiet. Sammenfatning af resultater og anbefalinger. Aarhus Universitet: DPU. Retrieved 8 june 2018 from http://edu.au.dk/aktuelt/nyhed/artikel/stress-truer-elevers-laering-og-trivsel/
Pike, C. (2002). Exploring the conceptual space of LEGO: Teaching and learning the psychology of creativity. *Psychology Learning & Teaching*, 2(2), 87–94. doi:10.2304/plat.2002.2.2.87
Regehr, C., Glancy, D., & Pitts, A. (2013). Interventions to reduce stress in university students: A review and meta-analysis. *Journal of Affective Disorders*, 148(1), 1–11.
Richter, L. (2015, January 19). Pres på uddannelsespræstationer gør studerende syge. *Information*. Retrieved from www.information.dk/indland/2015/01/pres-paa-uddannelsespraestationer-goer-studerende-syge.
Rogers, M. E., Creed, P. A., Searle, J., & Nicholls, S. E. (2016). Coping with medical training demands: Thinking of dropping out, or in it for the long haul. *Studies in Higher Education*, 41(9), 1715–1732. doi:10.1080/03075079.2014.999318
Schiønning, B. (2011, April 4). Studerende plages af stress. *DR*. Retrieved from www.dr.dk/nyheder/indland/studerende-plages-af-stress.
Tateo, L. (2014). Beyond the self and the environment: The psychological horizon. In K. R. Cabell & J. Valsiner (Eds.), *The catalyzing mind: Beyond models of causality* (pp. 223–237). New York, NY: Springer-Verlag. Retrieved from http://dx.doi.org/10.1007/978-1-4614-8821-7_12.

Tateo, L. (2015). Continuity and discontinuity of the educational context: Early leavers' in-between life stories. In G. Marsico, V. Dazzani, M. Ristum, & A. C. de Souza Bastos (Eds.), *Educational contexts and borders through a cultural lens* (pp. 29–52). New York: Springer International Publishing.

Wood, S. (2006). Views of the effectiveness of problem-based learning. *Nursing Times, 102*(21), 34–38.

Woods, D. R. (1987). *Problem based learning and problem solving*. Sydney: Higher Education Research and Development.

Chapter 9 Appendix

Questionnaire for the elicitation of ambivalence

Dear student,
   Could you please answer some simple questions about your academic experience? Please answer the first thing that comes to your mind. It should take just 5 minutes.

1) As student, I am_____, but_____
2) Problem-based learning is_____, but_____
3) Stress is_____, but _____
4) I live _____ stress, but _____
5) My course is_____
6) My age is _____
7) My semester is: _____
8) I am: male   female   LGBT
9) I live in: _____
10) I am interested in being part of the forthcoming study; you can contact me for an interview at (your email)

Chapter 10

Internship as liminal zone in education

Enrica Mele and Giuseppina Marsico

Introduction

In the current knowledge society, education assumes a very important role: knowledge and training represent some of the main drivers of social development and productivity. In fact, there has been a shift from education as a right, typical of industrial society, to education as a distinctive need in the post-industrial, *informational* society (Castells, 1996).

The new challenges posed by the social context have contributed to the reformulation of the concept of education and learning. Education is increasingly understood in a complex manner that includes the capability to make choices and reflect upon our own thinking.

The traditional vision of the training process – considered as a transmission of content and abilities from the trainer to the one who is learning – is gradually replaced by a conception of constructed formation, on the basis of which the educational process is seen as a space for elaborating and negotiating the meanings of all the actors involved (Carli, Grasso, & Paniccia, 2007).

The conception of a constructed formation thus refers to a vision of the human being as an active meaning maker through internalization and externalization processes (Valsiner, Lutsenko, & Antoniouk, 2018).

Formation in the current socio-cultural scenario, characterized by ever-changing and less durable skills required by the labor market, is a critical area characterized by fluctuation between the old system and the new one still to be built.

In line with an idea of constructed formation, an effort has been made by universities to articulate the theoretical dimension with practical knowledge, aiming to promote the development of skills and competencies that can be applied in practice by students.

This effort has led to the introduction of the internship in the academic curriculum. The internship represents a training device that promotes a connection between theoretical knowledge and practical as well as the professionalization of academic courses. This helps to fill the traditional gap between the educational and professional worlds, between the knowledge provided at the university and the following professionalism (Kaneklin, Scaratti, & Bruno, 2006).

Internships have been defined as settings designed to learn a practice. It is a situation in which students learn by doing, despite their actions have a small incidence on the work in the "real world" (Shön, 1987).

In this chapter, we focus on the internship in psychology, defined as practicum in the literature.

> The practicum is the first step on the path of professional development toward independent professional competence in psychology. The practicum comprises supervised training experiences, often called practicum or clerkships, which introduce students to the core competencies of the discipline, bringing classroom education to life in practice settings, and laying groundwork for further training in internship and beyond.
>
> (Hatcher & Lassiter, 2007, p. 49)

As a part of academic education at master's level, the practicum is the first supervised practical experience that allows students to integrate academic knowledge with professional practice in psychological services and develop new knowledge and skills.

Recently, attention to the practicum has taken shape through an emerging focus on defining and specifying professional competencies (Kaslow, 2004).

What does competence mean? There are various definitions covering different aspects of the construct. As often happens with complex concepts, there is no unanimous agreement. However, you can find some common elements among the different definitions. Broadly, we can say that over time, the construct of competence has evolved from an idea of a set of discrete and measurable elements (techniques, attitudes, knowledge, abilities) to a concept of competence understood as an organized set of procedures strictly related to professional tasks or situations. In other words, competence is seen as the effective mobilization of resources and abilities in a specific context. Two assumptions serve as the foundation of this current concept of competence. The first is that the context is an integral part of the competence, and thus, it does not exist separately from the conditions of its implementation. The second is the reflective nature of competence: a competent performance is characterized by thoughtful thinking and critical behavior as well as by the ability to understand where and how use some resources (Freda, Esposito, & Quaranta, 2015).

Defining the internship

Undoubtedly, internship could be defined in a number of ways. According to Davies (1990), the internship is a kind of experiential learning in which students take the opportunity to apply learned theories from an academic setting in a real-world situation. It offers an opportunity for students to integrate thinking and professional actions. In this way, internship fills the gap between university-learned theory and its practical usability (Fox, 2001). Other authors define internship more in terms of experimental learning (Pauze, Johnson, & Miller, 1989) or supervised work experience (McMahon & Quinn, 1995).

Even if the above-mentioned definitions stress more the academic or the professional side, the internship, can be perceived by the students as an opportunity and, at the same time, as a challenge to combine what they have learned at the university with what they are learning from the experience in psychological services.

The internship is, then, not only a physical location but also a psychological space in which the student, differently from the entire past academic course, has to assume responsibility for her own training project and the subjective construction of knowledge (Freda, 2008).

One of the main goals of practicum – during which students take part in unique, indefinite and sometimes conflicting professional practice – is to promote metacognition and metacompetence. This metaknowledge implies awareness of: a) the range and limits of what you know; b) your own intellectual strengths and weaknesses; c) how to use available skills and knowledge to solve a variety of tasks; d) how to acquire new or missing skills, or be able to judge if a task cannot be completed with current knowledge. Metacompetence similarly refers to the ability to judge the availability, usability and learnability of personal competencies. The development of metaknowledge and metacompetencies depends on self-awareness, self-reflection and self-assessment (Weinert, 2001).

This way of conceptualizing the internship implies the role of the trainee is one of an active meaning-maker who is in between what university offers and the competences required by professional contexts (Carli et al., 2007).

In particular, the perspective of cultural psychology of education (Marsico, 2017, 2018), which we adopt here, outlines how human beings are characterized by their ability to construct the meaning of experience: "Whatever we encounter in our lives we need to make sense of, rather than just to react to or act upon" (Valsiner, 2014, p. 25). Our aim is to explore the process of meaning making by psychology students from different countries that participate – as trainees – in various psychological services as part of their academic formation.

More specifically, in this work we intend to investigate the internship as a "liminal zone" (Marsico, 2018; Marsico, Dazzani, Ristum, & Bastos, 2015; Valsiner, 2014) located at the same time "inside and outside" the university, in an area in which many psychological and training processes take place.

Liminality and borders in education

From a cultural psychology perspective, liminality is the rule and not the exception of our living conditions. Humans are always in movement. They come from somewhere and go to somewhere else (Marsico & Valsiner, 2018). They constantly live in between their actual state and the future possible one.

According to anthropologist Victor Turner:

> Liminal entities are neither here nor there; they are betwixt and between the positions assigned and arrayed by law, custom, convention, and ceremonial. As such their ambiguous and indeterminate attributes are expressed by a rich variety of symbols in the many societies that ritualize social and cultural transitions.
>
> (Turner, 1969, p. 95)

The most significant implication of considering human ways of living as a permanent liminal condition is the implied focus on borders (Marsico, 2011, 2016). Borders – in analogy with membranes in biological organisms – are the structures "in-between" that unite the separated parts of the whole. Yet, *limen* is not just a line or a border, limiting one space or one time and another. It is, instead, a complex threshold that promotes and mediates transformation of one form or process into another. Any event of becoming presupposes the creation and operation of such delicate and vague border conditions (De Luca Picione & Valsiner, 2017; Stenner, Greco, & Motzkau, 2017).

As Valsiner (2014) pointed out, we are always and necessarily on the border between the two infinities (inner ◇ outer and future ◇ past). Therefore, our movements take place in a liminal zone. The general location of the human psyche is, then, exactly the zone of liminality at the intersection of infinities.

This chapter adds a new focus specifically on the liminality of education from a cultural psychology perspective. We try to localize the processes of education in the liminality of the Border Zone between the academic system and the professional world. In our ordinary educational discourses, education happens in the places designated for it – formal education "at university," technical competences "at the workplace." Learners, as in the case of internship, are supposed to *be within* these places in order to become educated, and of course, they are, but when looked upon from the perspective of their daily lives, these students are migrants between university and workplace.

Their real education involves the coordination of their experiences in every place they move through. Such coordination involves others who also organize their movements – professors, tutors, leaders of host institutions etc. – and requires an act of crossing the borders between different contexts in the process of education (Marsico, 2013).

Borders are partitions. They create demarcations and trace the specific border crossing areas. Yet, they both separate and unite (Marsico, Cabell, Valsiner, & Kharlamov, 2013); this makes it possible to identify some specific Border Zone in between spaces, social settings or, as in our case, educational contexts. After all, education, at any level, can be fully realized only in a Border Zone, which implies crossing the line between "here" and the "beyond" (Boesch, 1991). The "here-area" is the body of knowledge already known, the established knowledge, while the "beyond-area" is uncertain, unknown and opaque (Marsico, 2013). Liminality is thus the general condition of ontological indeterminacy (Greco & Stenner, 2017) at work in the occasion of the internship, which is a specific educational transition in which an existing set of processes, courses of action, systems of values and types of conduct is suspended while another is not fully in play.

This specific type of "in-betweenness" (Ristum, Bastos, Dazzani, & Marsico, 2015), which is the Border Zone we are scrutinizing in this chapter, is seen as the crucial part of the difficulties faced by psychology students when leaving university and going to professional services.

The research design: method and participants

The international research project here reported aimed to explore the main feelings and the meaning making processes of psychology students in Denmark, Italy, Spain and Brazil, during an internship in which they participate – as trainees – in practical experience with different psychological services.

With this purpose, we used a narrative semi-structured interview designed to explore the main cognitive, affective and social dimensions of the internship as experienced by the trainees.

During the interview, we also asked to the participants to do some tasks in order to stimulate their storytelling and their meaning making processes about the experience, as described below.

Considering that verbal language may not be sufficient to explore the affective dimension of personal experience (Valsiner, 2014), each trainee was invited to represent himself/herself at this stage of training (to become a psychologist) with a drawing. This request aimed to stimulate reflective thinking on the part of the trainee, on how he/she organizes and gives meaning to his/her relationship with the educational context and, more specifically, with the context of traineeship.

Trainees were also invited to bring a representative object of the internship experience to the interview as a starting point to stimulate the narrative.

In addition, in this research project we used the "Task of the flash cards" and the "Task of erasing the cards."[1] The trainee was asked to draw or write on flash cards the elements (people, situations, things) that he/she considers the most important aspects of the internship. We discussed the cards and then we asked him/her to imagine what the internship would be like if she or he had to delete these meaningful aspects from the experience. These tasks have been used to explore the most significant elements of internships from the trainee's point of view and to explore the experiences associated with the (imagined) elimination of the above aspects from his or her training practice.

The participants of the research were nine students from Denmark, Italy, Spain and Brazil undergoing their internship during their academic training in psychology course. A thematic analysis has been applied to the entire corpus of data, but here we discuss the first analysis of the data collected in Denmark and Italy.

More specifically, we analyzed five interviews: three Danish students and two Italian. The Danish students were undertaking the Master in General Psychology, Educational Psychology and Clinic Psychology. They were doing the internship with different psychological services: the University Clinic, the Municipality (Occupational Medicine section), a hospital Centre for Sexual Problems. The two Italian students were doing the Master in Clinical Psychology and participating in internships with two Mental Health Services.

We interviewed each participant while they were doing the internship,[2] at the middle–end of the experience.[3]

Some preliminary findings

The following main themes emerged from the thematic analyses we have performed.

Inside and outside the university: internship as a "liminal zone"

As previously mentioned, this research aimed to explore the experience of the internship by master's students in psychology in different countries. At this stage of their training, the students took part, as trainees, in activities with different psychological services (social service, hospital, mental care service, NGO, schools etc.) while still attending courses at the university. This section outlines the interviewees' processes of distinction making and attribution of meaning to the different contexts of their training experience.

Regarding the characteristics and aims of the different contexts of her training (the university and the internship place), a Danish student states:

> In the university the goal is to be educated, to be done, in the internship the goal is to be good as you can in the job.

In her vision, the internship place and the university do not share common goals:

> In the University, it's a lot of knowledge all the time in all direction. You're just learning everything and specialize afterwards. . . . In the internship, we are trying to understand the one thing we are working with. I think you can focus on what you are doing when you are on the internship, you keep the subject.

In her speech, the university allows her and the other students to learn many different things, from different subjects, and ultimately acquire an education, while in the internship, she has the opportunity to learn from the things she is working with, from the specific requests of the internship.

The place of the internship is often a service outside the university. As in the following excerpt, inside the university is considered as a safe and predictable place but is to some extent opposite to (external) reality; the place of the internship, by contrast, is more similar to a workplace, real and unpredictable, in which the professional practice takes place. A Danish student, regarding her internship experience, says:

> I have to experience and I have to cope with all kind of people, it would be more safe to be here doing things that we normally do. I had go out and practice and talking to real people about their problems.

Nevertheless, there are also cases in which the internship is undertaken within the university, as in the case of a Danish University Clinic:

> My internship isn't outside in the psychiatry, but it's here at University, in the Clinic.

The same student referred to her internship setting (a psychoanalytic one) by saying:

> I also heard it was really hard core, it was really strict and maybe stricter that it is outside in the reality.

In this case, unlike the previous statement, the internship place, located inside the University, is considered to some extent to be different to outside reality.

Internship as a liminal zone

As we have stated, an internship could be viewed as "in between" the academic training and professional practice.

In this view, the internship may be defined as a Border Zone that divides while simultaneously unifying inside and outside the university. This specific situation, of being a student entering psychological services for the first time in order to learn the practice, implies the idea of a two crossing contexts which intersect each other: the academic training at university and the professional practice of a workplace. The idea of a transit is well exemplified by the following from a Danish student:

> The object that represents my internship is the student card to come in and out of the clinic.

In this case, the student card acts as the "entry permit" for crossing a border. The card is a means for distinguishing her new experience from normal student life and also herself from other students. The card separates her from her other, previous experience, while also connecting her to the new one: the internship at the Clinic.

The internship placements, as zones between academic training and professional practice, are described in different manners by our participants. Irrespective of the scopes of the professional workplaces, the aims of internship (what internship should be) can be clear, vague or even negotiated with the trainee.

In this excerpt, a Danish student talks about a colloquium she did in order to enter the place of internship and to clarify her role there.

> I think I was the only one that had to go to a conversation to be accepted. I think all the other place don't have this kind of conversation. You just come around and you'll be there. It was nice to clarify what my job would be.

In this next excerpt, a trainee explains the scheduled process she should follow during the internship:

> We have the session with the client then . . . then we have this computer at our office where we not really transcribe . . . it's like a description of the process. So we just write down the themes and if there happen in our transference. And then, like, after approximately two sessions (with client) we talk about in to the supervision.

This Italian student instead outlines the lack of precise goals for their internship, which is lived as a less important experience during academic training:

> At the beginning of the internship, I was also following the courses at university, so I tried. . . . The psychologists there were available and they said "come when you could come." In the end, we finally arrange, even if I went there rarely and I mostly have been watched this group. Now I think . . . the internship is always a time cut between university engagements at this time.

Additionally, the degree of responsibility given to the trainees in different contexts is very different. We can find some contexts that give the trainee very little responsibility, keeping them in a peripheral position during the internships, as explained in the following excerpt from an Italian student:

> I take part at the first meeting as an observer, and I take part to the équipe meetings where they discuss to the clinical cases. . . . They showed me also some drawings, real drawings. . .

This excerpt shows how the student has only an indirect contact with the profession and she doesn't have the possibility to prove herself.

In another case, a Danish trainee notes how, after an initial difficult period when she was very doubtful about her knowledge, she gets some confidence:

> So it's the perfect balance between getting challenged but still safe.

Almost the opposite is the case of the trainee legitimate to progressively work as a professional and to have more and more responsibility. In this context, one of our Danish participants had the possibility to have a "first person" experience. She seems moving from the periphery to the center of the Border Zone.

> I was able to go there; I was from the university. From the outset, I was just following, beside. I'm also a group leader in that group helping making it work. So I have also been able to have the first meeting and now I am about to have my own client.

Despite all the differences relating to the purposes of internship, the responsibility given to the trainee and the competencies acknowledged, the internship is an important device for articulating theoretical (academic) knowledge with practical. In particular, the possibility of experiencing and facing some problems seems to have significant relevance.

In this case, an Italian student notes how the internship, even if she is just an observer, allows her to organize her knowledge relating to a particular situation. She tries to verify what she studied at the university:

> Thanks to the things that I was studying, I could understand better what they said (the psychologists), but while I was hearing I add other things.

In the following excerpt, another Danish trainee who has the possibility of working directly with the patient, combines what she studied in order to deal with the practice. She makes her own synthesis about what she has learned to face a situation in the internship:

> What I have learnt is really that you have your theoretical background and everything you have learned but you also have to use a lot of your experience with yourself, your personal life melts together with your job and your internship.

Talking about a situation in which a Danish trainee experiences some difficulties with a young client, she says:

> I knew how to do or you can say so. . . . I have my theoretical background that could help me but I also thought about my own prejudice about young people having these problems. And I also thought about that I actually could recognize these thoughts she had, not on the level she had them, but I could use my personal experience in my life because I am also young like her. I thought we have a good connection, my age and everything at that point are something that I could use to the therapy and not just something that was me.

On the border: where the real learning starts

This section outlines the role of the experience for the trainees in constructing meaningful professional learning.

One of the Danish trainee outlines how the internship experience, at the end of academic training, is for her a significant opportunity that provides the possibility of seeing what real work would be like and what it would mean to be a psychologist.

> I think some of the most meaningful . . . is the experience in general. I've learned a lot and in all kind of ways . . . just being like in a work space and also to see to find and see what you can do when you are done at university, what kind of work you are able to manage and . . . I think, I would like, if it have been possible to do more internships or so just follow some psychologist through the years I don't know, just to get him what you would say to be a psychologist.

However, she underlines that this experience is not enough to fill the lack of practical learning. She thinks that the best thing is having practical experience throughout the university years (and not only at the end), doing many internships or accompanying a psychologist though time. By incorporating the practical experience within the university course, it could be possible to fill the gap between reading about and talking with people, as demonstrated in the following excerpt:

> at university, we read a lot, we study a lot, we research, we do all kind of things but don't really talk to people, we need people, we just read about people.

The same Danish student, talking about learning in a professional practice, explains her vision with an interesting metaphor:

> When you have the license you have to learn how to drive a car. None of us is a good psychologist when we are graduated . . . when I'm . . . when I graduate that's when the practical learning starts.

The excerpt indicates where the participants locate the "real learning": on the outer border of the university. The internship is *de facto* a Border Zone for transit toward the profession.

Me in the present and in the future: becoming a psychologist

The processes of how the students represent themselves and live during this stage of their training to become psychologists (Kullasepp, 2006, 2011; Leijen &

Kullasepp, 2013) and their projection of themselves in the future are addressed in this section.

The interviewees' feelings and perceptions about themselves are very different.

In one case, an Italian girl says that she primarily perceives herself as a student compared to the other trainees in the internship context:

> The other girls are doing their specialization course, they are older and they hold the first request of the patient, I am the one that is still studying, I have not finished yet the University.

She adds:

> Before starting (the internship) I had very negative expectations. I wondered what I could do there? Then I did a work on myself because after all I am the trainee.

The student starts with a very negative representation of the internship but also of herself after many years of study at university.

Later on, this trainee underlines how becoming a psychologist is a very long and difficult path, but she relegates it to the end of her academic course. The experience of the professionalizing internship "disappears" and she as a student primarily wants to put an end to her academic course.

In addition, the other Italian student, while making the following drawing for answering to the question "how she represents herself," says:

> I don't know . . . I am a student, I have a lot of questions. . . . Now I can't see myself because I am a student yet. I am a student also because I imagine that the work as psychologist come later. . . . Now I don't have the tools to say I can do this.

Later on she also says (while discussing her drawing) (Figure 10.1):

> I can't see myself . . . but if I see the future it's shining it's strange this thing . . . even if you have to be brave . . . once you know your limit, your personal, methodological border, your border of knowledge. . . . In my opinion, you have to explore new horizon only if you feel safe. So now I would go on prudently just understand the border and then other worlds of the future.[4]

The trainee perceives the limits of the actual situation and projects herself into an imagined future. She seems to use the internship as a place to give herself some borders in order to push her in the future.

Figure 10.1 Drawing made by a participant

This dynamic is also well underlined in the following excerpt, in which she continues to explain her drawing:

> Since I see myself primarily as a student, it's unavoidable to take the books, they also represent a time limit, a border . . . also because the books force

you in a role, the book reminds you that you are a student and you can't do, rightly, a psychologist yet. It's like a protection.

In this extract, academic knowledge is perceived a safe but often quite rigid border.

Both of the Italian students, who have the role of observer in their internships, bring the vision that you can't start to think of yourself as a psychologist when you are at university.

In another comment, a Danish trainee underlines how in the internship you can experience yourself in a professional situation; in this new situation, not being like a student but instead acting like as a professional (even supervised) puts into question her identity, as exemplified in the following excerpt:

> I was really curious about how would be for me to be in this relationship which is professional and I am the therapist.

This new dynamic allows the trainee to create differentiations between the normal way of acting in ordinary life and "correct" professional practices. This process of becoming professional is described by a trainee as follows:

> I feel that it is interesting, I feel like I can't wait to but I am also a little bit afraid. I don't know, I just, I'm looking forward to it. I think it's interesting but I am also a bit afraid of it because I also want to be good at it; it just makes sense to me I feel privileged that I have the opportunity to know so many people in this kind of way.

She is in the process of self-definition (at the professional level), and the internship gives her a taste of what it means to enter into contact with people.

From the point of view of another Danish trainee, the experience of internship is just a taste and "*is not enough to consider herself as a psychologist.*" The participant feels she still has to learn how to be a psychologist and shows an ambivalent attitude toward her knowledge.

> We have knowledge that is not common knowledge . . . I don't know much about talking with people.

Related to her thoughts about the professional future, she says, "*I don't know what is gonna happen, it's a stressing time.*" She underlines an uncertainty about her future and professional trajectory.

For the two latter Danish students, the internship is a place and time in which they wonder if they want to be or are able to be a psychologist or not. The internship is conceived for as a test of their abilities, a test of what they have done over the years and if what they have learned in psychology will help them in what they should do.

> I was really nervous, I felt that I fail, it would be like a disaster for me.

> There is the period where I'm trying to figure out what I want to. . . . If I want to be a psychologist or not.

On the opposite side, in the following extract a Danish trainee represents herself as a worker. She enters as a university student and after a short period she is perceiving herself as a professional, not a student anymore. As in the following excerpt:

> Feeling not being a student but actually feeling like I am a psychologist. I have responsibility as an educated person. It's a job and everybody have to get along in some way.

Talking about herself in the future, she says: "*Internship has challenged me* as *I want to work* as a *clinical* psychologist."

As the different trainees have told us, perceptions of self at this stage of training, during this experience, are very different, including the role and the responsibilities they assume/they ascribed to in the internship context.

Personal style

Another theme related to the construction of the professional self has been referred to by some participants, especially the Danish ones, as "*finding your style*" and undergoing a process of identification with the professionals/psychologist in the internship.

One Danish student says:

> They are very good at their job and they are very different, so it gave you inspiration to find your own style, in your job. There are a lot of ways of doing our job.

Another Danish student, talking about their tutor and other professionals, says:

> They are very good but I also feel they are different from me and I don't think that my personal style as a therapist would be the same of them. I don't want to be like you. It's not that way. I also feel that I can be critical but in a healthy way.

It seems that internships allow students to observe how work is tailored in different ways depending on the person. Therefore, you should be able to find your own style. In this sense, the internship allows students to see "*embodied psychology*" at work.

In another interview with a Danish participant, we find at work the process of identification of the trainee with the tutor. In the student's words:

Not all people like us [me and my tutor: the psychologists in that context] because we are psychologists. There is some resistance.

After her identification with the supervisor, the student perceives herself as a possible disturbance inside the place of internship because she puts herself in an asymmetric role.

The internship seems to help her in defining who she is – in this ongoing process of constructing the professional identity – and her differences with others.

The others of the internship experience: tutor/supervisor, colleagues, patients/clients

Tutor/supervisor

Normally if there is a trainee, there is a tutor to supervise his or her actions. In many cases, we can find the construction of a personal relationship between the trainee and the tutor/supervisor, as expressed in the following excerpt:

> She is responsible for what I am doing. She is confident in me. She is giving me something, I really like her. She teaches me but she has also my back.

In some other cases, instead, the learning/supervising relationship is more distributed in the context, as in the following example:

> Go with him and see this, then tomorrow go with the other psychologist and see that other thing.

The functions of the tutor are many, as outlined by the trainees. It's a very important learning relationship that assumes different connotations.

The functions of the tutor, as pointed out by the trainees, could be synthetized as the following:

- Emotional support

  When I came to her and talk to her about my frustrations, she really calm me down.
  She gave me a space where I could just find some peace.

- Promoting reflection upon the practice

  So, and there is something which my supervisor then always asked me. What do you want to be supervised today? I can show some short film clips from the session which illustrate the issue that I want to get supervised.

In this case, the tutor lets the trainees select the relevant issues, making them build their own questions about the practice through their movie clips. The tutor encourages and welcomes the construction of the trainee's knowledge, giving her the responsibility of her construction.

This process of reflecting on the practice is something that the trainee brings with her to the session with the client, as in the following words:

> I am alone with the client but I can hear some . . . like my supervisor's voice.

- Help and Guidance

> It's really helpful to have like a guidance. . . . I think it would be really hard if I didn't have the supervision I would feel really alone.
> She points to this and that things that I have to consider.
> She also makes the things easier for me.

Colleagues

Colleagues are the other professionals of the internship place (as nurseries, social workers, doctors etc.). They also represent another source of learning, as in the following words:

> They have different perspectives and I also thought that I learn a lot about that. Talk to other professions and learn to communicate with other professions it's a part of being an educated psychologist. There are also nurseries, some doctors and we have to work together to find a solution for the patients and it also gave a lot of meaning, the different educated working together for one patient. There are differences but there is also a lot of help and togetherness too, through the colleagues.

They could also be other workers at the place of internship who push the trainee to demarcate the psychology profession from the other competences in the specific context, as in this case of administrative workers:

> I really don't understand why they don't understand the mind. Even though it's complicated with colleagues that time it's also a great experience.

Or the psychiatrists:

> The patients are followed more by the psychiatrists because they work with emergency.

Colleagues could be also students that share the common experience of internship and promote reflection on the practice during a supervision meeting, as in the following words:

> It's really helpful to have some students, some colleagues that are in the same situation as you. There are the tutor and the other student together to discuss, to help me and reflect on the issue I presented.

Patients or clients

Patients or clients elicited an emotional reaction and questions in one Italian trainee, as follows:

> I would like to work in the future in a preventive perspective because these patients have a dramatic history; some of them couldn't had some opportunities that I had instead.

In another excerpt, a Danish trainee states that the relationship with clients in the internship caused her to question herself and her abilities:

> At the beginning of internship, I get some confidence in myself, then I get really confused because the session that I had with citizens. I really did the feeling that I couldn't do anything, I couldn't see improvement and I had this feeling that I was just an everyday conversation and something that I could go to talk with everybody.

This other Danish trainee says that the contact with patients allowed her to develop a personal respect for others, for those that bring their problems and questions, towards whom she feels responsible *as an educated person*:

> It's a special thing to have respect to the one person who is sitting there, one feeling and it's not just something you read about it in a book and I have respect for. It's personal respect. You have something to get out every day and some people are counting on you and you have the responsibility to be there for them.

Concluding remarks

So far, we have discussed multiple components (personal, interpersonal and contextual) of the internships as accounted for by trainees from different countries. In this section, we try to build some theoretical reflections upon them.

First, internship refers to a student who is becoming a psychologist. It means that internship has to do with a *developing subject* in her move from one state to another (Figure 10.2).

Figure 10.2 exemplifies this transitional phase from state A (being a student) to state B (being a psychologist). The trainee lives in a fuzzy passage zone in which she is no longer A (not only a student) but is not yet B (a psychologist in full).

The fundamental presupposition of a transition is a socio-cultural relocation that is accompanied by the challenging, reworking or abandoning of previously valid identities, routines, knowledge and representations of reality (Simão, 2003; Zittoun, 2006).

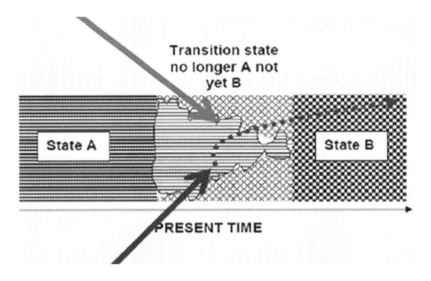

Figure 10.2 Transitional state
Valsiner & van der Veer, 2014, p. 152

The issue is further complicated by the fact that this "move towards" takes place in irreversible time and along an uncertain path, the borders of which are poorly defined. This is the case of the trainees, who have to deal with transformations in progress and the need to find new ways of thinking and acting in the specific institutional contexts in which they undertake their internships. Yet, change is slow. It is a gradual transition that takes place over a certain period of time and can be conceptualized in terms of "trajectory" (Marsico, 2012). In addition, this is not a solo journey. As the analysis of the interviews reveals, the internship implies entering a new social setting (the workplace) and interacting with actors different from the supervisor/tutor, including colleagues as well as patients/clients.

Each of these can be a source of support or of stress and disquietedness. Some of the excerpts presented above make evident the "scaffolding" role (Wood, Bruner, & Ross, 1976) taken by the supervisor/tutor, but also the ambivalent relationship with other professionals and challenging experiences with patients/clients. Internship, then, is primarily a very intense socio-emotional experience that somehow triggers personal and professional identity under construction. It's a dilemmatic field that deeply challenges the idea of who am I now and what I want to be in the future ("*I'm trying to figure out what I want to. . . . If I want to be a psychologist or not*"). This dilemma primarily has to do with a definition of the self at the present time in the educational/professional context of internship (Marsico & Tateo, 2018), but also with the projection of the self into the future.

Being and becoming are, then, the psychological dimensions at stake during the internship period.

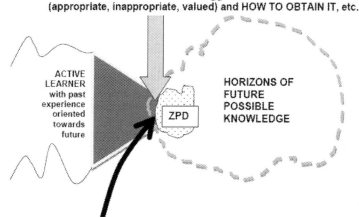

Figure 10.3 Internship as a zone of proximal development
Valsiner & van der Veer, 2014, p. 153

From a cultural psychology of education perspective (Marsico, 2017, 2018), the internship represents a Liminal Zone between what has already been learned and possible horizons of new knowledge. In Vygotskyan terms, we can legitimately call it a zone of proximal development (Vygotsky, 1933/1984).

As in Figure 10.3, the trainee is an active learner living a flux of experiences in the new professional setting. This happens under the constraints and guidance provided by the Macro-Social Context that sets what is the appropriate professional knowledge and how to get it as well as who are the Social Others (as in the case of tutors and colleagues in the professional services). Under this condition, the developing person moves beyond the established state into the area of acting and thinking that has not yet been actualized.

In this vein, the internship is a quintessential expression of a Liminal Zone in education, in between the individual psychosocial experience and the management of transitional episodes and *events of becoming*.

Notes

1 This methodology was inspired by an ongoing study conducted by Tatiana Valerio in Belo Jardim (Brazil) about the psychological dynamics associated with choosing a musical instrument.
2 This was the only formal requirement for taking part in the research.

3 The expected hours of internship are generally around 200–230 in the different countries.
4 One of the tasks we proposed to the participants was to think at herself/himself at this stage of training and make a drawing. All the methods used are described in the section "The research design: method and participants".

References

Boesch, E. (1991). *Symbolic action theory and cultural psychology*. Berlin, Germany: Springer – Verlag.

Carli, R., Grasso, M., & Paniccia, R. M. (2007). *La formazione alla psicologia clinica: Pensare emozioni* [The training to clinical psychology: Thinking emotions]. Milano: FrancoAngeli.

Castells, M. (1996). *The information age: Economy, society and culture: The rise of the network society* (Vol. 1). Malden, MA: Blackwell Publishers.

Davies, L. (1990). *Experience-based learning within the curriculum: A synthesis study*. Sheffield: CNAA.

De Luca Picione, R., & Valsiner, J. (2017). Psychological functions of semiotic borders in sense-making: Liminality of narrative processes. *Europe's Journal of Psychology*, *13*(3), 532–547. doi:10.5964/ejop.v13i3.1136

Fox, T. (2001). A sense of place. *Caterer and Hotelkeeper*, *189*(4160).

Freda, M. F. (2008). Tirocini intercorso per la laurea specialistica in psicologia clinica: la costruzione del setting formativo. *Psicologia scolastica*, *7*(1), 143–151.

Freda, M. F., Esposito, G., & Quaranta, T. (2015). Promoting mentalization in clinical psychology at Universities: A linguistic analysis of student accounts. *Europe's Journal of Psychology*, *11*(1), 39–49.

Greco, M., & Stenner, P. (2017). From paradox to pattern shift: Conceptualising liminal hotspots and their affective dynamics. *Theory & Psychology*, *27*(2), 147–166. doi:10.1177/0959354317693120

Hatcher, R. L., & Lassiter, K. D. (2007). Initial training in professional psychology: The practicum competencies outline. *Training and Education in Professional Psychology*, *1*(1), 49.

Kaneklin, C. L., Scaratti, G., & Bruno A. (2006). *La formazione universitaria. Pratiche possibili*. Roma: Carocci.

Kaslow, N. J. (2004). Competencies in professional psychology. *American Psychologist*, *59*(8), 774.

Kullasepp, K. (2006). Identity construction of psychology students: Professional role in the making. *European Journal of School Psychology*, *4*(2), 249–280.

Kullasepp, K. (2011). Creating my own way of being a psychologist. *The Japanese Journal of Personality*, *19*(3), 217–232.

Leijen, Ä., & Kullasepp, K. (2013). All roads lead to Rome: Developmental trajectories of student teachers' professional and personal identity development. *Journal of Constructivist Psychology*, *26*(2), 104–114. doi:10.1080/10720537.2013.759023

Marsico, G. (2011). The "non-cuttable" space in between: Context, boundaries and their natural fluidity. *IPBS: Integrative Psychological & Behavioral Science*, *45*, 185–193.

Marsico, G. (2012). The double uncertainty: Trajectories and professional identity in changing contexts. *Culture & Psychology*, *18*(1), 121–132.

Marsico, G. (2013). Moving between the social spaces: Conditions for boundaries crossing. In G. Marsico, K. Komatsu, & A. Iannaccone (Eds.), *Crossing boundaries. Intercontextual dynamics between family and school* (pp. 361–374). Charlotte, NC: Information Age Publishing.

Marsico, G. (2016). The borderland. *Culture & Psychology, 22*(2), 206–215. doi:10.1177/1354067X15601199

Marsico, G, (2017). Jerome S. Bruner: Manifesto for the future of education. *Infancia y Aprendizaje, Journal for the Study of Education and Development, 40*(4), 754–781. doi:10.1080/02103702.2017.1367597

Marsico, G. (2018). Development and education as crossing socio-cultural boundaries. In A. Rosa & J. Valsiner (Eds.), *The Cambridge handbook of sociocultural psychology* (2nd ed., pp. 302–316). Cambridge: Cambridge University Press.

Marsico, G., Cabell, K. R., Valsiner, J., & Kharlamov, N. A. (2013). Interobjectivity as a border: The fluid dynamics of "Betweenness". In G. Sammut, P. Daanen, & F. Moghaddam (Eds.), *Understanding the self and others: Explorations in intersubjectivity and interobjectivity* (pp. 51–65). London: Routledge.

Marsico, G., Dazzani, V., Ristum, M., & Bastos, A. C. (Eds.). (2015). *Educational contexts and borders through a cultural lens—Looking inside. Viewing outside.* Cultural Psychology of Education, 1, Geneva, Switzerland: Springer.

Marsico, G., & Tateo, L. (Eds.). (2018). *The emergence of self in the educational contexts.* Cultural Psychology of Education, 8, Cham, Switzerland: Springer.

Marsico, G., & Valsiner, J. (2018). *Beyond the mind: Cultural dynamics of the psyche.* Charlotte, NC: Information Age Publishing.

McMahon, U., & Quinn, U. (1995). Maximizing the hospitality management student work placement experience: A case study. *Education and Training, 37*(4), 13–17.

Pauze, E. F., Johnson, W. A., & Miller, J. L. (1989). Internship strategy for hospitality management programmes. *Hospitality Education and Research Journal, 13*(3), 301–307.

Ristum, M., Bastos, A. C., Dazzani, V., & Marsico, G. (2015). Experiencing the educational contexts: Insideness, outsideness, betweenness. In G. Marsico, V. Dazzani, M. Ristum, & A. C. Bastos (Eds.), *Educational contexts and borders through a cultural lens—Looking inside. Viewing outside* (pp. 157–160). Cultural Psychology of Education, 1, Geneva, Switzerland: Springer.

Shön, D. A. (1987). *Educating the reflective practitioner.* San Francisco: Jossey-Bass.

Simão, L. M. (2003). Beside rupture—Disquiet: Beyond the other—alterity. *Culture & Psychology, 9,* 449–459.

Stenner, P., Greco, M., & Motzkau, J. F. (2017). Introduction to the special issue on Liminal Hotspots. *Theory & Psychology, 27*(2), 141–146. doi:10.1177/0959354316687867

Turner, V. (1969). *The ritual process.* New York: Aldine De Gruyter.

Valsiner, J. (2014). *An invitation to cultural psychology.* London: Sage.

Valsiner, J., Lutsenko, A., & Antoniouk, A. A. (Eds.). (2018). *Sustainable futures for higher education: Cultivating knowledge makers.* Cultural Psychology of Education, 7, Cham, Switzerland: Springer.

Valsiner, J., & van der Veer, R. (2014). Encountering the border: Vygotsky's zona blizaishego razvytya and its implications for theory of development. In A. Yasnitsky, R. van der Veer, & M. Ferrari (Eds.), *The Cambridge handbook of cultural-historical psychology* (pp. 148–173). Cambridge: Cambridge University Press.

Vygotsky, L. S. (1933/1984). Krizis semi let. In L. S. Vygotsky (Ed.), *Sobranie sochinenii. Vol. 4. Detskaia psikhologia* (pp. 376–385). Moscow: Pedagogika.

Weinert, F. E. (2001). Concept of competence: A conceptual clarification. In D. S. Rychen & L. H. Salganik (Eds.), *Defining and selecting key competencies* (pp. 45–65). Ashland, OH, US: Hogrefe & Huber Publishers.

Wood, D. J., Bruner, J., & Ross, G. (1976). The role of tutoring in problem solving. *The Journal of Child Psychology and Psychiatry, 17*(2), 89–100.

Zittoun, T. (2006). *Transitions: Development through symbolic resources*. Charlotte, NC: Information Age Publishing.

Afterword on educational dilemmas

Luca Tateo

I started planning this collective volume in the wake of widespread debate about the psychological discomfort of students all over the world. Across grades and nations, it seemed that students were experiencing growing levels of stress. During the same period, my personal observations were making me think of some kind of paradoxical situation. Traveling to different countries, from Europe to South America to Asia, I could observe a number of different educational contexts and living conditions in schools and universities. I was particularly surprised to listen to omnipresent discourses about university students' stress in Nordic countries, where the study environment and the work/life rhythms seemed honestly very easy and supportive – even luxurious, or I would say privileged – compared to other countries, including Italy, my place of origin. It appeared immediately clear that the material conditions of study were not the only issue in creating discomfort. In some universities, in which the study environments were much more uncomfortable and the curricula more difficult, students appeared more active and committed, and the discourse about stress was not so visible.

Moreover, I could observe that innovation was not the prerogative of some "advanced" educational systems, and that conservativism was present everywhere. My personal experience was that the positive and negative attributes of educational contexts were distributed in leopard spots across countries and cultures. In the same way, besides the standardization efforts, educational approaches, values and ideologies developed a number of different local *edu-systems* (the equivalent of eco-systems in life sciences) with their own local solutions to problems. I realized that such diversity could not be an obstacle, as is somehow implicit in the idea of standardization. With these ideas in mind, I started to look for colleagues who were interested in presenting and discussing such diversity. I invited them to contribute to this volume in a form that was free from some of the obnoxious constraints of current academic publishing, caged by disciplinary barriers and orthodoxies. Hopefully, we succeeded in this challenge.

However, during the editing of the book, I came to the conclusion that the current debate was not critical enough. Reading the contributions of this volume and drawing on the enormous corpus of studies in the cultural psychology of education, I slowly realized how the ideology of education itself is much more problematic than we account for. So, I now feel the need to briefly add some further reflections post-factum that I hope the reader will take as hints for future research. I will do this in the form of short paths, leaving to the reader the joy of developing them empirically.

Path 1: The process of education is a dilemmatic field. I always wondered what the relationship between education and human development is. I think that development is inevitable, as its opposite is the death of the organism. However, the forms of human development are culturally mediated. We like to think that human development is a linear progression; so does the process of education. We tend to forget that at every step of the process of education, something is produced and something else is discarded. We also tend to think about making choices as taking one path in a bifurcated branch, while the alternatives disappear. I suggest that the process of education does not look like a tree of choices but rather a dilemma. When we make a choice, the alternatives do not disappear; they remain as elements of the field and create a system of forces and tensions. We think that education is about producing knowledge and filling gaps of ignorance. What if education is also about creating gaps of knowledge and producing ignorance? Why do we always assume that what we produce is better than what we disrupt? For whom, for what sake, for what purpose and in what conditions? A dilemmatic field is a space/time in which every alternative path carries a valid meaning for someone in some respect, so there is no monological, ready-made, once-and-for-all solution in the process of education. The same elements that create productive conditions can at the same time create discomfort. There is no magic blue pill that can "cure" this, as the medicalization of education seems to promise.

Path 2: The process of education is cogenetic. An *edu-system* is composed of a number of sub-parts, which come into existence and disappear together. For instance, in defining what "schooling" is, one also defines what is "not schooling", that is, all the intermediate forms of "para-curricular", "extra-curricular" and "leisure" activities whose borders are fuzzy and continuously moving. Indeed, often innovation in the process of education comes exactly from this border zone. Another example are the definitions of "school", "family" and "community". Several works in cultural psychology discuss the border zones between these social contexts, which in turn can be defined only in relation to each other. A further example of cogenetic logic in the process of education are the "study" and "non-study" forms of "on-the-job training", "internship", etc. Hybridization is possible only if we think in terms of cogenetic logic. In the studies in this volume, one can see how the "well-being" and "non-well-being" of students emerge together and constitute sub-parts of an *edu-system* in which only extreme variations of their relationship actually lead to serious discomfort. Are we operating for the elimination of the conditions of "non-well-being" (impossible in terms of cogenetic logic), or are we operating on the border zone, simply including forms of temporary efforts of learning in the field of "discomfort" (the basic operation of medicalization)? Is academic writing a joy or a pain? Of course, we must answer: both!

Path 3: The process of education is value-laden. Every human collective produces a system of acceptable and non-acceptable forms of development. According to path 2, when we define something, we imply the opposite and the conditions of the transition. Setting learning goals, accountable standards or acceptable behaviors immediately creates an opposite set of non-desirable goals, non-accountable dimensions and disruptive behaviors. At the same time, it defines the conditions for transiting from "non-A(cceptable)" to "A(cceptable)". Can we hypothesize that educational discomfort is related to values? Can we, for instance, argue that value-laden standards produce the conditions for a dissonance between those values and personal goals or expectations, that the person must repair, using specific forms of "non-A" to "A" transition? How are these conditions related to discomfort? In addition, cultural psychology has demonstrated the relevance of values in education and development, but value-laden processes are also power-based. How can cogenetic logic help, for instance, to illuminate colonization and decolonization dynamics in education?

On the one hand, we are witnessing times of recrudescent intolerance, racism, blind defense of wealthy (and mostly white) privileges, nationalism, neo-fascist groups, aggressiveness and bellicosity. On the other hand, none of the problems human collectivity must face, from climate change to migration, from neocolonialism to water supplies, can be solved through the limited resources of a nation alone. There is no adamant truth in human action: in its dilemmatic nature, every path we take implies gains and losses for someone. The process of education is a fundamental arena, where these dilemmas are often played for the first time in ontogenesis. We must be aware and respectful of the fact that every choice humans make falls within a dilemmatic field. So, educational interventions that apparently aim at social inclusion of some groups (e.g. migrants) can reproduce social inequalities, assimilate diversity and perpetuate discrimination. The process of education can be used to build peace and prosperity but also to prepare war and oppression. A dilemmatic field means that there is no human being, no human collective and no human culture which is "worth" more than another.

July 28, 2018, on the border between Croatia and Bosnia-Herzegovina

Index

Note: Page numbers in *italics* indicate figures; page numbers in **bold** indicate tables.

Aalborg Municipality 148, *148*
Aalborg University 132, 136, 146, 148, *148*, 151, 156, *166*
academic environments 148, *148*, 149
academic freedom: curricular 32–33; ecological 35–36; instructional 33–34; intrinsic education 31–36; leisure 36–37; participatory 34; role 36; types 24, 32; valuative 34–35; *see also* intrinsic education
accountability, dilemmas of 91
advocacy, recognition discourse of mental health 88–89
ambivalence questionnaire 153, 170
amyotrophic lateral sclerosis 2
anchor points 100
Anker, Markus 104
anxiety: analysis of 106; existential phenomenology and 131–132; stress 105; studies of 103; university experience and 98–99
Arendt, Hannah 121
Aristotle 27, 34, 36–37
Asimov, Isaac 25–26
Asperger's disorder 88
Aspies 88
Attention Deficit Disorder (ADD) 83
attention deficit hyperactivity disorder (ADHD) 6, 80, 83
authoritarian, teaching style 23
authority, dilemmas of 83
automatization 37

Bartleby the Scrivener (Melville) 120
beautiful suffering 89–90

Beckett, Samuel 117, 118–119
behavioral responses to stress 101
behaviorism 22–23
Biesta, Gert 48, 49, 114, 117
Big Magic: Creative Living Beyond Fear (Gilbert) 113
Bildung: case of Andrea 132–133; concept of 130, 137n1; existential phenomenology of education and 130–132; ideals and meaning behind 130–131, 137n2; perspective of university student 132
Biographer's Tale, The (Byatt) 119
biomedical discourses of student mental health: affordances of 78–80; from agents to patients 80–81; clarity and legitimacy 79; dilemmas of 82–83; dilemmas of authority 83; dilemmas of chronicity 82–83; eclipsing alternative responses 81; finally getting an answer 78–80; pre-empting blame 79–80; resisting medicalization 80–82; resources and control 79; surveillance medicine and self-monitoring subject 81–82
bodybuilding competition *4*
borders, educational 174–175
Border Zone, internship as 174–175, 177, 179, 180
bounded indeterminacy 10
Bruner, J. S.: sense 100; meaning 102; scaffolding *188*
bukatsu: corporal punishment survey 140–141; downward collectivism 143–144; extracurricular school

"sports" activities 139–140, 144n1; projective praise 144; questions on corporal punishment **141**; rates of corporal punishment *142*; results of study 141–142; situations of corporal punishment from teachers or coaches **142**; word 139
burnout, studies of 103–104
BuzzFeed (website) 78, 90
Byatt, A.S. 119

Canadian Mental Health Association 78
capsulated mother-child 66
Castle Bridge School 16, *17*, 20n2
Centre for Cultural Psychology 1
Cesaro, Michele 98, 108n1
Cheeke, Robert *4*
children: death of child *2*; first-grader problems in Japan 70–72; growing up in Japan's collectivist culture 72–73; hesitation to attend preschool 66–67; "*o'juken*" entrance exams for private elementary school 68–70; with special needs 1, 6, 60, 66; *see also* Japan
children's world, Japanese phrase 64
chronicity, dilemmas of 82–83
circulatory system 77
CISS (Coping Inventory for Stressful Situations) 104, 105, 106–107; Avoidance scale 106, 107; Distraction scale 106, 107; Emotion scale 106, 107; Maneuver scale 106, 107; Social Diversion scale 106, 107
Clackamas High School *4*
classroom management 22–24; punishment and rewards 22; student responsibility *vs* unconditional obedience 34; teachers defining 22; *see also* intrinsic education
Clinton Presidential Library *3*
cogenetic logic: of internship 194; systemic 6–9; thought experiment 14–17; window of possibilities and 9–13, 19
cogenetic system: case of socially guided development *7*; diachronic perspective *10*; features of 7–8
collectivism: downward 143–144; first-grader problems 72, 73; Japanese preschool facilities 58–59; repressive 143–144; upward 145n4

competence, definitions 172
competition, in higher education 45–47
competitive state 41; term 50
contemplative pedagogies in higher education 53
coping skills 101
corner setting activities, kindergartens in USA 61, *62*, *63*, 64
corporal punishment: background in Japan 143; Japan's schools and 140; questions on **141**; rates of *142*; student suffering, from teachers or coaches **142**; survey on 140–141; survey results 141–142; *see also bukatsu*
corporative truth seeking, university ideal 130–131, 136–137
Counseling Center, University of Salerno 98, 103, 104, 108n1
counseling university students: analysis of results 106–108; CISS (Coping Inventory for Stressful Situations) 104, 105, 106–107; Global Severity Index (GSI) 104, 105, 107; identity transition 99–101; objectives of research 104; participants of research 104–105; post-intervention of psychological counseling 107; research 104–107; Rosenberg Self-Esteem Scale 105, 107; stress of 101–104; tools and procedures in research 105; university experience and 98–99; *see also* university students
creative authorship, type of intrinsic education 27, 28–29
crisis and resolution, concept of 99, 108n2
critical authorship, type of intrinsic education 27, 29–31
cultural integration, university students 100
cultural psychology 1; developmental and educational trajectories 5; education 173; liminality and borders in education 173–175; *see also* internship
curricular academic freedom 32–33
Curricular Map 33
curriculum, Chinese school system 8, 9

Danish Writers' Academy 123
day care: basic daily schedule *58*; Japanese system 56–58; *see also* Japan
democratic: participation 25; teaching style 23

depression: analysis of 106; higher education students 135–136; stress 105
Derrida, Jacques 115, 118, 119, 121
development: childhood death 2; cogenetic and temporality 9–13; cultural psychology of 5; educational trajectories 14–16; hypothetical trajectories of human 5, 5–6; idea of inevitability of 4; locus of in education *13*; Steven Hawking 2–3; Valsiner's concept of 10
dilemmas: of accountability 91; of authority 83; of chronicity 82–83; of normativity 87–88; of performativity 92; process of education 194, 195
discomfort: nature of 114–119; of writing 112–114; *see also* writing
distress 101, 104
drama pedagogues 28
dyslexia 30

ecological right for education 35–36
economic logics, student mental health 86
education: cogenetic system 194; dilemmatic field 194, 195; forms of in human communities 18–19; ideology of 193–194; inclusive 53; instrumental goals of 24–25; learning society 121; liminality and borders in 173–175; locus of development in *13*; neoliberalisation of 47–50; ontological 27; polyphony of 18; positive 52–53; process of 1; school, in preschool facilities 68; value-laden system 195; *see also* internship
educational dilemmas, worldwide 17–19
educational intervention, imagined child 13, *14*
edu-systems 193, 194
elementary school: entrance examinations for private 68–70; Japanese first-grader problems 70–72; *see also* Japan
elitism 26
emotional self, shaping 86–87
equality 50
ESPN.com 90
eustress 101
excellence 6, 48, 115
existential phenomenology, education and Bildung 130–132
expectations, in higher education 44–45

Facebook 115
fascism 23
first-grader problems, Japanese children 70–72
Frances, Allen 80
Frank, Art 80

Gibbs, Simon 49
Gilbert, Elizabeth 113
Global Severity Index (GSI) 104, 105, 107
Golden Notebook, The (Lessing) 112
Guerrero, Eddie 35

habitus, sociological concept of 128, 130, 133, 137n2
Han, Byung-Chul 120–121
Hawking, Steven 2–3, *3*, 6
Heathcote, Dorothy 28, 29, 37n2
higher education: contemplative pedagogies in 53; existential phenomenology 130–132; expectations and performance 44–45; first semester students in deep water 134–135; infantilisation of 51, 53–54; learnification of 48, 49; motivation for field of study 126–129; nature of discomfort in 114–119; need of reflected normative ideals 129–132; neoliberalisation of 48; neoliberal takeover of 53; non-educational invasion of 51, 54; performance and competition 45–47; *see also* university students; writing
hikikomori (social withdrawal) 56, 67
horizon sign, concept of 152
Huffington Post (website) 78, 90
human collective: development trajectories 4, *4*; diagnosis of sclerosis 6; window of acceptability 3–4; window of possibilities 6–7
Human Condition, The (Arendt) 121
human development, hypothetical trajectories of 5, 5–6

identity repositioning 100
identity transition of university students 99–101
inclusive education 53
inclusive separation 8

infantilisation: campus life 52; of higher education 51, 53–54, 165, 167; suggesting inverse movement of 149
instructional academic freedom 33–34
instrumental education: intrinsic *vs* 24–31; magic learning pill and 26; necessity-based society and 37; purposes of 25–26; ubiquity of 36–37
internship: on the border and real learning 180; as Border Zone 174–175, 177, 179, 180; cogenetic logic of 194; colleagues experience 186; competence and 172; defining 172–173; drawing by a participant in 181, *182*; hours of 176, 190n3; inside and outside the university 176–177; introduction in academic curriculum 171; as liminal zone 177–179, 189; macro-social context of 189, *189*; patient or client experience 187; personal style 184–185; as practicum for psychology 172; research design 175–176; seeing self becoming psychologist 180–184; transitional state for trainee 187, *188*; tutor/supervisor experience 185–186; as zone of proximal development *189*
intervention *14*
intrinsic education: academic rights and freedoms 31–36; conditions for 31–36; creative authorship as type 27, 28–29; critical authorship as type 27, 29–31; curriculum 27; genuine 24; instrumental *vs* 24–31; ontological 27
irreversibility, principle of 1–6

Japan: April-born pressure of older children 64–66; basic daily schedule in day care centers and kindergartens 58; children's world 64; children with lack of anonymity 73; collectivism in preschool facilities 58–59; cooperativeness in 61; corporal punishment background in 143; downward collectivism 143–144; first-grader problems 70–72; group setting activities 59; hesitation to attend preschool 66–67; hikikomori (social withdrawal) 56, 67; individualizing collective culture 72–73; Juken exam for entrance to high school 68–70; *mimamori* (watch and protect) in 60; "*o'juken*" entrance exams for private elementary school 68–70; preschool facilities 56; projective praise 144; school education in preschool facilities 68; stressed leader 64–66; utilizing children's relationships with others 59–61; young child education and care in 56–58; *see also bukatsu*
Juken, entrance exam for high school in Japan 68–70
Jutel, Annemarie 79

Kemp, Peter 130
kindergartens, basic daily schedule in Japan 58; *see also* Japan

Labaree, David 24–25
laissez-faire, teaching style 23
language, therapeutic discourse for mental health 84–85
La Red Mágica (LRM) 29–31
Latin-American Community Center (LACC) 29–31, 35
leaders, April-born older children as 64–66
learnification, higher education 48, 49
learning for the sake of learning 26
learning society 121
Lego-Logo Club 35
leisure: academic freedom 36–37, 38n8; leisure-based society 37, 38n8
Lessing, Doris 112, 124
Lewin, Kurt 23, 147
Lewis, Tyson 113, 120, 121, 122
liminality 173–175
Llambías, Pablo 123
Lunde Larsen, Esben 42–43, 50

Mad or Normal (television show) 82
magic learning pill 26, 37n1
mainstream schools, classroom management 22–24
Marsico, Giuseppina 6
Mason, Elaine 3
Matusov, Eugene 29
May-born/April-born or, children as leaders 64–66
medicalization: definition 80; from agents to patients 80–81; pre-empting blame for mental health 79–80; resisting

80–82; surveillance and self-monitoring subject 81–82; *see also* mental health
Melville, Herman 120
mental health: consciousness raising 77; constructing 77–78; diagnose-and-treat logic 78; forms of 92–94; meaning-making around 93; medical constructions 78, 94n2; methods 78; situating the inquiry 76–78; term 78; wellness 76, 83, 86; *see also* biomedical discourses of student mental health; recognition discourses of student mental health; therapeutic discourses of student mental health
Mental Health Commission of Canada 76
military training, Chinese schools 8–9, *8*
mimamori (watch and protect) Japanese preschool 60
motivation: case of student preparing for professional life 132–133; field of study for university students 126–129
music pirating 30

nature/nurture 9
Nazism 23
neoliberalisation: of education 48–50; neoliberal takeover of higher education 53
Netflix 89
New York Times (newspaper) 30
normativity, dilemmas of 87–88

obsessive compulsive personality disorder 79

participatory academic freedom 34
perfectionism 46, 47
performance: competition in higher education 45–47; expectations in higher education 44–45
performativity, dilemmas of 92
phobic anxiety 105, 106
poiesis 34
polyphony of education 18
positive education, term 52–53
post-intervention of psychological counseling 107
potentiality: actualization and 120–121; studying as dwelling in 121–122
practicing psychologist 155, 167n4
praxis 34, 122, 136

"Prisoners of War Camp, The" (Heathcote) 28
problem-based learning (PBL): Aalborg University and 146–147; field of meaning 156–159; first semester students 134–135; map of meaning field "PBL is . . . but" *157*; themes about **156**; *see also* students' experiences
Profession (Asimov) 25–26
projective praise 144
psychology: embodied 184; goals of practicum 173; intern becoming psychologist 187, *188*; internship as practicum in 172; liminality and borders in education 173–175; *see also* internship
psychology students: case of Andrea maximizing strategy of 132–133; circular processes of scientific inquiry 133–134; first semester, in deep water 134–135; motivation and grade point averages 126–129; practices managing education 129–132; stress, fear of failing and emotional drama 135–136
psychopathology, SCL90-R 105
puppy therapy 76
Putting a Name to It (Jutel) 79

recognition discourses of student mental health: affordances of 88–89; appearance *vs* reality 90–91; critiques of 89–91; dilemmas of accountability 91; dilemmas of performativity 92; "I wanna be proud of who I am" 88–89; problem-saturated descriptions 90; us *vs* them 90
resilience: notion of 51; students lacking 50
responsibility, student 23, 34–35
robotics 37
role, academic freedom 36
Rose, Nikolas 80, 85
Rosenberg Self-Esteem Scale 105, 107
Roskilde University 146, 148, *148*

school, word 36–37
school education: Japanese first-grader problems 70–72; Japanese preschool facilities introducing 68
scientific inquiry: circular processes of 133–134; first semester students in deep water 134–135

SCL90-R 105
self-actualization 24, 37
self-esteem 103; Rosenberg Self-Esteem Scale 105, 107
self-management: mental health 85
self-realization 24, 37
self-regulated learning (SRL), notion of 49
self-responsible learner 49
self-transcendence 24
self-understandings, mental health 84–85
sense 100, 102
Shanghai public middle school: library 148, *148*; photos of military training *8*
sick role, notion of 89
Smedley, Ron 37n2
Snapchat 115
social constructivism 18
social efficiency 25
social justice 25, 50
social meanings 102
social mobility 25
social sciences, themata 9
social withdrawal (*hikikomori*) 56, 67
society, leisure-based 37, 38n8
somatization 105, 106
special needs, children with 1, 6, 60, 66
State Educational Grants (SU) 127
stress: activation and performance level 103, 108n4; agency and 160; behavioral responses to 101; burnout 103–104; fear of failing and emotional drama of students 135–136; lacking resilience 50–51; mental state crisis of students 52–53; neoliberal condition of education 47–50; personal relating to **162**, *163*; physical responses to 101, 108n3; Rosenberg's test 105, 107; student individualisation 49; themes about **159**; university experience and 98–99; university life and 41–43; university students and 101–104; vulnerable students 51–52; *see also* students' experiences
stress factors 101
student: responsibility 23, 34–35; *see also* mental health; university students
students' experiences: ambivalence questionnaire 153, 170; condition of being a university student 152–156; discourse about stress and pressure 159–164; examples of environments 148, *148*, 149, 151; exploration of field

of meaning 147–148; field of meaning 150; in higher education 146–147; limitations and potentialities of study 164–165; map of meaning field "as a student, I am ... but" *154*; map of meaning field "PBL is ... but" *157*; map of meaning field "personal relation with stress" *163*; map of meaning field "stress is ... but" *161*; methodology of study 152; participants in study 151; pilot study of 150–165; problem-based learning approach (PBL) in 156–159; stress in 146–147, 149–150; themes about being a student **153**; themes about personal related to stress **162**; themes about PBL **156**; themes about stress **159**; under pressure 146–147, 149–150
Study Progress Reform, Danish government 43

teaching styles 23
technological unemployment 37
telecommunication 37
temporal logic 9
therapeutic discourses of student mental health: affordances of 84–85; critiques of 85–87; dilemmas of 87–88; dilemmas of normativity 87–88; economic logics 86; language to express and relate 85; self-understandings 84–85; shaping the emotional self 86–87; strategies for self-management 85
thought experiment, cogenetic logic at school 14–17
Three Looms Waiting (documentary) 37n2
Turner, Victor 174
Twilight (series of novels/films) 92
Twitter 115

United States, corner setting activities in kindergartens 61, *62*, *63*, 64
university: ideal of corporative truth seeking 130–131, 136–137; psycho-social transition 101–102
University of Calgary 78, 84
University of Copenhagen 150
University of Salerno 98, 104
university students: burnout 103–104; cultural integration of 100; Danish study 41; engagement of 48–49; everyday life and struggles of 43–47;

expectations and performance 44–45; first semester students in deep water 134–135; future of higher education 52–54; identity transition with 99–101; individualisation notions 49; lacking resilience 50–51; life cycle 98, 99; mental health 42, 43, 52, 53; motivation for field of study 126–129; neoliberalisation of education 47–50; performance and anxiety 103, 108n4; performance and competition, 45–47; self-esteem and grades 46–47; stress, fear of failing and emotional drama 135–136; stress and 101–104; stress of life 41–43, 47; vulnerability to stress 51–52; well-being 42, 43, 46–47, 49–50, 52, 53; *see also* students' experiences

Valerio, Tatiana 189n1
valuative academic freedom 34–35
Villaneuva, Steve 35–36
Vygotsky's zone of proximal development 1, 9, 19

wellness, student mental health 76, 83, 86
What's Happened to the University (Furedi) 51
window of possibilities 5, 6; cogenetic logic and 9–13; thought experiment 14–17; zone of proximal development *15*
Worstward Ho (Beckett) 118
writing: blank page 115; (im)potentiality 120–123; joy and discomfort of 112–114; learning by 123–124; nature of discomfort 114–119; paradox of learning 117; paradox of learning to write 115–118; paradox of writing itself 118–119; relationship between potentiality and actualization 120–121; as studying 122–123; studying as dwelling in potentiality 121–122
Writing and Difference (Derrida) 118

zona blizhaishego razvitia (ZBR) 19n1; cogenetic aspect of 11–12; epistemological power of 12; potential of 16, 18; temporal dimension of 14; Vygotsky's 10–11
Zone of Freedom of Movement (ZFM) 10
Zone of Promoted Actions (ZPA) 10
zone of proximal development: concept of 10; Vygotsky 1, 9, 19; windows of possibilities in *15*
Zuckerman, Julie 16

Printed in the United States
By Bookmasters